184

4

88

387

3

CORRIDGE.

THE COMPLETE GUIDE TO COUNTRY LIVING

THE
COMPLETE
GUIDE TO
COUNTRY
LIVING

A Discursive Dictionary

SUZANNE BEEDELL

in association with Barbara Hargreaves

David & Charles

Newton Abbot   London   North Pomfret(Vt)

AUTHOR'S NOTE

I would like to thank first of all my collaborator, Barbara Hargreaves, for her advice and help throughout and her specialist sections on Dogs, Shooting, Fishing and Deer; my assistant, Ginette Leach, for her help with all the research and typing, her specialist knowledge of horses, and general knowledge of country life; Robin Godber of the NFU for his help with farming matters, and many others unnamed who have helped with all kinds of odds and ends of information.

S.B.

British Library Cataloguing in Publication Data
Beedell, Suzanne
   The complete guide to country living.
   1. Country life—Great Britain—Dictionaries
   I. Title II. Hargreaves, Barbara
   942'.00973'4   S522.G7

ISBN 0–7153–7665–9

© Suzanne Beedell & Barbara Hargreaves 1979

Photoset and printed in Great Britain
by Redwood Burn Limited, Trowbridge & Esher
for David & Charles (Publishers) Limited
Brunel House Newton Abbot Devon

Published in the United States of America
by David & Charles Inc
North Pomfret Vermont 05053 USA

INTRODUCTION

From A to W (it never reaches X, Y or Z) the book is arranged alphabetically, and where there were any problems, commonsense has been applied. For instance, a slow worm is not a snake, it is a lizard, but it has been included under '*Snakes*' because the main purpose of that section is to help someone who has found a snakelike creature to identify it quickly, especially as one species of snake is dangerous.

To make things easier for the reader, there is direct cross-referencing in the text—for instance '*Heavy Horses*' see '*Farmhorses*', under which latter heading the subject is dealt with. Strictly speaking, they are heavy horses, but most people who do not know about them call them farmhorses.

Books suggested as further reading are in print, and association and other addresses are correct at the time of writing, but things change and we apologize in advance for such changes which have come too late for this book.

Throughout we have included matters which seem to bear directly on country living. Some are omitted which you may feel should have been included, but the book could not run to several volumes, and they are all, at best, borderline cases. Wine-, cider- and liqueur-making have been included, because they come directly from country produce; beer and ginger beer have been left out because there is nothing specially country about them. They can be made just as well in the middle of any city. Barbecues belong in town as well as country gardens. The peripheral country sports, such as archery, climbing, caving, orienteering, and fell walking, are omitted because they are done by townspeople as well as country people and strictly speaking have nothing to do with *living* in the country.

Legal matters noted herein are correct at the time of writing, but laws change, and we cannot stress too heavily that these entries are for guidance only and that a solicitor must be consulted if any action is contemplated. Likewise, there is no one-and-only right way to do anything; experts often differ; opinions differ. That's life, but the expert advice in this book won't take you very far wrong in any direction.

A

Access There is a right of access to and from property through existing gateways. If a gateway is boarded up, the planning authority could say that access had been abandoned. Then they might do something which affected your access and claim that it no longer existed. Therefore it is much better to close an entrance in such a way that it can be re-opened if necessary; either by locking the gate or by installing a gate with spikes or barbed wire on top which is virtually unclimbable. A gate with upright bars is much harder to climb than one with horizontal bars. There is also right of access from private property to any adjoining public highway, except a motorway. The National Parks and Access to the Countryside Act, 1949, allows local planning authorities to negotiate access to open country, foreshore, rivers and woodlands. (See also *Boundaries*, *Rights of Way*, *Footpaths* and *Trespass*.)

Acres Now legally a thing of the past, the acre has gone metric. Nevertheless, the use of the acre as the unit of land measurement is ingrained among country people, and all except the very newest deeds and maps are marked in acres. In the United States the acre continues to be the standard of measurement. The British and American standard acre is 43,560 sq ft or 4,840 sq yd, in any shape. It is possible to judge by eye the approximate acreage of smaller fields; very big fields being hard to judge. A soccer pitch is $1\frac{3}{4}$ acres, so, by eye, fit soccer pitches into your field and work it out from that.

The acre has always been a somewhat variable measurement in different parts of the British Isles, so make sure when dealing with locals that you are both talking about the same standard acre. For instance, in western Ireland the standard acre is about $1\frac{3}{5}$ of the English standard acre. (See also *Hectare*.)

Adders See *Snakes*.

Adult Education Centres Throughout the country these run excellent courses in every subject and craft under the sun. The year starts in September as at school, and a prospectus of courses may be found in your local library or local paper. The popular courses become fully booked very quickly, so do not waste time once they are announced.

Agas See *Solid-fuel Stoves*.

Agricultural Advisory Services The Agricultural Development and Advisory Service maintains central and regional offices in each county (see Yellow Pages) and employs officers to advise on all aspects of horticulture and agriculture. They will help with problems large and small and are the first people to consult before starting any agricultural or horticultural project of which you have no prior experience, or if you run into difficulties with crops or stock.

Agricultural Shows Agricultural shows are held at national, regional, county and even market-town level. Soaring costs have resulted in many smaller shows disappearing and in permanent showgrounds being set up for the major shows; the Royal Show has been held at Stoneleigh, near Kenilworth, for many years now. Agricultural shows provide opportunities for every imaginable facet of country life to be exhibited. There are competitive classes for all kinds of livestock, produce and crafts, educational and craft exhibits, and shops selling everything from combine harvesters to country clothes. The flower sections are always superb.

All the country organizations and clubs have tents where members can meet and refresh themselves; hospitality to customers

7

and others goes on round the clock, and when you tire of meeting your friends there are always sheepdog trials, show jumping, and parades of winning livestock going on in the rings.

Awards won at agricultural shows count for much among country people and standards are very high. At the regional and national shows, livestock breeders come from all over the world in search of high-class stock. Contact your County Agricultural Society (Yellow Pages) for schedules of classes and entry forms.

Algae *In Ponds* The thick green soup which appears in ponds is made up of single-celled green plants—algae—which thrive in sunlight. To clear a pond without adding chemical algicides, introduce water plants such as water lilies, with leaves that float on the surface. These shade out some sunlight and so help to clear the water. Duck weed quickly covers the whole surface of a pond, and algae does not thrive beneath it. The duck weed can be flushed off with a hose when the algae has gone, although the latter will soon return once the cover is removed. In fact algae does no harm to anything except the look of the water, and fish love it.

In Swimming Pools If the water is properly chlorinated algae should not be a problem, but chemical algicides can be bought from suppliers of swimming-pool chemicals.

On Stone Paving and Garden Seats Treat with deosan hypochloride. Simply add a teacupful of domestic chlorine to a watering can full of water, and sprinkle the area to be cleaned. After an hour brush hard with a yard broom and repeat the treatment in a day or two if necessary.

Further Reading: Building Research Establishment leaflet No 139, *Control of Lichens, Moulds and Similar Growths* (HMSO).

Ancient Lights Under the Prescription Act, a right to the use of light for a dwelling house or other building is obtained by the enjoyment of it for twenty years without interruption. Obstruction of light must be enough to constitute a nuisance if there is to be any chance of a successful action to obtain an injunction to abate that nuisance. The building of houses or other buildings where they could deprive a house of light, or crops (such as market-garden or greenhouse crops) of sufficient light could be enough to justify action. Check with your local planning officer. If he is not helpful, consult a solicitor.

Ancient Monuments An 'ancient monument' on your land, scheduled by the Ancient Monuments Act, could be anything from an earthwork to a watermill. Should it require repair or upkeep then there are various grants avail-

The Pharos at Dover is the oldest lighthouse in Britain. Tile courses every few feet are certain indication of Roman building

able. Annual acknowledgement payments are made by the Department of the Environment to help ensure the survival of easily destroyed field monuments, such as tumuli, which appear on the Register of Land charges.

Buildings scheduled as ancient monuments may be eligible for grants from the Historic Buildings Council, or from the local authorities under the LA (Historic Buildings) Act, 1962, or under Section 3 of the Ancient Monuments Act, 1931. The latter empowers local authorities to make grants even if they are not the owners of the property.

The Commissioners of Works are empowered to make regulations regarding access to, and the admission fees for, ancient monuments in their charge. They can also enter land (after giving fourteen days' notice) in order to inspect ancient monuments. But they may not enter houses or gardens, or dig without the owner's permission, or the permission of anyone else who may be affected by the digging.

The fact that access has been granted to visit or look at an ancient monument does *not* create a right of way, no matter for how long the access has been allowed. (See also *Grants* and *Historic Buildings*.)

Useful Addresses: Ancient Monuments Secretariat, Department of the Environment, Fortress House, 25 Savile Row, London W1X 2HE; The Society for the Protection of Ancient Buildings, 55 Great Ormond Street, London WC1N 3JA; Ancient Monuments Society, 33 Ladbroke Square, London W11; Historic Monuments Centre, 36 Parliament Street, London SW1.

Further Reading: Sectional List No 27, *Ancient Monuments and Historic Buildings* (HMSO).

Angling See *Fishing*.

Animals *Straying Animals* Since the Animals Act, 1971, came into effect, the rule is that when livestock stray onto someone else's land, the owner of the livestock is liable for any damage they cause.

If the livestock are detained, the owner is liable for any expense incurred, but notice must be given to the police and the owner (if known) within forty-eight hours. The right of detention ceases when compensation is offered for expenses or damage. If no one claims them after fourteen days, the livestock may be sold. The detainer may deduct from the proceeds any costs or expenses arising, but must look after the stock properly.

While there is no Common Law liability to erect fences, the owner of the livestock has a duty to keep them in and putting up fences is plainly the best way. Where a landowner has a contractual duty to maintain fences, then the owner of livestock kept in the field would not be liable for damage if his livestock strayed because the fences were not maintained.

The Act lays down that livestock straying from the highway, provided they are lawfully on the highway (in other words being moved along it), do not render their owners liable to damage or expenses arising out of their trespassing. But where negligence by those in charge of the livestock can be proved, the owner *is* liable. If the livestock stray from their own pastures, or from their owner's land, onto the highway, and then onto your land, the owner is liable because they were on the highway unlawfully. The Animals Act places the liability firmly on the owner of the livestock straying onto the highway and applies the ordinary rules of negligence, which must be proved. Owners of livestock should insure themselves against claims for damages.

One exception applies to livestock grazing lawfully on common or traditionally unfenced land. Obviously it would be unreasonable to expect owners of livestock in such circumstances to accept the same liabilities as those applying to livestock on enclosed land.

Attack by Animals The spread of safari and wild game parks throughout the United Kingdom has necessitated some tighter regulations which are also contained in the Animals Act. Dangerous species are defined as those not usually domesticated in the British Isles and which, when fully grown, require restraint. As a rule, the keepers of such animals are liable for damage.

Trespassers who enter and are injured by a dangerous animal—one of the specified species—cannot claim damage if the animal was not kept there for protective purposes, or, if it was, if it was not unreasonable to have kept it there for that purpose. Where an animal is not specified as coming from a dangerous species, but even so can be dangerous, its keeper would only be liable if he knew all along that it could cause severe damage unless restrained. For instance, bulls, horses and dogs can be dangerous and the owner's only defence would be to plead that the injured party was at fault, or that he did not know that his animal was dangerous.

An interesting point is that a guard dog may be held to be unreasonably employed as such if it was known by its keeper to be savage.

The keeper of a dog which damages livestock or kills them is liable for damages, as a rule. An exception is where the livestock were themselves trespassing on the dog's owner's land, or where the fault lies with the owner of the livestock. (See also *Guard Dogs, Licences, Rights of Way* and *Trespass*, and individual species and *Sheep Worrying*.)

Welfare Addresses: Blue Cross, 1 Hugh Street, London SW1 has a home for horses and donkeys at Northiam, Sussex; Animal Welfare Trust, 47 Whitehall Street, London SW1; RSPCA, The Manor House, Horsham, Sussex. Check under 'Animal Welfare Societies' in the Yellow Pages for local addresses.

Further Reading: Field Fisher, T. *Animals and the Law* (Oxford University Press).

Ants and Anthills Ants, indoors, are more of a nuisance than a danger, as they do not carry disease. They do invade kitchens and larders in search of food, especially sugar. They may also come indoors for drops of spilled moisture, and, once they get in, more and more follow and crawl all over the larder. A puff of insecticide dust in the crevices in door and window frames, through which they usually enter, will discourage them. Should ants be a real problem, follow them back to their nest, which will usually be under a paving stone, in a flower bed, or in a rockery. Pour petrol, boiling water or liquid derris into the opened up nest.

On the credit side, ants eat the larvae of fruit and house flies, and some caterpillars. Chinese orchardists value ants so much that they make little bamboo bridges for them to travel from tree to tree. Ants dislike certain plants, especially mint, tansy and pennyroyal, so plant these wherever ants enter your house.

Aphids (green fly) dislike spearmint, stinging nettles or nasturtiums, so these plants also discourage the ants who can find no aphids upon them. Ants literally farm and spread aphids for the honeydew which they excrete and build nests in the soil of flower beds, disturbing and sometimes killing plants by burrowing among their roots. In frames and greenhouses they feed on newly sewn seeds and swarm to eat ripe fruit.

Spread out large anthills and treat them with Murphy chlordane worm killer, which kills the ants but is also dangerous to domestic animals. No grazing animal should be allowed in the area for at least three weeks until there has been enough rain to wash the chemical into the soil. BHC powder or liquid may also be used according to makers' instructions, but not where food crops are to be grown, particularly roots.

The large red ants which live in woods can inflict a painful sting. Eradicate these as above.

Further Reading: Ministry of Agriculture leaflet AL 366, *Ants Indoors* (HMSO); Brian, M. V., *Ants* (Collins); Wragg, D., *The Ant World!* (Penguin).

Apiaries See *Bees*.

Apples See *Orchards*.

Arbitration Arbitration is commonly used to settle a difference between two parties about value. Insurance policies may contain arbitration clauses. Arbitrators may be called in to decide the value of certain assets when taking over a property. Arbitration may also be used to settle such things as boundary disputes. By written agreement between the parties the matter is submitted to an arbitrator whose decision both will accept as binding. At the same time an agreement is made about costs. If no such agreement is made, the arbitrator will decide how they shall be borne. He fixes his own fee. Anyone can act as an arbitrator provided both parties agree as above. There is an official panel of arbitrators and referees, all officers of the high court.

Useful Address: The Institute of Arbitrators, 10 Norfolk Street, London WC2. Write to the Clerk for information and guidance.

Architects An architect will do as much or as little as he is asked to do. He will draw up plans for buildings, conversions or additions according to your ideas, making suggestions based on his knowledge of materials, methods, costs and planning requirements. He will see plans through the local authority planning department, will arrange for builders and contractors, and will supervise the work. It depends entirely on your briefing.

In this country it is best if construction work is done in spring and summer, so always give your architect as long as possible to do his preliminary work. Three months is not excessive, especially as, when the architect's work is done, plans must be passed by local authorities and builders and contractors must be contacted and booked.

Ask your architect to tell you clearly, in writing, before starting, what his fees are.

Useful Address: Royal Institute of British Architects, 66 Portland Place, London W1N 4 AD. Check under 'Architects' in Yellow Pages for local names and addresses.

Associations' and Societies' addresses Addresses are listed under individual headings in the Yellow Pages of the telephone directory, eg, Animal Welfare contains RSPCA. Under Associations, Social, Cultural and General, there are many societies which do not fit in anywhere else.

Your local reference library has an up-to-date list of association addresses.

The addresses below are correct at the time of writing, but do change frequently.

Amalgamated Weavers Association, 74 Corporation Street, Manchester

Ancient Monuments Secretariat, Fortress House, 25 Savile Row, London W1X 2HE

Ancient Monuments Society, 33 Ladbroke Square, London W11

Association of British Tree Surgeons and Arborists, 11 Wings Road, Upper Hale, Farnham, Surrey

Association for the Preservation of Rural Scotland, 1 Thistle Court, Edinburgh EH2 1DE

Association of Weavers, Spinners and Dyers, Fivebays, 10 Stancliffe Avenue, Marford, Wrexham

Blue Cross, 1 Hugh Street, London SW1

British Beekeepers Association, 55 Chipstead Lane, Riverhead, Sevenoaks, Kent

British Butterfly Conservation Society, Tudor House, Quorn, Leics

British Deer Society, Riverside House, Heytesbury, Warminster

British Ecological Society, Monks Wood Experimental Station, Abbots Ripton, Cambridge PE17 2LS

11

Associations' and Societies' addresses

British Field Sports Society, 26 Caxton Street, London SW1H 0RG

British Ornithologists Union, Zoological Society of London, Regents Park, London NW1

British Rabbit Council, 7 Kirkgate, Newark, Peterborough

British Safety Council, 62/64 Chancellors Road, London S6

British Society of Dowsers, High Street, Eydon, Daventry, Northants

British Speliological Association, 4 Kingston Avenue, Acklam, Middlesborough, Cleveland TS7 6RS

British Waterways Board, Melbury House, Melbury Terrace, London NW1 6JX

British Wool Marketing Board, Kew Bridge House, Brentford, Middx

The Building Centre, 26 Store Street, London WC1

Central Association of Agricultural Valuers, Estate Office, New College, Oxford

Central Rights of Way Committee, Suite 4, 166 Shaftesbury Avenue, London WC2

Civic Trust, 17 Carlton House Terrace, London SW1Y 5AW

Commons, Open Spaces and Footpaths Preservation Society, 199 Shaftesbury Avenue, London WC2H 7RS

Council for Nature, Zoological Gardens, Regents Park, London NW1 4RY

Council for the Protection of Rural England, 4 Hobart Place, London SW1

Country Landowners Association, 16 Belgrave Square, London SW1

Countryside Commission, John Dower House, Crescent Place, Cheltenham, GL50 3RA

Countryside Commission for Scotland, Battleby, Redgorton, Perth, PH1 3EW

Crafts Advisory Committee, 12 Waterloo Place, London SW17

Department of the Environment, 2 Marsham Street, London, SW1P 3EB

Forestry Commission, 231 Corstorphine Road, Edinburgh EH12

The Heavy Horse Preservation Society, Old Rectory, Claypit Street, Whitchurch, Shropshire

Historic Buildings Council for England, 25 Savile Row, London W1X 2HE

Historic Monuments Centre, 36 Parliament Street, London SW1

Inland Waterways Association, 114 Regents Park Road, London NW1

Institute of Arbitrators, 10 Norfolk Street, London WC2

Institute of Biology, 41 Queensgate, London SW1

Institute of Landscape Architects, 66 Portman Place, London W1

International Gun Dog League, 1 Clarges Street, Piccadilly, London W1

Jacob's Sheep Society, St Leonards, Tring, Herts

Kennel Club, 1 Clarges Street, Piccadilly, London W1

Leather Institute, 82 Borough High Street, London SE1

Mammal Society of the British Isles, c/o Institute of Biology (see above)

Manorial Register, Historical Manuscripts Commission, Quality House, Quality Court, Chancery Lane, London WC2

Master Thatchers Association c/o G. E. Dunkley, 25 Little Lane, Yardley Hastings, Northants

Ministry of Agriculture, Fisheries and Food, Whitehall Place, London SW1

Mushroom Growers Association, Agriculture House, 23 Knightsbridge, London SW1

National Master Farriers and Blacksmiths Association, 674 Leeds Road, Lofthouse Gate, Wakefield

National Sheep Association, Groves, Tring, Herts

National Trust for Places of Historic Interest or Beauty, 42 Queen Annes Gate, London SW1H 9AS

National Trust for Scotland, 5 Charlotte Square, Edinburgh EH2 4DU

Nature Conservancy Council, 19 Belgrave Square, London SW1

Noise Abatement Society, 6 Old Bond Street, London W1

Norfolk Reed Growers Association, 15 Chaplefield East, Norwich

Ordnance Survey, Romsey Road, Maybush, Southampton

Pheasant Trust, Great Witchingham, Norwich

Poultry Club of Great Britain, 72 Springfield, Great Dunmow, Essex

Ramblers Association, 1/4 Crawford Mews, London W1H 1PT

Royal Archaeological Institute of Great Britain, c/o London Museum, Kensington Palace, London W8

Royal Institute of British Architects, 66 Portman Place, London W1N 4AD

Royal Institute of Chartered Surveyors, 29 Lincolns Inn Fields, London WC2

Royal Society For the Prevention of Cruelty to Animals—all local addresses under Animal Welfare in Yellow Pages.

Royal Society for the Protection of Birds, Sandy, Bedfordshire

Scottish Rights of Way Society, 32 Rutland Square, Edinburgh

Society for the Promotion of Nature Conservation, 2 The Green, Nettleham, Lincs LN2 2NR

Society for the Protection of Ancient Buildings, 55 Great Ormond Street, London WC1N 3JA

Swimming Pool and Allied Trades Association, 74 London Road, Croydon, Surrey

The Tree Council, Room 202, 17/19 Rochester Road, London SW1

The Wildfowlers Association of Great Britain and Ireland, 104 Watergate Street, Chester

Wildfowl Trust, New Grounds, Slimbridge, Glos

Attics Many old houses have floored-in attic spaces under the rafters. Later houses may have large unfloored attic spaces and some modern houses have usable attics. Access may be through a trap door. Fold-away attic

Open staircase to an attic room

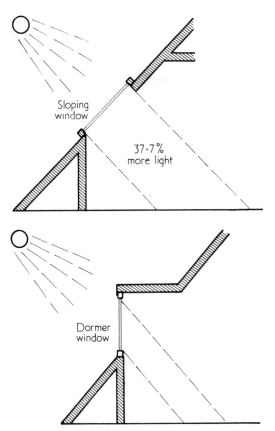
Fig 1

Sloping window

37·7% more light

Dormer window

13

Attic conversion with Velux sloping roof window

ladders can be bought but these are not suitable for everyday use. An architect or builder will tell you if a staircase can be put in, or even simple wooden steps. A trap door is unsafe, especially for children. Let in light by installing either dormer or sloping roof windows (Fig 1). Dormers let in less light, but give more headroom and a direct outlook. Sloping roof windows let in more light but allow little outlook, especially in a shallow pitched roof. Both can be fitted into any type of roof and complete kits can be bought. Fit ordinary windows into gable ends. To give enough light the window area should be at least 10 per cent of the floor area.

Get an architect, surveyor or builder to check that the timbers and walls will support the considerable extra weight of flooring. The joists of the ceiling below make a perfect bed

for the floor which can be of boards, butted together and nailed to the joists, or of sheets of chipboard nailed directly to the joists. Chipboard makes a good base floor for carpeting or vinyl or any other type of modern floor covering, or it can be sealed with a good proprietary sealer and left as it is. It may be difficult to get whole sheets of chipboard up to the top of the house, but timber merchants will cut them down into convenient sizes. Should an existing floor be too rough, surface it with sheet hardboard, butted and nailed into place.

Before resurfacing walls or the undersides of the roof, do any electrical wiring which may be necessary. Be sure that this is done to professional standards.

Again bearing in mind the problems of added weight, face up the underside of the roof and any walls. Do not use sheet polystyrene to insulate the roof as it adds considerably to fire risk. Glass fibre or mineral wool quilt is far better. The whole or part of the wall and ceiling surfaces may be panelled with very thin groove-and-tongue boarding, and this gives a good-looking and permanent finish which, after being well sealed with polyeurethane sealer, will normally never need decorating. It is easy to install, being cut to fit board by board and each board secretnailed into place over the rafters and wall timbers, or onto battens attached to masonry or brick walls.

Much cheaper, quite easy to install and with very good insulating properties is 'gyproc' paper-faced gypsum plaster board which comes in sheets. This can be cut to fit, using a sharp knife to score one side of the board (Figs 2 a and b). Nailed to the timbers or thistlebonded to masonry walls, with joins taped over and finished with plaster, it forms a perfect surface for modern decorative paints, papers or other wall coverings.

Build partitions to hide water tanks, but leave easy access. Chimneys passing through attic spaces should be carefully checked to see

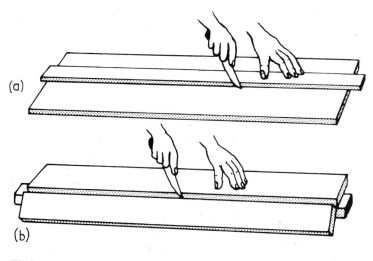

(a) Score the board deeply with a knife, using a straightedge

(b) Place a length of wood under the board. Press down sharply on the board which will snap. Cut through the paper backing with a knife.

Fig 2

that all pointing is perfect and that no smoke can enter the room.

Old timbers and beams can be cleaned up and left as decorative features of a room. In really old houses the attic beams are often of considerable interest as it is from these that an expert can best tell the date of construction. (See also *House Dating*.)

Useful Addresses: Loft Conversions—Crescourt Loft Conversions Ltd, Roebuck Lane, West Bromwich, West Midlands; Velux Sloping Roof Windows, Head Office, Helford Road, Glenrothes, East Fife KY7 49R.

Auctioneers All market towns have at least one firm of auctioneers who do a wide range of business from the local livestock market to the sale of farms and houses and their contents. There is a tendency for one particular firm to dominate each district, but there is nothing which says that you cannot employ an outside firm if you so wish. Auctioneers work on a commission basis and are governed by the code of practice laid down by their society.

In many towns, on market day, there will be what amounts to a junk auction. This is a very good way to get rid of all kinds of unsaleable rubbish, from old pots and pans to broken-down washing machines, antique tools and even heaps of scrap metal. Bargains abound. At the end of most farm sales of livestock and machinery, surplus furniture, tools and general odds and ends will be sold, and here too there are bargains to be found.

If you wish to sell your property or stock by auction, your auctioneer should give you the best advice as to time, place, etc. Auctioneers tend to specialize, so pick the right one for your purpose as he should know how to give your property its best chance. Be sure that any antique or unusual items are properly valued before the sale. A local auctioneer may not always have the specialist knowledge to do that, but should know someone who has. The better firms may charge you more, but will take matters entirely into their own hands, if you so wish, and attend to every detail including widespread advertising in the right places. (See also *Estate Agents*.)

Useful Address: Royal Institute of Chartered Surveyors, 29 Lincolns Inn Fields, London WC2.

Aviaries See *Birds*..

B

Badgers (*Meles meles*) Badgers are popular animals, except with gamekeepers, and many people enjoy badger-watching. The animal is almost entirely nocturnal, very shy and lives underground, usually in woodland, but sometimes on sea cliffs and other open places. It is common on mainland areas of the British Isles, but not in the north of Scotland. Badgers live in setts like large rabbit warrens, often in sandy banks, but the entrance holes are about a foot wide to accommodate the much larger animal. They use a nearby tree as a scratching post, and one way of deciding if a sett is occupied is to find the scratching tree and see if it has been used recently. The sensitive nose of a badger warns him of human presence and he will not come out of his sett if he is the slightest bit suspicious. Check the wind direction when still well away from the sett, by burning a twist of paper or lighting a cigarette to see which way the smoke goes. Approach the sett quietly from downwind. Settle out of sight and contain yourself in silence. Late June to early September, from dusk till dawn, are the best badger-watching times.

In the house badgers are boisterous and mischievous and they do not make good house pets. They become too trusting and cannot be returned to the wild as they are vulnerable to both human and animal predators. They are not easy to house train, and do not always get on with domestic dogs and cats. Hand-reared badgers all too often end up as inmates of zoos.

Badgers can bite very hard indeed and this also makes them unsuitable pets if they are to

Badger with one cub

come into contact with strangers or children. So have a care if you are brought an orphan cub to rear, and think of the problems ahead. Young badgers are most endearing creatures and heartbreak can be the end product.

Badgers are protected by law and the Badgers Act 1973 prohibits their indiscriminate killing, protects them against cruelty and forbids the use of steel tongs to extricate them from their setts. No one may take or kill badgers without a licence from the Ministry of Agriculture.

Badgers can be carriers of bovine TB and, should a colony be suspected of infecting cattle with TB, then one of them will be caught and tested, and, if positive, the whole colony will be destroyed. This whole process is carried out by Ministry of Agriculture officials and personnel. Landowners should not take action themselves but should contact their local animal health office. Any carcases found should be left *untouched* and the Ministry notified to enable them to carry out general tests for TB.

The recent rabies scare has highlighted the fact that, should the disease reach this country, badgers would inevitably become carriers and would probably have to be exterminated, along with most of our indigenous wild animals.

Further Reading: Forestry Commission leaflet No 68, *Badger Gates* (HMSO); Forestry Commission leaflet No 103, *Badgers in Woodland* (HMSO); Lewis, R., *Mister Badger* (Research Publishing); Ratcliffe, E. J., *Through the Badger Gate* (G. Bell & Son).

Barbed Wire See *Boundaries; Fencing.*

Barking Dogs See *Nuisances.*

Basket-making This is an easy and satisfying craft by which you can make all kinds of useful containers for garden and house.
Hard Basketry Made from any hard twig, one-year-old material without shoots which will

bend round your fist. Even brambles can be used provided the thorns are rubbed off with a handful of rags. Brambles, elm-bole shoots and peeled willow rods can be used immediately, but other twigs should be collected in the autumn and tied into bundles and left out in the open till they have become leathery. They must not dry out completely or they will become brittle, so the time outside rather depends on the weather. It may be anything from a month to three months.

Use bramble, clematis, dogwood, elm, honeysuckle, ivy, hazel, larch, lime, privet, rose, sloe, snowberry, broom, or willow, especially that cultivated specially for the purpose which can be bought from craft shops, or, if you live in the right area, at willow auctions.
Soft Basketry Made from rushes, reeds, sedges and thick grass. These must be cut in July or August and allowed to dry, but not to bleach, before being gathered into bundles and stored in a dry place. Before use, they must be damped down.
Tools A bodkin, in other words an old screwdriver sharpened to a point, garden secateurs, a Stanley knife, an old metal file on a handle to use as a 'rapping iron', a pair of round-nosed pliers and a measuring tape, a bradawl and some clothes pegs.

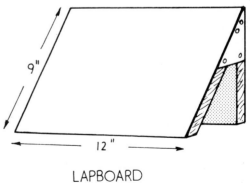

LAPBOARD

Fig 3

Make a lapboard out of two pieces of soft wood to which the basket can be pinned or

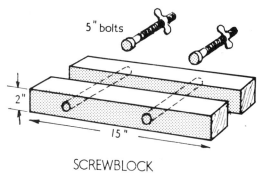

5" bolts

2"

15"

SCREWBLOCK

Fig 4

Three sleeping pipistrelles, our commonest bat

tied while working on sides and borders (Fig 3). An old flat iron makes a useful weight for holding the basket down while you work. Also make a screwblock for holding cane for square work (Fig 4).

It is best for a beginner to have some instruction from an expert, or a short course of classes, though if you are prepared to learn from your mistakes go it alone using a good book.

Materials from: W. Gadsby & Son (Burrowbridge) Ltd, Basket Works, Lyng Road, Bridgwater, Somerset. Check under 'Basket Suppliers' in Yellow Pages.

Further Reading: Dryad publishes a series of books about *Basketry*, *Rushwork*, etc; Wright, D., *Modern Basketry from the Start* (David & Charles); *Hedgerow Baskets*, WI leaflet; Maynard, B. *Basketry* (G. Bell & Son).

Bats Bats are nocturnal flying mammals, of which there are fourteen British species. All are insectivorous and do nothing but good. Bats do have ugly faces but are marvellously adapted creatures. The one thing that a bat will never do is get entangled in your hair, and yet this is a widespread belief. They are total masters of their own natural sound-location system and have instant reflex action to it. They are not blind, and their presence in belfries or anywhere else has nothing to do with stupidity. In fact bats are naturally cave dwellers, and use belfries, lofts and other dark and sheltered places as substitute homes.

There is no need to destroy bats and in fact they should be conserved because, due to residual insecticides, they are declining. The greater horseshoe bat and the mouse-eared bat are protected under the Conservation of Wild Creatures and Wild Plants Act, 1975.

If you must get rid of bats, wait until they are all out on a warm, late summer evening, *not* early summer when young may be left inside, and block up their entry holes. They just go away and roost elsewhere. If this is not feasible, smoke them out, using a bee smoker with corrugated paper, and puff it into all cracks and crevices.

It is a fact that bats will keep the timbers in their roosting area absolutely free of wood-boring beetles and insects of all kinds. This can be a major advantage in an old house where woodworm infestation is a problem.

Further Reading: *Focus on Bats*, from the

Society for the Promotion of Nature Conservation, 2 The Green, Nettleham, Lincoln LN2 2NR (with SAE); Yalden and Morris, *Lives of Bats* (David & Charles).

Beachcombing after high tide has scoured away the shingle

Beachcombing

> As I was walking by the ocean,
> To my surprise and my emotion,
> I found a message in a bottle,
> From a sailor on a South Sea Isle!

Unlikely, but where I live on the channel coast one frequently finds messages in bottles

thrown overboard from ferries by travelling schoolchildren. There is a fascination about beachcombing because it is the simplest form of treasure hunting. All you have to do is to walk along the high-tide lines, and from my childhood I must have scuffed through several hundred miles of dried seaweed, cuttle-fish bones, bits of plastic, tarry rope, electric light bulbs, old shoes (never in pairs), and rotting fruit. I have some green glass net-floats picked up on the Chesil Bank and a hard hat from an oil rig from North Norfolk. I have some fascinating pieces of distorted plastic. There is no better place to find sea-smoothed pieces of wood, both cut and natural. These things are there in plenty and nobody minds you taking them. I have also had large tins of paint, splendid baulks of timber, and once there were telegraph poles by the dozen, quite useless to me! And here the trouble starts, for in fact everything of any value belongs to someone else. If it has come from a wreck (and it is not a wreck so long as a man, a cat, or a dog survives upon it) the owner has a year and a day in which to lay claim to it. Otherwise it belongs to the Crown or to someone to whom the Crown has granted a 'franchise of wreck'. Technically therefore you should report to the coastguard or police everything of value that you find. If, in fact, what you have found is neither flotsam (goods floated away from a wreck), nor jetsam (deliberately thrown overboard), nor ligan (thrown over and marked with a buoy), it might be that it is Treasure Trove and covered by the laws relating to that. (See also *Treasure Trove*.)

Further Reading: Hickin, *Beachcombing for Beginners* (David & Charles); Soper, *Shell Book of Beachcombing* (David & Charles).

Beagling See *Dogs* and *Hunting*.

Beams Beams and other timbers which have been exposed by removing old plaster can be cleaned up and left exposed, and beams

already visible may need cleaning. First check that the timbers are sound. If there are a lot of worm holes and any evidence such as fresh wood dust or live woodworm, check to make sure that the timbers do not need renewing. Do this by digging here and there with the point of a strong penknife to discover if the timber is hard, or soft and cheesy. Or using a fine bit, drill into the timbers. If the beam has gone in the middle, after the bit has penetrated the first inch or so, which is usually hard, it will run in much more easily, and brown dust rather than curly greenish wood shavings will come out of the drill hole. Old timbers may have suffered badly from death watch beetle, which makes a much bigger hole than the ordinary woodworm, and be absolutely riddled and soft inside.

If on examination you find that beams and joists have shrunk apart, or cracked or rotted at the joins, then take expert advice on strengthening and replacement. A frequent danger point is where warped beams have pulled their mortices away from the joist tenons. Joist tenons must be firmly seated or the floors they carry may move or collapse. The most satisfactory way is usually to reinforce the beam on the inside with a piece of timber wide enough to reseat the joists. These pieces can be cut to fit the joists and then fixed to the beam with iron pins (Fig 5).

Should the timbers be sound enough and

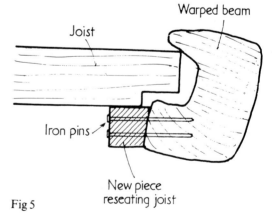

Fig 5

Joist

Warped beam

Iron pins

New piece
reseating joist

Finely curved Elizabethan lintel beam scarred with key marks where plaster was added later. A bricked up 'clomb' oven and Flemish mouldings on the lower sides of the joists above

attractive enough to be left uncovered, then clean them up with a wire brush. Pull out any old nails, and chip or cut away any soft spots. Use an electric drill, if possible, with a coarse sander disc to clean up bad spots. Do not remove old adze marks or try to reduce the surface to a totally smooth state; that would take away all the character from the beam.

Give all timbers a couple of coats of insecticide brushed well into all cracks and crevices. Then fill any cracks and holes with a good wood filler. Wood fillers for boats, etc, can be bought in different colours, or you can mix in a little stain to make a colour match if you intend to stain the beam.

Modern polyeurethane sealers, matt or sheen finish, can be used on timbers which are to be left unstained, or put on as a last coat over stain to protect it. To be really traditional use beeswax. Put half a pound of beeswax into an old saucepan, and melt it, add *pure* turpentine (not turps substitute) very carefully because this is an inflammable mixture, and stir until it has the consistency of thick custard. This mixture is then painted on to the wood with a rag and left to dry. Rub the dry polish to a semi-shiny finish. (See also *House Dating* and *Woodworm*.)

Further Reading: *Notes on the Repair and Preservation of Timber Work in Ancient Build-*ings, No LI (HMSO); Beedell, S., *Converting a Cottage* (Sphere); Edmunds, R., *Your Country Cottage* (David & Charles); Richardson, S. A., *Protecting Buildings* (David & Charles).

Beaters See *Shooting*.

Bees Beekeeping is a fascinating hobby which will certainly pay for itself. There are many books about beekeeping and beginners should buy one of these and take advice from

an established beekeeper. In fact, to help a beekeeper in all aspects of his work is the best possible way to learn and will help you to decide whether or not to go in for the quite expensive purchase of equipment and bees. Join your local beekeepers' association (the local library should know the address) from which you may be able to buy secondhand equipment and certainly a lot of knowledge.

The police have a 'swarm list' and if they are notified of a swarm they will contact a beekeeper on their list to go and collect it.

If you do react violently to bee stings then it is best not to keep bees for you will inevitably be stung. How much depends on a lot of things; the temper of your bees, the clothes you are wearing (white overalls are better than dark—cross bees will sting the black spots on a spotted dog and leave the white ones alone!). If your reaction is slight then stings are only an annoyance.

If you think your bees have foul brood disease notify the local divisional office of the Ministry of Agriculture immediately. They have a diagnosis service for adult bee diseases. If the disease is confirmed, destruction of the infected bees, combs and equipment will normally be required. In special cases it can be treated with an antibiotic by the Ministry's officer. All contact colonies must be similarly treated. (See also *Stings* and *Honey*.)

Useful Addresses: British Beekeepers Association, Owen Meyer, 55 Chipstead Lane, Riverhead, Sevenoaks, Kent; British National Honey Show, Hon Gen Sec M. Bond, 14 Southgate, Beaminster, Dorset.

Further Reading: *The British Bee Journal*, 46 Queen Street, Geddington, Kettering, Northants; Whitehead, S. B., *Honey Bees and Their Management* (Faber); Manley, *Beekeeping in Great Britain* (Faber); More, *The Bee Book* (David & Charles); HMSO publications No 9, *Beekeeping*; No 100, *Diseases of Bees*; No 206 *Swarming of Bees*; No 144, *Beehives*; AL 283, *Advice to Intending Beekeepers*;

AL 412, *Feeding Bees*, and many other booklets on: *Preparation of Liquid Honey*; *Mead and Mead Making* and *Wax for Show*, from the British National Honey Show (address above).

Beetles There are about 3,700 species of beetle in the British Isles and not one of them is dangerous to man, although several bite. The ladybird can give a little nip and the green blister beetle may emit a substance which causes little skin blisters. The devil's coach horse, with its fearsome two-horned head, can also deliver a painful bite. What most people call cockroaches (which are not beetles) are not cockroaches at all, but churchyard beetles. These live in cracks and crevices and come out at night to scavenge bits of food.

The wood-boring beetles (commonly known as woodworms, of which there are five species) do the most damage, both to furniture and house timbers.

Colorado beetles are extremely dangerous to certain crops. Others, such as ladybirds, are of the utmost value in controlling insect pests.

There is no point whatsoever in destroying harmless beetles which all have their places in a balanced ecology. If there are too many in your house, evict them. Destroy them with pesticides only when necessary. In the case of bad infestations, contact your local pest control officer through the local council. He will attend to things and, in most cases, his services are free. (See also *Colorado Beetle*, *Pests*; *Pesticides* and *Woodworm*.)

Bellringing A pastime enjoyed by its devotees, but not on the whole by the uninitiated general public for whom the changes being rung are a meaningless racket. To live near a church with an enthusiastic team of amateur bellringers can be torture. However, if it appeals to you, approach your local vicar, who will introduce you to whomever is in charge. You can't beat them, so join them!

Many women enjoy bellringing. There is much lore to do with 'campanology'.

Just as a matter of interest:

No of Bells	No of Changes Possible	Name
4	24	Singles
5	120	Doubles
6	720	Minor
7	5,040	Triples
8	40,320	Major
9	362,880	Caters
10	3,628,800	Royal
11	39,916,800	Cinques
12	479,001,600	Maxims

(which would take 74 years!)

These names are always preceded by the name of the method; thus on five bells the method known as 'Grandsire' could be 'Grandsire Doubles'; the same method on eleven bells would be 'Grandsire Cinques'. To ring an ambitious set of changes can take a

very long time and a lot of hard work and concentration, and lead to the consumption of a lot of beer!

Besoms To make a besom, which is an extremely good tool for brushing up dead leaves, you need: (1) an old broom handle, 1–1½yd (1–1.5m) long according to your height, or an ash, lime or hazel pole, the same size; (2) a bundle of birch twigs gathered in the autumn and left over the winter to season. Cut these from the crown of the tree so that they are nice and whippy. They should be between 24in and 1yd (600mm and 1m) long; (3) some thin strips of willow, hazel or oak for binding, or if you find it easier to handle, some pliable wire; (4) a 4in (100mm) wooden peg.

Arrange a good armful of twigs so that the longest ones are in the middle. Bounce the non-sweeping end of the bunch on the ground so that the twigs are knocked level. Then bind it tightly with willow strips or wire in two places. Put the first tie 6in (150mm) down from the level end of the bunch, and the second 4in (100mm) below that. Then point the handle at one end and pre-drill a $\frac{1}{3}$in (10mm) hole through it, 6in (150mm) from the pointed end. Force this handle right through the middle of the bound end of the bunch of twigs until it is beyond both sets of binding. Push

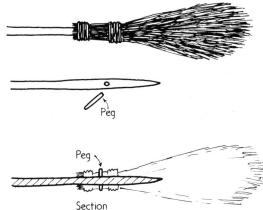

Fig 6

23

the peg through the twigs and through the hole (Fig 6).

Practice makes perfect!

Binoculars The figures on binoculars denote, first, the magnification factor, and, second, the size of the objective lens which controls the amount of light gathered. Thus 7 × 50 gives medium magnification but plenty of light, so such glasses would be useful in dull conditions, in woodland, or at dusk or dawn, as well as in normal daylight. At 8 × 40 there is more magnification with less, but reasonable, light-gathering power, enough for daylight conditions; 10 × 40 gives excellent magnification in reasonable light conditions, and 10 × 50 gives excellent magnification in all light conditions. For bird-watching high magnification is important, but the more powerful, the more expensive, especially if the glasses are to be compact and light.

Expensive glasses have better quality lenses, give brighter and clearer images, and are probably less likely to let in rain. Definitely, as with all optical instruments, you get what you pay for. If you do buy a pair of 7 × 50s in the lower price ranges, be selective, the quality of the image can vary enormously. The writer has a pair of 7 × 50s which were very cheap but which, as general purpose glasses, give a clear and undistorted image.

Always buy binoculars with a centre focus-

ing wheel, and one separately focusing eye-piece. To focus, remove your spectacles if worn and shut the eye on the separately (Fig 7) focusing side. Focus the glasses for the other eye using the centre wheel, then shut that eye and open the other on the separate focus eyepiece and focus that without moving the centre wheel. Open both eyes and the focus should be perfect.

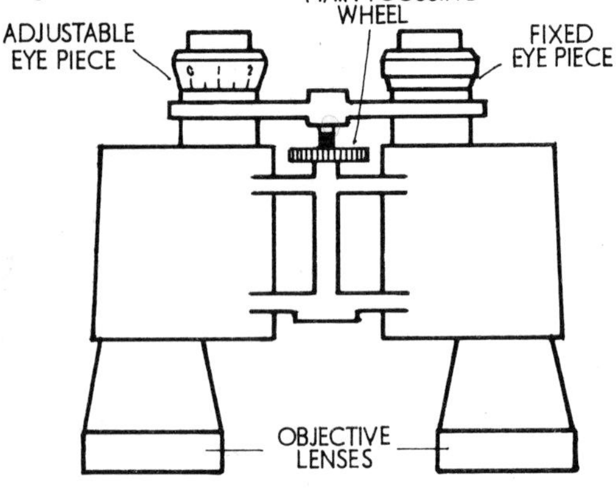

Birds *Attracting Birds to Your Garden* Encourage all the berry-bearing shrubs and trees to grow—yew, rowan, hawthorn, cotoneaster, berberis, spindle, dogwood, ivy, elder, guelder rose and honeysuckle. For seed, leave sunflowers, cornflowers, asters, scabious, evening primrose and antirrhinums, Michaelmas daisies, thistles, teasels, ragwort and nettles. Leave attractive nest sites—tumbledown walls, old sheds with broken panes and holes in them, and inside the sheds piles of odds and ends and suitable ledges

Fig 8

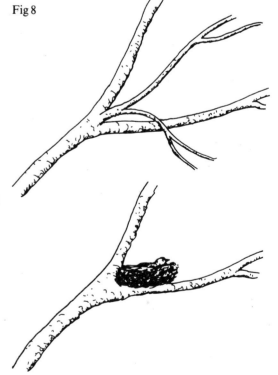

Fig 7

ADJUSTABLE EYE PIECE

MAIN FOCUSING WHEEL

FIXED EYE PIECE

OBJECTIVE LENSES

Mistle thrush

Bird Baths Ornamental bird baths should be at least 10in (300mm) wide and 2in (50mm) deep. Any shallow container will do. Be sure you keep the water topped up, bathing birds soon scatter it far and wide.

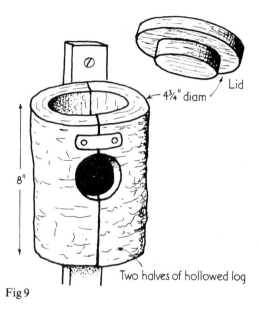

Lid

4¾" diam

8"

Two halves of hollowed log

Fig 9

where robins, wrens, blackbirds and others are likely to nest. Allow hedges and trees to thicken up, and cut or prune only in early spring or late autumn so that the nests remain undisturbed. With a pair of secateurs cut out twigs and small branches to make fork nest sites (Fig 8). Brambles and gorse attract small birds such as linnets and hedge sparrows. Reed or sedge attracts reed buntings and sedge warblers. These, and wild celery and millet, will grow in a mass by one corner of a garden pond. Hole nesters like decaying trees. Start a few holes with a brace and a big bit, and woodpeckers or nuthatches may take over. A pond should have a gently sloping edge where birds can drink or bathe and a little mud will be much appreciated by swallows and martins in a dry season.

Small holes in sheds, about 1in (30mm) in diameter, will encourage nesting tits, slightly bigger ones let swallows in. Some birds like to nest in creeper, and half a coconut, with a drain hole, pushed well in, might look interesting to a spotted flycatcher.

If you prefer thrushes to flowers and vegetables, then encourage snails by leaning the odd piece of wet plank against a damp, dark wall. Cats and neat tidy gardens are unattractive to nesting birds.

Nest Boxes An upright box with a hole no more than 1½in (40mm) in diameter (Fig 9) will be used by tits and other small birds, but not by sparrows, robins or larger species. See the table below for appropriate sizes for larger species. Many birds prefer open-plan homes (Fig 10). Even a shallow tray set up inside an old shed, under the roof, is favoured by many types, especially blackbirds.

Kestrels will use boxes mounted high on a building or tall pole, with a short pole above as a perch (Fig 11). Prime boxes to attract woodpeckers with dry sawdust and a few beetles and grubs (Fig 12).

Starlings and sparrows may take over nest boxes. They are ebullient, imitative and beautiful birds and not altogether to be despised. (Fig 13).

Always put a batten on the tree or post to which the nest box can be attached so that

Birds

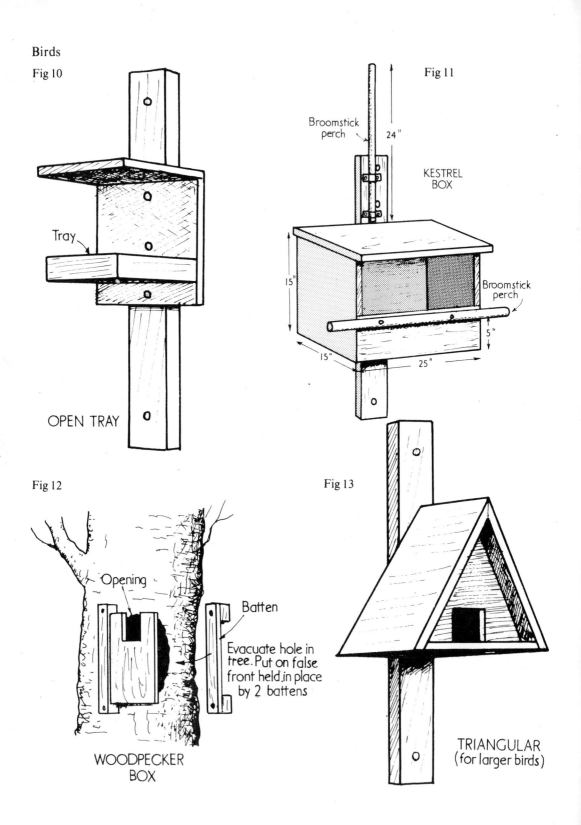

Fig 10

Tray

OPEN TRAY

Fig 11

Broomstick
perch

24"

KESTREL
BOX

Broomstick
perch

15"

15"

5"

25"

Fig 12

Opening

Batten

Evacuate hole in
tree. Put on false
front held in place
by 2 battens

WOODPECKER
BOX

Fig 13

TRIANGULAR
(for larger birds)

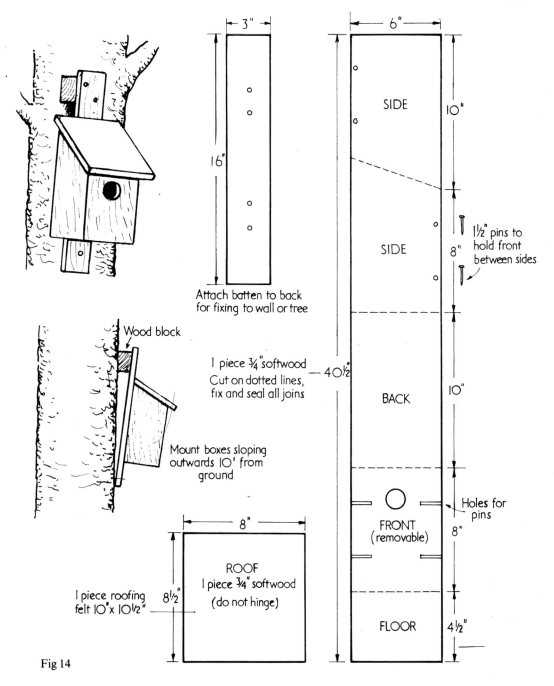

3"

16"

Attach batten to back
for fixing to wall or tree

Wood block

1 piece ¾" softwood
Cut on dotted lines,
fix and seal all joins

Mount boxes sloping
outwards 10' from
ground

8"

ROOF
1 piece ¾" softwood
(do not hinge)

1 piece roofing
felt 10" x 10½"

8½"

6"

SIDE

10"

SIDE

8"

1½" pins to
hold front
between sides

BACK

10"

— 40½"

FRONT
(removable)

Holes for
pins

8"

FLOOR

4½"

Fig 14

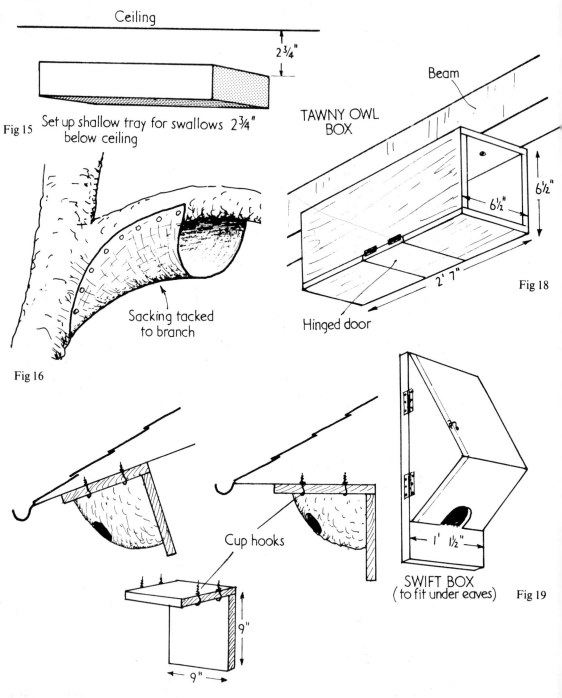

Ceiling

2¾"

Fig 15 Set up shallow tray for swallows 2¾"
below ceiling

Fig 16 Sacking tacked
to branch

TAWNY OWL
BOX

Beam

6½"

6½"

2' 7"

Hinged door

Fig 18

Cup hooks

9"

9"

SWIFT BOX
(to fit under eaves)

1' 1½"

Fig 19

Fig 17 Right angled boards for house
martins to build against

water will not hold up between tree and box. Position boxes firmly, not lower than 6ft (2m) from the ground, so that the entrances face away from the prevailing wind, and in the arc from north through east to south east, sloping slightly outwards from top to bottom (Fig 14) so that rain cannot enter. The adult bird must have a clear flight path to the entrance. Do not hinge the roof; fix it securely to the sides and seal the gaps with Sealastik. Make the box front removable for cleaning purposes. Nesting birds should be left alone and an opening lid invites disturbance. Always drill a small hole in the floor for ventilation and drainage. Cover the roof with roofing felt turned down over the edges (Figs 15, 16, 17, 18 and 19).

Put up boxes in autumn so that they weather in by the spring and can be used as roost and shelter boxes during the winter. Put in a little dry moss to encourage nesting, and hang up some straw, feathers (after treatment with bug powder), wool (cotton or sheep), string, dog, cat or horse hairs, in a dry place in little net bags (greengrocers use them for fruit). Under the bird table is as good as anywhere.

After the young birds have flown, clean the box and dust it with Coopers Poultry Aerosol to get rid of parasites. Put in some fresh moss and hope for a second brood!

Bird Tables Build the table out of the reach of cats, on a post or bracket, or hung from a tree. A roof is not essential but will protect special food from rain or snow (Fig 20).

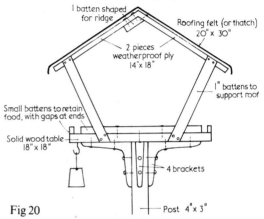

Fig 20

Titbells Any cup-shaped object in which small holes can be bored will do. Put a hole in the bottom for string and one at each side at the top for a hanging perch (Fig 21).

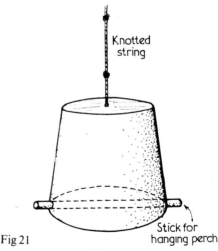

Fig 21

Feeding Birds Fill the cup with scraps and seed and pour hot liquid fat over it. When it has set, hang it upside down. Skewer peanuts, complete with shells, on a piece of wire, twist a curl over at the bottom to keep the nuts on

29

Nuthatch at a bird table

and another at the top to make a hanging ring. Collect rowan and elderberries and haws in late summer and autumn, store them spread out in a dry place, and put them out for the birds when really bad weather comes. The heads of weed seeds, thistle, teazle, ragwort and stinging nettles, hung up in muslin bags in the dry, will also keep well for midwinter feeding.

Make up 'bird pudding' from seeds, nuts, cheese, oatmeal, cake and bread scraps, rice, potato, etc, all mixed together in a bowl. Pour hot fat over it (any old waste dripping will do) and leave it to set. Put it out in chunks. As a guide, for each 1lb (500g) of scrap mixture, use ½lb (250g) of melted fat.

Birds will eat what they like and reject what they don't, but be a little careful with coconut. Never use shredded coconut, it is indigestible, and don't put up coconut halves in the nesting

season; young birds cannot digest it and it will kill them if fed to them by their parents.

Useful Address: The Royal Society for the Protection of Birds, The Lodge, Sandy, Bedfordshire will send you lists of nestboxes, bird tables, hoppers, etc, and will, on request, provide all kinds of information about birds, bird-watching, etc.

Further Reading: Soper, Tony, *The Bird Table Book* and *New Bird Table Book* (David & Charles).

Aviaries Except for the rearing of game birds and ornamental waterfowl, which will in due course be released to live wild, there can be no possible excuse for building aviaries in our bird-filled countryside. The keeping and breeding of tropical birds in aviaries is not within the scope of this book, neither is the breeding of budgerigars, canaries, etc. Pigeons and doves are dealt with under a separate heading. Very occasionally you may succeed in rearing damaged fledglings, or even in saving damaged adult birds, which cannot be released to take their chance (Fig 22). If you wish to build an aviary for these, choose a site facing south and protected from north winds. The side of a building is ideal. The aviary must be of a fair size, 4yd (3.5m) long by 2yd (1.75m) deep, 3yd (2.75m) high at the back slope, sloping to 2¾yd (2.5m) high at the front. Use 2in (50mm) deal quartering for the framework, ½in (12mm) wire netting for the mesh, and weather-boarding for a shelter at one end. Make the floor of concrete with a smoothly screeded surface for easy cleaning and disinfecting. Board in one end and 3ft (1m) of the front. Roof over half the roof area and cover it with roofing felt. Treat all timber with creosote or wood preservative before erecting. Include a wire-mesh door in the front framework. Perching branches may be put in when the job is finished, and nesting or shelter boxes put up inside the covered area. To shelter areas without excluding light, tack heavy-duty, clear polythene on the outside.

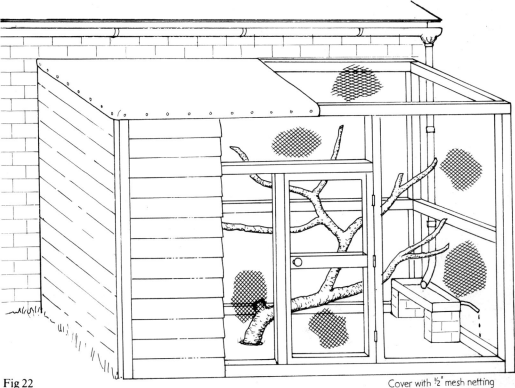

Fig 22   Cover with ½" mesh netting

If you have a suitable small shed or out-building, then it is only necessary to add a wire-mesh area to it with suitable access for the birds through a door or window, and outside access for yourself.

Further reading: Le Roi, D., *Budgerigars and Other Cage Birds* (Kaye & Ward, 'Pets of Today' series).

First Aid for Birds, Fledglings, etc The kindest thing to do to an obviously dying bird, or one severely oiled or damaged, is to kill it. Kill a large bird by wringing its neck, or by holding it by the legs and swinging the head hard against a brick wall. To kill smaller birds, press the thumb hard against the left side of the breast. This should stop the heart. It is unpleasant, but sometimes necessary.

Exhausted birds should be put in a place where they can rest without danger from cats,

dogs, or wild predators, with water and food, and released as soon as they have recovered. Deal with flesh wounds by gently mopping them with a little warm water and a drop or two of Dettol. Broken bones, if recently broken, can be splinted together using thin sticks (even cocktail sticks may do) and tape, but the bird will have to be kept safely and fed until the joint has mended. This may take some time and you should consult the nearest expert (the nearest ornithological society will tell you who he or she is). Providing the right food may present some problems, especially if you are dealing with waders or seabirds. Adult songbirds will survive on bird seed, insect eaters will do so on soaked brown bread for a few feeds. Birds of prey need chopped raw meat and roughage. Seabirds need pieces of raw fish and will probably have to be force fed to begin with.

31

Spotted woodpecker taking seeds and nuts from the hand

Fledglings are frequently picked up as abandoned when, in fact, they are nothing of the kind. If a fledgling has managed to flop out of its nest and fly a few yards, it must be strong and recently fed, and its parents will not be far away, however desolate the baby may seem. Leave it well alone, or return it to where it was found. Should you be stuck with one, you will need to feed it about ten times a day on 'soft-bill food' sold by pet shops, with a little egg yolk mashed into it. You must also catch small moths and flies and chop up some earthworms to balance the diet! Before long you will feel like the foster parent of a cuckoo!

Keep fledglings in an open-fronted box with 1in (30mm) wire netting across the front. If the old nest is available, put that in to make them feel at home, and fix the box firmly in a tree where it cannot be got at by cats. If the parents are still about, they may feed the fledglings through the wire.

Further Reading: Fitter, R. S. R., *Collins Guide to Bird Watching* (Collins); RSPCA pamphlet, *Oil Pollution of Sea and River Birds*; The British Trust for Ornithology, Tring, Herts, *Field Guide*; Tottenham, Katherine, *Bird Doctor*.

Keeping Away Predators It is easy to prevent cats climbing tree trunks by putting a wire netting collar round the trees. Cats climb by hanging on with their front claws and pushing with their back feet. If they have to let go up front, they fall off. To keep dogs away from low, or ground, nests, sprinkle a circle of fox repellent round them.

Foxes roam mostly at night, and an oil lamp hung in a tree, and moved occasionally to another site, helps to keep them off. Fox repellents may also keep them away from nests. Anything which looks like a trap, even a bit of metal tacked to a stick and put near a hole in a hedge, and frequently handled so that it smells of humans, deters them. Foxes

swim well and attack ornamental water fowl on islands in ponds and lakes. Ducks and members of the crow family are insatiably curious, and seem hypnotized by odd behaviour on the part of foxes. Foxes know this and act oddly to attract their prey. Beatrix Potter obviously knew this when she wrote *Jemima Puddleduck*.

Grey squirrels destroy nests and eat nestlings. There is no cure but shooting. Stoats and weasels, although they may destroy nests, keep so many other pests under control, rats, mice, etc, that on balance they do good and should not be destroyed. Badgers do no harm at all to birds. Rats do little damage, but field mice may destroy or take over the nests of small birds. Hedgehogs are insectivorous and do little damage to birds.

The magpie and jay are the only professional bird-egg hunters. Jays are shy and usually restricted to woodlands, but magpies can be thorough pests. It may seem harsh, but do destroy any magpie nests you find, prefer-

Nesting swans taken from 50ft (15.24m) away with a long lens; even so the cob was getting very aggressive

ably in April before the birds are hatched out. This keeps the population within limits. There is no danger of it being reduced too much.

Sparrows and starlings monopolize food supplies and nesting sites wherever attempts are being made to encourage other species. Put wire over drainpipes which sparrows love, destroy eggs and nests. They are the most numerous species in the world, so don't worry about doing this. The same applies to starlings; however much you discourage them, there will always be plenty around.

Owls and hawks do little damage to other birds in relation to that done by magpies, cats, etc, and should *not* be regarded as a menace. All species are less common than they were, and should therefore be encouraged, *never* destroyed.

Bird-Watching What may begin as just keeping an eye on what goes on in your garden and

Young cuckoo being fed by its tiny foster parent

around your home, may end up as a full-time hobby or job which could take you from Greenland to the Galapagos. There are hundreds of books about birds. To list them all here is really impossible.

Useful Addresses: The Royal Society for the Protection of Birds, Sandy, Bedfordshire; Nature Conservancy, 19 Belgrave Square, London SW1; The National Trust, 42 Queen Annes Gate, London SW1; The Wildfowl Trust, The New Grounds, Slimbridge, Glos; The Council for Nature, Zoological Gardens, Regents Park, London NW1 will send you current addresses of local natural history societies.

Further Reading: Fitter, R. S. R., *Collins Guide to Bird Watching* (Collins); Gooders, *The Bird-Watchers' Book* (David & Charles).

Photographing Birds The one essential for bird photographs is to get close enough; either by photographing from a hide, enticing birds near to a hidden camera in a house or outbuilding, or by using very long lenses.

A bird table or bath not more than 3yd (approx 3m) from a window should attract plenty of subjects. Birds like to perch near at hand before alighting on either, so provide a convenient natural perching twig with nothing behind it for several yards, and set up your camera focused on that. An open window, with curtains drawn across, makes a good 'hide'. Set the camera up on a tripod with the lens poking through the window, and the curtains held above and below it with bulldog clips or clothes pegs. A 135mm lens, or a zoom lens set at that, will give excellent results, bringing birds 3yd (approx 3m) away and nearer into close up. Set the aperture so that only the bird, not the background, is in sharp focus. Using a 135mm lens at about $2\frac{3}{4}$yd (2.5m) at f11 would be about right. Of course the exposure should be fast to freeze any slight movement. The faster the shutter speed the wider the aperture and the narrower the depth of field which will be in exact focus.

Most SLR cameras will only take electronic flash at $\frac{1}{60}$ of a second. This is slow, so movement may be blurred, also it means that apertures will be small if the subject is near the camera, and therefore the depth of field will be great and too much background detail may come up. By making sure that the subject is at least 3yd (approx 3m) from the camera, a wider aperture may be used (consult your flash tables) keeping the bird only in sharp focus. A camera which can synchronize flash pictures at fast shutter speeds is ideal for this work, as you can stay close to the subject, stop movement, use a big enough aperture to blur out the background, and still not overexpose.

The same principles apply when photographing from a hide. Erect your hide as near as possible to the subject, have a helper, and, when you have got into the hide, send him noisily away so that the bird, who cannot count, will think you have both gone.

To photograph birds at a distance, very long lenses and tripods to hold the apparatus still will be essential if pictures are to be successful. A 1,000mm lens can give wonderful results if properly used.

It is now illegal to disturb, by photography or otherwise, birds on or near a nest which are scheduled in Schedule I of the Protection of Birds Act (about fifty of the more rare birds) without a special licence from the Nature Conservancy Council. Although it is legal to photograph nesting birds of common species, even this should only be done by a really skilled photographer using the correct equipment—otherwise the birds may desert.

Further Reading: Beedell, S., *The Amateur's Guide to Leisure-Time Photography* (Bartholomew); Hoskings, E. and Newberry, C., *Bird Photography as a Hobby*; Warham, J., *Technique of Bird Photography*.

Tape Recording Birdsong The songs of birds are varied and individual. Mimics such as starlings can reproduce anything they hear, from squealing pigs to Siamese cats. Chaffinches have a basic song, and add to it by imitation as they grow from fledglings, thus developing and perpetuating a local chaffinch vocabulary or dialect. Therefore, after your preliminary efforts to get used to your equipment, set out to record the songs of specific species or types, or even the sounds of a particular habitat such as an estuary. Birds sing very fast and can understand themselves! Slow down your recorded song and a much more intelligible and often melodious sound comes out.

Mains tape recorders can be adapted with a vibrator convertor for use from car batteries using long cables, and excellent battery machines are available. The faster the tape runs the better the recording will be, but running costs and capital expense will be greater. Best speed is probably 15in (381mm) per second, but half that, $7\frac{1}{2}$in (190mm) per second, is adequate for most work. Swiss-made Nagra 1ll, the Fi-cord, also Swiss, or the German Uher 400 are the best, but the most expensive, portable recorders.

The human hearing system is stereophonic and can therefore pinpoint direction and distance of sound. The tape recorder with a standard microphone cannot do this, it just picks up a jumble of every sound within its range. It is sometimes possible to hang an ordinary mike on a long cable beside a nest, but you will certainly need something better than this. A parabolic reflector is the answer. This collects sounds at up to forty times the distance of an ordinary microphone. It is set up facing the sound to be recorded, and the microphone is attached centrally, facing inwards, to pick up and transmit all the reflected sound (Fig 23). To make true stereophonic recordings, set up another parabolic reflector and mike, a few feet to one side of the first. Practise to find the best positions. Grampian make suitable parabolic reflectors. The type of hand-held directional microphone, used by the BBC for outside broadcasts such as golf matches, is also suitable but very expensive. It is a cigar-shaped object of wire mesh with a pistol grip, and is capable of picking up and isolating low

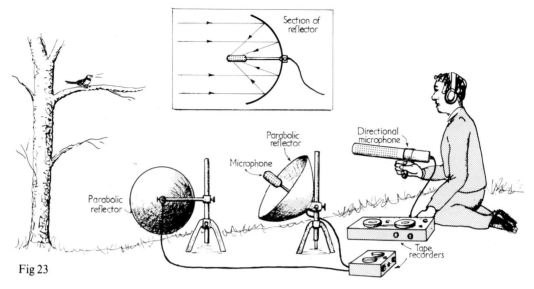

Fig 23

volume sounds at considerable distances from the operator.

When recording, always wear headphones plugged into the loudspeaker output socket of the recorder so that you can hear what is actually being recorded.

There is endless scope here for a marvellous hobby which will take you into the heart of the life of the countryside.

Further Reading: Simms, Eric, *Voices of the Wild* (Putnam)

The Law and Bird Protection Birds, other than game birds for which there are special laws (see page 124), are protected by the Protection of Birds Acts. These Acts protect wild birds, their nests and eggs at all times, with certain exceptions. It is an offence for any person to kill, injure or destroy the nest of any wild bird while the nest is in use, or to take or destroy the egg of a wild bird, or to disturb a bird while it is on or near a nest containing eggs or unflown young.

Licences may be issued to take or kill birds for scientific, educational, or other purposes. Certain harmful birds can be killed at any time; their eggs may be destroyed by 'authorized persons'. This includes owners and occupiers acting on land in their occupation. This list includes woodpigeons, carrion crows and others, but may be altered by the Home Secretary at any time. So check with your local police station before you start killing any birds.

The close season for wildfowl usually extends from 1 February to 31 August.

Egg stealing can be punished with fines up to £25, even from so-called deserted nests, and wild birds' eggs, even blown ones, must not be sold. It is legal to sell some gulls' eggs for eating, or for feeding certain types of poultry, and to sell the eggs of wild ducks, geese, or swans if they are intended for hatching.

Certain methods of killing or catching birds are illegal: most sorts of traps, poisoned or drugged bait, explosives, birdlime, nets, live bird decoys, certain large-bore shotguns, gas or electrical devices to frighten birds. It is also illegal to ring birds unless you have a licence. Check this with the British Trust for Ornithology.

The Acts apply to England, Wales and Scotland. Separate legislation is in operation in Northern Ireland and the Irish Republic.

Without reprinting the Acts in their entirety it is impossible to give full information here. Think in terms of a blanket protection, with some exceptions for harmful species. The full schedules and details may be found in *Stones Justices Guide* in your local library.

As it is against the law to take birds' eggs, there is little to be said on this subject. However, observing nests is part of bird-watching and identification can be made by noting the size, colour and shape of eggs and checking with any good bird book. But please *do not handle the eggs at all*. (See also *Ducks*, *Geese*, *Pigeons* and *Poultry*.)

Further Reading: The Royal Society for the Protection of Birds leaflet, *Wild Birds and the Law*.

Blackberries See *Fruit*.

Blacksmiths See *Wrought Iron*.

Blueberries See *Fruit*.

Bonfires Never build bonfires where the flames could set light to hedges, fences, buildings, or run through dried grass or weeds. The sideways reach and heat from a good fire in a breeze is surprising, and bits of smouldering ash and sparks may blow a long way. A bonfire can get out of control very quickly, water is rarely available on the spot, and it may be too hot to beat out. Never light a fire upwind of buildings or anything inflammable, nor when smoke can blow into houses, or all over the neighbour's washing. Never leave a bonfire to burn without frequent attention, or at night. A fire may appear to be out, but can flare up hours later as material dries out. Build fires in a special bonfire area, preferably with low brick walls on three sides, or a wire cage, or even an old dustbin with holes in the sides. Spread the ashes on garden soil in thin layers as they are a source of valuable potash.

Legally, if you allow the escape of fire from a bonfire so that it causes damage to another's property, you are liable and even though he makes a claim on his insurance company, they will in turn claim against you. If a neighbour continually burns rubbish where it constitutes a nuisance, you could apply to the county court judge to make a Declaratory Judgment and thus get the nuisance abated. However such cases are expensive, so just be careful with your own fires, and your neighbours will reciprocate.

To build a bonfire, make a centre of inflammable material such as old newspapers, wood shavings, dried grass or straw, under a wigwam of dry twigs. Gradually increase the size of the twigs, leaving a tunnel at the bottom for air to get in on the windward side, but be sure that the higher layers are fairly closely built. Put waste oil on the fire before lighting it, but don't chuck paraffin onto a lighted fire as it may blow back at you. Petrol should never be brought anywhere near bonfires. The secret is to get a good hot fire going and add to it continually. If you have a lot of weeds or green plants to burn, wait till the fire is dying down a bit and stack them all over the top, making a fairly close pile. This will dry out and eventually flare up and burn. Revisit such a bonfire every half hour or so to pile it all up into the middle again. (See also *Safety* and *Fires*.)

Boots and Wellingtons Always remove dirt

Using a boot beetle

37

and mud from boots and shoes, and if they are wet, stand them to dry out naturally in a warm airy place, but *not* right on top of a stove or radiator. Special bags of crystals which absorb moisture can be bought to put inside boots or wellingtons and these help to keep the insides dry. These bags must then be dried out, *not* in a gas oven, for re-use. Scrunched up newspapers or tissues also help to dry out damp boots.

Always keep riding boots on their trees.

Treat outdoor boots occasionally with a good application of dubbin, allow it to soak in well, and then polish them with ordinary polish or cream. This feeds the leather and helps to keep it supple and waterproof. Very effective silicone aerosol sprays can also be bought which help to make boots water-repellent, but remember that silicone does not feed the leather in any way, and therefore every so often they should be cleaned off and given a feed of dubbin or any good leather oil or cream, if they are to last for years, which they will do if properly looked after.

To mend a hole in an otherwise good wellington boot, use a self-vulcanating rubber-tyre patch from a puncture kit put on with Woolworth's magic rubber. Put a coat of adhesive on the boot, leave it till tacky, and then press the patch on firmly.

Keeping feet warm inside wellingtons is a matter of wearing loose woolly socks, special wellington socks and lambswool insoles. Wellingtons should always be bought a size too big, as tight boots, even over thick socks, make the feet cold. (See also *Leathercare*.)

Boundaries Refer any serious boundary dispute to a solicitor. There is no law which states that you have to fence your property or maintain its boundaries to keep anyone or anything out. But along public highways you must fence to keep your own livestock in.

Hedges and Ditches On ordnance maps the boundary lines are almost always taken to be the centre of the fences or hedges. This means that a ditch is normally part of the field on the ditch side of the hedge. However, because of the presumption that a man would dig a ditch on the very edge of his property and throw the spoil back on his own land, in the absence of a definite direction in the deeds it is assumed that the far side of the ditch from the hedge is the boundary, but this ancient presumption is only rarely brought into play, and normally the deeds do make a definite statement (Fig 24).

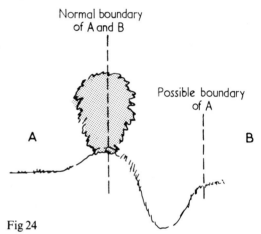

Fig 24

Hedge without a Ditch If both owners have kept the hedge trimmed then the boundary is in the middle: if one owner only has trimmed the hedge, then the far side away from him is the boundary (Figs 25 and 26).

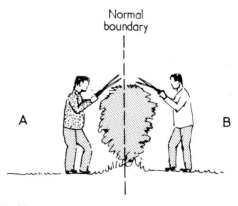

Fig 25

Fig 26

A's boundary

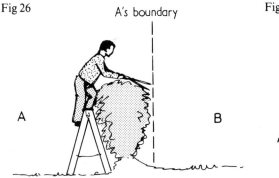

A
B

Post and Rails or Wire The posts are on the owner's side, so the boundary is on the side of the rails or wire, and upkeep is the responsibility of the owner of the posts (Fig 27).

Fig 27   A's boundary and fence

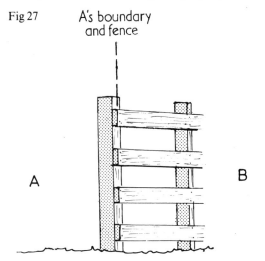

A
B

Walls The owner is the person who erected it, or his assignees. The outer surface away from his land is the boundary. Buttresses are usually on the owner's side because he will have been the one responsible for the upkeep and will have buttressed it on his side to support it. If a wall falls down and has to be demolished, the owner alone may decide with what to replace it, or whether to replace it at all. There is no onus on him to replace it for the benefit of a neighbour with either a like structure or a different one (Fig 28).

Fig 28

A's boundary and wall

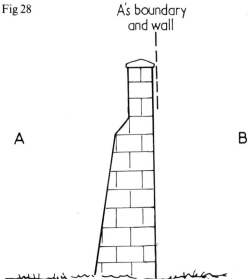

A
B

If a neighbour undermines or damages your wall or fence from his side, or if you wish to get at it from his side, you may not go into his property to repair it without permission.

He may not, by operations on his land, detract from the natural support of your wall so that is is endangered, but you have no legal right to keep him at any specified distance from it, and should he be causing damage the onus of proof to a court would be on you.

Watercourses Be they stream or ditches, on your land or along your boundaries, they must be kept in order.

Overhanging Trees This is a constant source of trouble. You only have a right to cut back

Fig 29

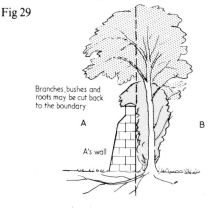

Branches, bushes and roots may be cut back to the boundary

A
B

A's wall

39

Bracken

branches and roots to the extent of your own boundaries (Fig 29). Your neighbour cannot prevent you from entering his land to cut back either roots or branches, provided you have given him notice of your intention to do so. Any branches you cut off do, however, belong to him. There is not, as is commonly believed, any time or way in which the right of branches to overhang the property of another can be established. (See also *Rights of Way* and *Riparian Rights*).

Further Reading: Evans, *Law for Gardens and Small Estates* (David & Charles); Fox, *Countryside and the Law* (David & Charles).

Bracken Eradication of this persistent plant can best be done by ploughing or rotavating. However this must be done thoroughly, and there will be regrowth until the plant is completely destroyed. If you have a rotary mower, then frequent cutting, combined with dressings of lime and fertilizers to encourage grass, will get rid of it in a grassy area.

Spraying with sulphuric acid when it first appears, and again if there is a second growth, should do the trick. But be careful to see that neither domestic nor wild animals, nor you yourself, come into contact with the acid. A dressing of sodium chlorate will also kill bracken and other growth where it is applied. This is an expensive weed killer, and can also kill or damage stock which ingest it.

Further Reading: Ministry of Agriculture leaflet No AL 190, *Bracken and Its Control* (HMSO).

Brass Rubbing There are many monumental brasses in our parish churches and the taking of copies of these by rubbing is very simple. First ask permission from the parson. There may be a fee to pay, and an appointment to make. From a good shop, buy a roll of architects' detail paper, ½in (12mm) wide masking tape (*not* Sellotape), a stick of black heelball, black acorn crayon, and a black crayon pencil

Dusting off. Note heel ball, masking tape, roll of paper and soft brush

Rubbing lightly, carefully keeping within the edges. Note the rivets in neck and hands, and scratch marks elsewhere

40

home and lay it out on a wooden table top. Then, working with a crayon and a crayon pencil, clean up any blemishes, scratches, etc, and darken the rubbing where necessary. With practice a very good clear image can be

The finished rubbing of the brass of Christina Phelyp in Herne Church, Kent. She was the wife of Henry VIII's goldsmith. The hand pose is an East Anglian convention indicating prayer. The white part of the cloak probably had an inset of some other metal, long since stolen

Rolling up

for finishing. You will also need a clean duster.

First dust the brass to remove all grit and dirt. Lay a sheet of paper over the brass, allowing plenty of spare top and bottom, and secure it in position with little tabs of masking tape. Press through the paper along the edges of the brass, making a slight crease. Then, holding the heelball firmly in your palm and fingers, begin carefully to rub across the paper inside the creases. The trick is not to go over the edges of the brass onto the stone, nor to rub so hard that the edges of the design are blurred, and yet to get a complete image of the brass. Once the whole brass has been transferred to the paper, roll it up carefully and replace any mats, pews, etc. Take the rubbing

Finishing off at home with Acorn crayons and crayon pencils

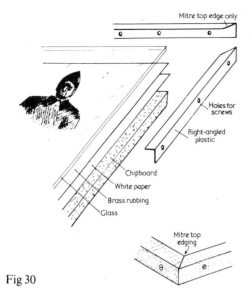

Mitre top edge only

Holes for screws

Right-angled plastic

Chipboard
White paper
Brass rubbing
Glass

Mitre top edging

Fig 30

made from most brasses. There is no way of removing mistakes in a rubbing except by painting them out with opaque white paint, and this always shows, so just try hard not to make any!

Finished rubbings may be hung on modern black plastic poster hangers, framed, or cut out and mounted on hessian or wall board with paperhanger's paste. A roller is essential to do a decent job of mounting. The size of frame to carry the weight of glass for big rubbings makes framing very expensive, but they can be made into panels. Use a piece of chipboard, with a layer of white paper on it, then the rubbing, then a sheet of glass. Screw right-angled black plastic to the side edges of the chipboard at 6in (150mm) intervals (Fig 30).

Further Reading: Beedell, S., *Brasses and Brass Rubbing* (Bartholomews); Cook, Malcolm, *Discovering Brasses* (Shire); Victoria & Albert Museum publication, 1968, *Brass Rubbings* (HMSO).

Bricks *Cleaning and Repointing* Clean plaster off old bricks with a stiff wire brush, or with a

hammer and chisel. To remove stains and blemishes, rub with a piece of brick of the same type. Builders' merchants sell special brick cleaners. Before repointing, chip out any damaged plaster. Use crushed brick to 'self colour' mortar. When repointing brickwork as a decorative indoor feature, do not use mortar which is too light in colour, and do not leave the pointing 'proud' above the surface. This gives altogether too hard an effect.

Bricks may be bought from builders' merchants, but, if you live anywhere near a brick works, look out for overbaked or second-quality bricks being sold off cheaply. These are excellent for garden walls, etc, and they do for rebuilding old fireplaces, chimney breasts and decorative work generally, as their colours are more interesting than those of best building bricks!

Further Reading: Beedell, S., *The Wall Handbook* (MacDonald).

Overdone repointed bricks

Bridleways The law imposes on the highway authority the duty of ensuring that every bridleway shall be maintained at a width of at least 8ft (2.5m), except that where a gate crosses a bridleway this need only be 5ft (1.5m) between the posts. This is not quite the same thing as saying that all bridleways must be 8ft (2.5m) wide, but nevertheless that is considered to be the correct minimum width.

The public has right of way on foot, horseback, or on bicycles, but not in cars or on motorbikes. (See also *Rights of Way* and *Footpaths*.)

Bulbs Bulb culture is fully covered in gardening books, but daffodil and narcissus bulbs planted at random in gardens, orchards, on banks and under trees, look splendid. Remember you will not be able to cut the grass with a lawn mower until they have died right back.

Just take a double handful of bulbs and scatter them gently on the ground. Then plant each bulb exactly where it has fallen. When the bulbs grow, the flowers will be in random spacing, an effect which is very difficult to achieve in any other way.

Further Reading: Doerflinger, *The Bulb Book* (David & Charles).

Bulls Contrary to general belief, the law does not regard a bull as a dangerous animal. It is classed with cows and sheep. There is no general law which says that you cannot run a bull in a field to which the public has access or right of way. But most counties have a byelaw which says: 'No person, being the occupier of a field or enclosure through which there is a public path, may permit any bull exceeding the age of twelve months to be at large.' In other words he *must* be tethered. Some counties (check this at your County Hall) also have a byelaw that this should not apply to any bull which is at large in any field or enclosure in which cows or heifers are also at large.

The liability created by the first byelaw is a criminal liability. The owner of a bull which has attacked someone can only be under a civil liability when the person injured can establish that the owner knew, or should have known, that the bull was dangerous.

Bulls are by their very nature unpredictable and dangerous. Even the best tempered animal can suddenly attack. Normally a bull running with heifers or cows is perfectly safe and quiet, but should you have a dog (on a lead of course) or even noisy children with you, be careful. As a general rule, keep away from bulls and always have an eye to the quickest way out of the field.

Cows, when freshly calved, are nervous and occasionally will attack anyone who goes too close. In general cows, heifers and bullocks are harmless although they may come rushing up and will follow you about, and sometimes are bold enough to push and nuzzle at you. A bit of arm or stick waving and general shooing will usually keep them at a distance. However, I have seen cattle attack a noisy dog which barked at them, and this might happen, especially if there were calves about.

Bulrushes (*Typha latifolia*) Apart from the use of big spikes in flower arrangements, and as habitat for some marsh birds, they can be a bit of a nuisance as they clog sluggish streams and ponds very quickly. The early shoots of the flower heads, as they first appear, can be cut, boiled and eaten with salt and butter, rather like sweet corn. Bulrushes must be pulled up or dug out, or, if in deeper water, cut below the surface. If this is done whenever they appear, it will eventually kill them off.

Butter If you have a house cow then some of the milk can be made into butter and cheese (see page 49). Small electric churns can be bought to do this job, but there is an art to butter making. Dairy equipment suppliers will send you leaflets and the publications listed overleaf will tell you all you need to know.

Peacock butterfly

Useful Addresses: Dairy Equipment Suppliers: Clares Carlton Ltd, 7 Winchester Avenue, Denny, Stirlingshire, Scotland, and Wells, Somerset BA5 1SQ.

Further Reading: Ministry of Agriculture leaflet No AL 437, *Farmhouse Butter Making* (HMSO); Street, L., and Singer, A., *Backyard Dairy Book* (Whole Earth Tools, Bottisham, Cambridgeshire).

Butterflies The butterfly population has been hit very hard by chemical insecticides, and by the general tidiness of our agriculture which has destroyed the weedy habitats of many species. While the caterpillars of some species (such as cabbage white) can occasionally be the most destructive and terrible pest, attaining almost the scale of a biblical plague, butterflies generally are to be encouraged for their sheer beauty. If you like butterflies, grow a buddleia tree, plenty of phlox, Sweet William, and Michaelmas daisies, and leave some areas of unsprayed weeds.

It is easy to breed butterflies provided you have the right plants for them. All that is necessary is a small breeding cage and some pupae. If you have a greenhouse the pupae can be hatched in that without using a cage. (See also *Moths*.)

Useful Addresses: The British Butterfly Conservation Society, Tudor House, Quorn, Leics; Hugh Newman, The Butterfly Farm Ltd, Bexley, Kent; Worldwide Butterflies, 21 Brighton Square, Brighton, Sussex; Thomson & Morgan, London Road, Ipswich, Suffolk—both these two supply pupae cages, advice and instructions on breeding butterflies.

Further Reading: Newman, L. Hugh, *Create a Butterfly Garden* (Cedar); Newman, L. Hugh, *Looking at Butterflies* (Collins); Higgins and Riley, *Butterflies of Britain and Europe* (Collins); Forestry Commission leaflet No 65, *Butterflies in Woodlands* (HMSO).

C

Calor Gas What we generally call 'calor gas'—butane and propane in heavy bottles or cylinders—can be used for any purpose for which mains gas is used, provided the proper adaptors and equipment are installed. The law requires that propane in cylinders may not be stored inside buildings, but butane in cylinders is absolutely safe indoors if properly used. The important factor is always to make sure that connection to a new cylinder is correctly and tightly made. Thousands of people use bottled gas domestically without any trouble, and it is the normal gas fuel of many caravan and boat owners. The occasional accidents are almost always due to misuse and not to faulty gear, and are no more common than accidents from mains gas supplies.

Your local suppliers have catalogues of all stoves, refrigerators, fires, lamps, etc.

Cookers using bottled gas take a little getting used to, for one has to learn the heat adjustment by experience.

There are small portable appliances of all kinds which run off throw-away cylinders—hand lamps with incandescent bulbs which give as much light as paraffin pressure lamps; blow torches which are much safer and easier to handle than the old-fashioned blowlamps; there are larger portable heaters which fit directly on top of a container bottle; single and multiple picnic and camping stoves of all sizes, and small refrigerators are available. (See also *Lighting*.)

Useful Address: Calor Gas Ltd, Calor House, Windsor Road, Slough SL1 2EG.

Camomile Lawns See *Herbs*.

Canals Our canals, so long abandoned, are not neglected any more, as it is now realized

The lock at Fort Augustus on the Caledonian canal

Canal in disuse, near Rye

that they can still provide a network of re-creational areas for fishing, boating, wildlife habitat, and a peaceful means of getting from one place to another. Many miles have been cleared and brought back into limited use, locks have been repaired, and pressure has been put on the appropriate authorities to keep them in order. The canal boat holiday has become very popular indeed, so quite a big industry with some lobbying power now exists. Should you have a canal running through your property, or wish to help either practically or financially with the work of canal clearance and maintenance, ask at

46

your local library, or find out if there is a canal society in your area, or contact: The Inland Waterways Association Ltd, 114 Regents Park Road, London NW1 8UQ, or British Waterways Board, Melbury House, Melbury Terrace, London NW1 6JX.

Further Reading: Burton, A., *The Canal Builders* (Eyre Methuen).

Caravans There is nothing to prevent you from storing or parking a modern or traditional caravan on your property provided it is not lived in. No type of caravan site, either for single vans, or for letting purposes, may be set up without planning permission for which

you must apply in the first instance to your local authority. The granting of permission, even for a single van, will depend on available facilities, mains water, electricity, drainage, etc, and on the amenity value of the site, the reactions of other local residents, and the general planning policies of the area.

Cats Cats are very self sufficient because they spend a lot of time outdoors and, by their nature, fend for themselves. There are some dangers in this. Firstly, unless you are breeding cats, in which case they must be restrained, all cats are best neutered. Males wander for miles after females, and females attract a host of suitors and produce litter after litter of ever-scruffier kittens. Both male and female cats should be neutered before they are six months old. The male is best done at about three months. The female operation is rather more serious and is done under a general anaesthetic, but the cat usually recovers very quickly indeed.

Other dangers to country cats are foxes which take the odd unwary animal at night; poison put out to catch other animals such as

Caravans permanently parked in an orchard, used as summerhouses

rats, and traps for rabbits, etc. The so-called 'humane trap', which closes round the body, is in fact far more lethal and damaging to cats than was the old-fashioned gin which rarely did more than bruise a leg; gamekeepers do not like cats who go after young pheasants.

Some town cats become definitely disorientated in the country and take time to settle down. They may find themselves on the territory of another cat, which can cause lots of fights and arguments. Give a cat new to the country plenty of food so he does not need to hunt, and plenty of love, and keep him at home for a while. Cats in the country will inevitably catch birds and animals, it is their nature, and there is nothing to be done about it, however distressing it may be. They also keep down rats, mice, shrews and voles.

Cats Up Trees and Poles The feline tendency to get up and refuse to come down causes a lot of trouble. They find poles difficult, but most cats will descend if left long enough, although kittens may not summon up the courage. Give them time; they will neither fall off, nor

47

Song catnapping

starve for a few hours. The only final answer, with or without a ladder, is to climb to the rescue. Wear a pair of thick gloves because frightened cats struggle fearfully.

Lost Cats Check first with any local trappers that they have visited their traps. Cats go after mice in grain-drying silos, so ask any neighbouring farmers who have these if they would please check. Your cat may have slipped in and be unable to get out. Always leave a baulk of timber floating in any big water tanks, cats can swim but cannot get out if the water level is low. Water butts should be covered for the same reason.

Report lost cats to the police, especially if you find one. Tell your local vet and the milkman, the postman, the newspaper boy, and the man who drives the milk collecting lorry. In fact tell everyone who travels round the district.

Breeding Cats The necessary cages will have

to be built, and at certain times the cats must be confined. Pedigree stud males usually have to be confined all the time, for they will wander and can also be extremely aggressive towards other domestic males.

Further Reading: Henderson and Coffey, *Cats and Cat Care: an International Encyclopaedia* (David & Charles); Loxton, *Caring for Your Cat* (David & Charles); Schneck and Norris, *Collins A to Z of Cat Care* (Collins).

Cattle Grids Should a trespasser break his ankle on your cattle grid, he would not be protected by law, but should a visiting friend do the same thing, he would be protected if it could be proved that the cattle grid was faulty, as there is a common duty of care towards persons lawfully on any land. There should always be a notice saying 'Warning—Cattle Grid'.

The point of a cattle grid is that it allows cars, tractors, etc, to pass without the necessity of stopping to open gates, while stock will not cross it because their feet go through the gaps. Cattle grids are frequently used where the public have a right of way across areas where stock is kept. The owner need not then worry about gates being left open and stock escaping. Once installed, they need little or no maintenance. There must always be a side gate which can be opened to allow hooved animals through when necessary. A plank across the middle jammed between two bars will allow hedgehogs, etc, to cross.

Cellars What better place than a dry cellar in which to store your homemade wine, to keep your enormous deep freeze, or to convert into a rumpus room or private disco for the kids. The key word is 'dry'. Old cellars being below ground level are rarely so, and ground water may be seeping in all over the place. Check thoroughly that no downpipes from the roof are emptying straight into the ground outside instead of into proper drains, and see that ground level concrete gutters are not

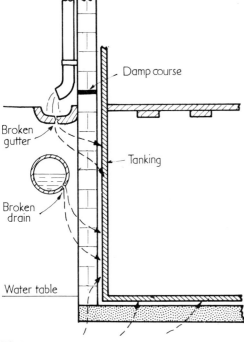

Fig 31

 Water table

cracked and are carrying water away properly (Fig 31). Check that no underground drains are broken and leaking—bright green dye is specially sold by builder's merchants for this purpose. Pour this into each sink or bath in the house and into each lavatory (one at a time), flush away, wait a while, and watch in the cellar to see what happens. Should colour appear then the faulty drain will have to be dug out and replaced.

Having done everything possible from outside, if the cellar is still damp then it can be 'tanked', in other words completely lined with bitumen, floors and walls. Heavy-duty polyeurethane might do the trick in mild cases, but you should take the advice of a builder. Tanking, if your house has no damp courses, or poor ones, may only result in the damp in the cellar walls rising up into the rest of the house.

If the cellar is bone dry, scrub the walls down thoroughly with a wire brush and clean

off all loose whitewash before putting on several coats of a modern wall paint. If any kind of wallboard, or panelling, is to be installed, then it will have to be 'battened out' and a good cavity left for an air flow to keep the walls dry.

Further Reading: Beedell, S., *The Wall Book* (MacDonald & Janes); Beedell, S., *Converting a Cottage* (Sphere Books); Department of the Environment *Guides to Good Building* (HMSO) No 21, and *Watertight Basements* Nos 51 and 52.

Cesspits See *Drains*.

Cheese Semi-hard, soft, acid cured, and cream cheese can be made at home with a minimum of equipment and you can produce some pretty good equivalents to Coulommier, Pont L'Eveque, and other named cheeses, and a whole variety of delicious cream cheeses.

Moulds for cheese making (wooden, tinned steel, or plastic) presses, thermometers, and all other equipment, starters, rennet and

Fig 32

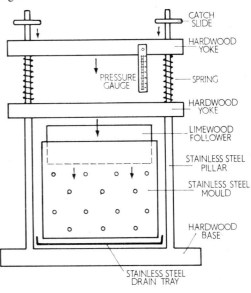

anatto may be bought from special suppliers (Fig 32).

Materials from: Clares (Wells) Ltd, Wells, Somerset (all equipment); Dairy Dept, Somerset Farm Institute, Cannington, Somerset (starters and rennet); W. H. Boddington & Co Ltd, Station Road, Horsmonden, Sussex (plastic cheese moulds); W. M. Godfrey & Partners, Brenchley, Kent (dairy equipment); County Farm Institute Dairy Departments (see phone directory).

Further Reading: Seymour, J. S., *Self Sufficiency* (Faber); Ministry of Agriculture leaflets, No 458 *Soft Cheese*, and No 222 *Cream Cheese* (HMSO); WI *Cheese* leaflet.

Cherries See *Fruit* and *Orchards*.

Chestnuts See *Nuts*.

Chickens See *Poultry*.

Chimneys See *Fireplaces*.

Cider Cider is the fermented juice of apples. Small sugar-and-tannin rich apples are grown specially for cider-making and are not much use for anything else. They are left to fall or are shaken from the trees, raked up into heaps and taken away to the cider-makers. If you have some of these, use them to make your own cider, although, actually, any apples can be used. Let them weather out of doors, spread out on racks' in the sun if possible. When they have shrivelled a little, but not begun to rot, they are ready for use. Discard brown or mouldy fruit. Beat and crush and chop the apples, and press the juice out of them. Wine-makers' suppliers sell small cider presses suitable for home use. When making only a small quantity, apples can be put through a mincer and the juice pressed out by squeezing the pulp inside a clean linen or hessian bag. Put the juice in fermentation jars, or larger containers, with air locks, and ferment

to a finish. If fermentation is not spontaneous after four days, then add a teaspoonful of dried yeast, started in a little of the very slightly warmed juice, with a teaspoonful of sugar. Add this to the juice in the fermentation jar. The cider will be dry. Bottle it and sweeten just before drinking by adding about ¼lb (113g) granulated sugar per gallon (4.5 litres), or a few teaspoonfuls per bottle. Drink shortly after sweetening, or the added sugar may start a fresh fermentation which might burst the bottles.

A light cider can be made just like other country wines by mincing apples into a bucket and covering them with boiling water. Mash this together for a couple of days, strain off the juice, add 2lb (908g) sugar and put into a fermentation jar. Add ½oz (14g) dried yeast, started in some of the warm juice. Ferment to a finish and bottle. To get a sparkling cider, rack off the liquid before fermentation has finished, and bottle it when clear, tying down the corks. (See also *Wine-making*.)

Useful Address: Loftus & Co Ltd, Charlotte Street, London (for materials).

Clay Pigeons See *Shooting*.

Clydesdales See *Farmhorses*.

Cob Nuts See *Nuts*.

Cockroaches There are nine species of cockroach living in Britain. The only ones you need bother about are those which settle in warm kitchens, such as the common cockroach (Fig 33), and cause damage by chewing food. Much more of a town than country pest, they can be eliminated by puffing insecticides into the crevices where they live. A really serious infestation would need the attention of the local authority's pest-control officer.

Further Reading: Ministry of Agriculture leaflet AL 383, *Cockroaches* (HMSO).

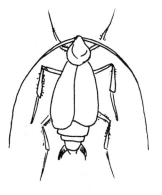

Fig 33

Colorado Beetle This beetle is ½in (12mm) long with black and yellow stripes longways, on its wing cases. The larvae are red with black spots and have black heads and legs and can be confused with the larvae of the ladybird. These larvae eat potato leaves and, as each female beetle lays up to 800 eggs at a time, the damage is colossal. So far we have been successful in keeping them out of Britain! There was an infestation in Kent in 1976, but it is hoped that it has been dealt with. Should you see anything resembling either the beetle or its larvae, kill it, put it in a safe container such as a screw-top pill bottle, and take it immediately to the nearest police station. This is the *law* (Fig 34).

Fig 34

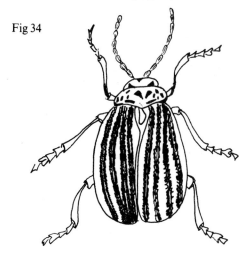

Common Land Contrary to popular belief the public does not own common land. All common land belongs to someone. This someone used to be the lord of the manor but is now usually a local authority in towns, or a private individual or company in the country. The public has legal access to common land within a borough or urban district for air or exercise, and in the country this is also now being accepted as usual. There is a right of access to National Trust commons and those where the owner has made a deed granting access, and to some large commons such as Epping Forest and many others covered by special acts of parliament.

Driving motor cars, lighting fires and camping are almost always forbidden.

However, local people have had rights since medieval times to take away or allow their animals to take away, by grazing, the products of the lord's waste land which was the original common. These rights still exist and there are six basic rights of common.

1 Common of pasture—which enables commoners to graze their animals.

2 Turbary—the right to extract peat or turf for fuel.

3 Estovers—the right to take small pieces of wood for fuel or fence repair.

4 Piscary—the right to take fish from lakes or streams.

5 Pannage (or Mast)—enables pig owners to graze their stock on fallen beech nuts or acorns.

6 Common in the Soil—the right to take stones, minerals and coal from common land.

Between 1750 and 1850 landowners enclosed vast tracts of common land for their own use, until, in the 1860s and 1870s, bills were passed to restrict further enclosures and maintain common land. In 1965 the Commons Registration Act was passed. All common lands are shown on maps kept by the county councils, with details of ownership and rights of access, set up as a result of the 1965 Commons Registration Act.

Compost

There are no commons in Scotland. (See also *Footpaths*.)

Compost To make compost it is no use just throwing all your vegetable waste into a heap. Compost is properly rotted down organic material from kitchen and garden, including leaf mould, and is best made in a bin (Fig 35), 4ft

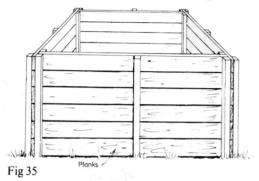

Fig 35   Planks

(1.22m) square. Use corner posts with slats of timber between, or plastic, or wire meshing; or you could buy a ready-made bin. First put in a 6in (150mm) layer of plant waste, lawn mowings, cabbage leaves, etc. Leave out diseased plants, weeds and tough grass such as ground elder and couch, and anything with really woody stems as it will not rot. Give it a good sprinkling of water and add a thin layer of straw. Then add a sprinkling of compost activator (from garden shops) and a thin layer of soil or bonfire ash if you have it. Repeat these layers until the heap is about 4ft (about 1m) high. After a couple of months, fork the whole thing over—ideally into another bin beside the first, putting the less rotted material into the middle. The heap will be quite hot inside, enough to kill weed seeds, and too much rain makes it soggy, so protect it with a polythene sheet in really wet weather. A compost heap made in autumn should be ready next spring. Fork it into the topsoil at the rate of one bucket per full square yard. When planting roses or deep-rooted bushes, fork some compost into the bottom of the hole to supply humus.

52

Further Reading: Shewell-Cooper, *Compost Gardening* (David & Charles).

Conservation *Listed Buildings* Under the Town and Country Planning Act, 1971, the Secretary of State for the Environment has a duty to compile a list of buildings of special historical or architectural interest. Most buildings built before 1700 and many built up to 1840 which are still in any sort of shape are listed. Later buildings must be good examples of architectural style, or good illustrations of planning or social history, or have technical innovations, group value, or association with well known characters or events.

Anyone may submit suggestions to the Chief Inspector of Historic Buildings, Department of the Environment, 25 Savile Row, London W1X 2HE.

Once a building is listed, demolition, alteration, or extension requires the consent of the local planning authority. If the local authority itself wishes to demolish listed buildings, it must obtain permission from the Secretary of State.

These are the basic requirements, but there are others to do with repair, damage, etc. If you need further information, check with your local amenity society if there is one, or with the Department of the Environment.

Conservation Areas Whole areas may be declared conservation areas by local planning authorities, or by the Secretary of State. The latter has this power in case local authorities themselves do not wish to frustrate their own redevelopment plans.

A local amenity society may work to get an area declared a conservation area through either channel. When this has been done, no building may be demolished without the consent of the appropriate authority.

Trees in conservation areas may not be lopped, felled or cut in any way without six weeks' notice being given to the local authority who must maintain a register open to public inspection. During that time it may be

An unusual job, returning an errant channel buoy to the sea

decided to impose a 'Tree Preservation Order' for long-term protection. Only a local authority can make a tree preservation order. (See also *Ancient Monuments*; *Grants*; *Historic Buildings* and *Trees*.)

Further Reading: *Ask* (Amenity Society Know-how) Ed David Fletcher, produced by Civic Trust for the North West, 56 Oxford Street, Manchester MI 6EU.

Contractors and Plant Hire It is possible to hire machinery, from wheelbarrows to bulldozers, with or without operators, to do almost any job from mixing concrete to sanding wood-block floors or cutting down trees, and your Yellow Pages will guide you.

When hiring machinery be sure to check exactly what it costs, whether or not the price includes delivery and collection, and whether or not it is covered for breakage while you are using it, or for damage caused by it if it is faulty. Get all this in writing if you can. When hiring a contractor and his own men and machinery, again be very sure that you know exactly what he is going to charge you, at what rate, and have it in writing. Especially

for small (by their standard) jobs, contractors are notoriously unreliable on keeping appointments. The trouble is they often get sidetracked on to other jobs which have conveniently cropped up nearer the place where the machinery is in use than your own establishment. There is little you can do about this except to keep on chasing the contractor.

Conversions Almost any building can be converted into a home, and almost any sound building is worth converting. The shapes imposed on rooms by oast houses, windmills and the like can be put to splendid use. Architects are used to being asked to design a home within such frameworks, incorporating the owner's ideas.

When considering the purchase of a building for conversion, check first of all with the local planning authority that there is no reason why you should be refused permission to convert. It could be that, all unknown to you, a new motorway or development is in the offing. Check next on the availity of mains services, water, telephone and electricity, or the possibility of well-water supplies. Have a surveyor check the building to make sure that it will stand conversion without the enormous

53

Converted oast house

expense of replacing worm-riddled timbers, etc; that, if it is stone or brick, it is not damp beyond the possibility of easy cure; that it will stand the strain of additional construction, roofing, etc. Check access and rights of way, both for yourself and other people. A public footpath right through your garden could turn out to be a nuisance!

Remember to insure your property as soon as you acquire it. Accidents such as fires can happen during conversion.

Before work can be begun, the local planning authority will want full plans and details of what you are going to do, and must approve them. (See also *Attics, Conservation* and *Home Improvement Grants*.)

Further Reading: Edmunds, R, *Your Country Cottage* (David & Charles); Beedell, S., *Converting a Cottage* (Sphere Books).

Corn Dollies The corn mother, mell baby,

kirn child, kirn doll, mell mother, Devonshire neks, Midland mares, Welsh hags and flags, harvest queens for Scotland, Bridget cross from Ireland, are all names for types of corn dollies associated with ancient pagan festivals centred round Ceres, the Earth Mother, goddess of all earth-grown things. Rituals involving corn dollies ensured that the corn spirit remained in the earth, or that the devils went off to your neighbours. Nowadays corn dolly-making is a decorative and satisfying craft for nimble fingers.

Made from freshly cut wheat stalks (rye, barley or oats are not so good), this has to be an autumn craft. Begin on the first Monday of August. Find a wheat field and cut a few

Converted watermill

54

Catherine's first corn dollie. Work with fairly green corn, which is not brittle. Pour boiling water over the finished dollie and hang it up to dry and it will turn to a nice pale blonde colour

First stages

straws just above the first knuckle down from the ear. Strip off the sheath, and then cut off some of the ears, with a slanting cut; retain some straws with ears.

To make a very simple NEK. Choose five good clean shining straws and tie them together in a uniform bundle, just below the ears, and weave these in rotation across each other, crossing the two adjacent straws each time with the last straw of the previous pair. To join in straws, cut the ends slanting and slide the new one into the old one.

Pack the inside of the dolly with odd pieces of straw, or even a wire if the shape has to be bent and stay bent. Fasten off ends neatly by tucking them away.

To keep straw to use later, prepare it, let it dry out and store it in a dry place. Before use, roll the straws up in a damp cloth and leave them for a few hours to become supple.

I made a complete mess of my first attempts at corn dollies, but my young daughter made really remarkable dollies with no instruction and no difficulty the very first time she tried.

Further Reading: Nott, M., *Corn Dollies*, WI leaflet; Sandford, L., and Davis, P., *Corn Dollies and How to Make them*, WI booklet.

Cottages (Tied) A tied cottage is one occupied by an employee who, in turn, is required to occupy that cottage as an essential condition of his employment, but he is not in fact an ordinary tenant. It is a service tenancy. Should you cease to employ him, he then becomes a statutory tenant, subject to the normal provisions of the Rent Act. If he will not relinquish his tenancy, and you need the cottage for an incoming worker, then the only way to get him out is to prove to the local authority that the incoming worker is going to suffer hardship if he cannot have the cottage. The onus is then on the local authority to rehouse the old tenant. Consult your solicitor with any problems.

By the same token, should you let a vacant tied cottage to an ordinary tenant, it ceases to be a tied cottage and the case is subject to the Rent Act. A vacant cottage, which has not been a tied cottage, becomes one if it is used to house an employee.

These arrangements do mean that both incoming and outgoing worker and employer have fair protection, and hardship can be avoided all round.

Couch Grass See *Weeds*.

Countryside Codes There are many so-called country codes, and all clubs and associations to do with the country produce them. All of them may be summed up very briefly indeed.

Do not behave anywhere in the country, however wild and unpopulated it may seem, as you would not behave in your neighbour's house and garden in town, or expect him to behave in yours.

The freedom of yourself and others to go where you will on private or public land depends not upon right, but upon lawful and considerate behaviour and control of your vehicles and animals.

Every inch of land, even under water, and everything man made or planted upon it, or reared on it or in it belongs to someone. Even those things which grow and live wild are widely protected by law. So damage nothing, uproot nothing, kill nothing.

Countryside Commission The Countryside Commission is responsible for countryside policy throughout England and Wales, and 'The conservation and enhancement of the natural beauty and amenity of the countryside and of open air recreation in the countryside.' (Countryside Act, 1968).

Address: John Dower House, Crescent Place, Cheltenham GL50 3RA.

Covenants Covenants often exist in respect of such things as drainage, provision of rights of way, restriction on usage of land, erection of fences, even provision of cottages, and it is as well to make sure when buying a property that these covenants will not one day let you in for a lot of expense, or prevent you from doing something you intended to do with, or on, your property. Covenants often exist for things which no longer apply, but, unfortunately, although you can if you like ignore them, they are still enforceable by law if somebody cares to try, unless the covenant has been discharged or modified. This can only be done by applying to the Lands Tribunal. Section 84 of the Law of Property Act, 1925, provides for the restriction or total discharge of covenants on the ground '. . . that by reason of changes in the character of the property or the neighbourhood . . . the restriction ought to be deemed obsolete, etc, etc'.

Consult a solicitor for full details. There is no way that any covenant may be discharged by mutual agreement; it must be by the full process of the law (and the expenses thereof!).

Cows (House) Unless you have previous milking experience do not buy an in-calf or freshly calved heifer (that is, with her first calf) because she will have to be trained to be milked, and if you are also a trainee the situation is impossible.

If you have previous experience, then a heifer is a best buy because she will not, with any luck, have anything wrong with her. If you buy a second (or third or fourth) calver, then she is being sold because her owner has a reason for parting with her. This could be that there is something wrong. She may have a damaged quarter; she may not produce much milk; she may be difficult to get in calf; she may be subject to mastitis; she may just not take to machine milking. As dairy farmers must only keep cows which are an economic proposition, a low yielder, or an older cow without any other faults may be on the market, and would do you well enough as a house cow where enormous quantitites of milk could only be an embarrassment. A

Jerseys are a good type of house cow

breeder with a high reputation, or a local farmer you know well and can trust, will probably do his best for you.

You must learn to milk by hand, and to try to do this on a freshly calved cow is asking for trouble. However, her udder could be damaged by not being milked out, so get someone who can milk to help you for the first week or two, until the agony has gone out of your hands and pins and needles no longer wake you in the night. If your cow has a calf at foot who is allowed to take his fill, the udder will be unevenly milked and twice a day the cow must be tied up and milked dry, so there may not be much left. It is therefore best to get rid of the calf and take all the milk yourself.

Although small milking machines can be bought, it is still necessary to know how to hand-milk to be able to milk a cow out properly.

There must be enough grazing available for

the cow all summer, fresh drinking water and a bit of shade, and for the winter a dry and draught-proof loose box where she will live almost all the time. You also need a shed for storing hay, straw and cattle cake, and the cost of these is considerable. In fact it is unlikely that your milk will come cheap.

The animal will come in season some time after calving, but need not be got in calf the first time, in fact the longer she is kept waiting, the longer she will milk. However, after about six months she should be got in calf. A call to your nearest artificial insemination centre will produce the necessary 'bull'. Normally cows indicate that they are in season by riding one another, but a lone cow will be restless, noisy, have a slight discharge from swollen hind parts, and her milk yield will drop temporarily.

An attractive Jersey with big brown eyes and a gentle disposition makes a wonderful house cow, producing plenty of very creamy milk. Dexters, small and high-yielding are also very popular as house cows. Kerrys also produce plenty of rich milk from poorish pastures.

Further Reading: Russell, Kenneth, *The Herdsman's Book*, (Farming Press (Books)); *The Farmer's Weekly* magazine and *The Farmer and Stockbreeder* contain plenty of breeders' advertisements.

Coypus (*Myocastor coypus*) These are outsize rodents up to 2½ft (762mm) long which always live near fresh water. Now established wild in Britain in Norfolk and Suffolk, they were originally farmed for their fur (nutria) and the progenitors escaped. They reached pest proportions and stringent trapping campaigns were launched to contain them in the Broads area. Unfortunately, the creatures break down river banks by burrowing and go into the fields to eat sugar beet. Their liking for the roots of reeds, rushes and sedges, has done a useful job in some parts of the Broads by keeping these encroaching weeds under control, but they take even this too far and reduce some areas to bare mud.

Efforts are now being made to exterminate the creature altogether and occupiers must by law inform the Ministry of Agriculture of any coypus at large on their land, and must try to trap and destroy them. The Ministry will help with advice and the loan of traps.

Further Reading: Ministry of Agriculture leaflet No AL 479, *Coypus* (HMSO).

Crab Apples See *Fruit*.

Cranberries See *Fruit*.

Crayfish Crayfish grow up to about 4in (100mm) long and live in hard-water rivers—those which flow from and through the chalk country of Britain. They like clean, well oxygenated water. Because they are all too easy to catch, they may be scarce in some places, but abound where the fishing is privately owned

or protected. By the way, it is an offence to take crayfish from private water without permission. Crayfish are nocturnal, spending the day beneath rocks and in burrows in the banks, but will respond to bait set near to them (Fig 36).

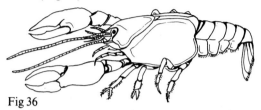

Fig 36

There are various ways to catch them, all involving baiting with raw liver or bad raw meat. A piece of meat or liver tied firmly to a string and dropped in the river close to the bank where you see the crayfish, will result in him grabbing the bait. Hoist him out. To catch them in numbers, tie a bunch of sticks, like pea sticks, into a bundle weighted in the middle with enough stones to hold it on the bottom, and push a lump or two of meat well into the sticks. Leave the bundle on the river bottom for a while; crayfish will crawl into it to get at the meat. Or make a flat net with a piece of wire or plastic netting on a metal hoop or frame (shape immaterial). Bait this in the middle, lower it on a string tied to a pole to a likely place in the river. After a quarter of an hour it should have crayfish clinging to it.

Repeat the fishing processes till you have all the crayfish you want. Drop them into boiling salted water, cook for ten minutes, drain, and, when quite cold, eat with mayonnaise and salad.

Cream-making Put fresh milk into a shallow pan or bowl and stand it in a cool place overnight. Skim off the cream with a saucer or a special skimmer from a dairy supplier (see *Cheese*). Heat it in a double saucepan to 180°F (82°C), and then stand the top half in another saucepan of cold water until the cream has cooled. Renew the cold water if the cream does not cool quickly enough. Pour it into a sealed jar and store it in the fridge.

Sour skimmed milk with a starter (see *Cheese*) and use it for bread- and scone-making.

To make Devonshire or clotted cream, set the milk till the cream has risen, then put the cream pan in another pan of water, bring the water to the boil and let it simmer gently for forty minutes. Remove the cream pan and put it in a cool place for sixteen to twenty-four hours. Skim off the cream and use it as soon as possible. It will keep for a few days in a sterile jar in the fridge.

True Devonshire cream is usually made by standing the cream pan at the cool end of a kitchen stove overnight. The very low heat cooks the cream to a very rich and buttery texture. If you have a solid fuel stove, then make your clotted cream this way. A little experimentation will teach you the exact temperature to aim at. (See also *Butter* and *Cheese*.)

Further Reading: HMSO Advisory leaflets, AL 495, *Cream* and AL 438, *Clotted Cream*.

Crickets (*Acheta domestica*) The rythmic 'plink plink' of the cricket is familiar to anyone who has lived in an old house with cellars where there were central-heating boilers. I lived somewhere where they used to come out and rasp away in full view, obviously enjoying the warmth. In the same house a turn-out of cupboards which contained hundreds of old magazines and papers in bundles, and where hot water pipes ran, resulted in dozens of crickets scattering in all directions. Yet to find a single chirping cricket can be quite impossible. The nearer you get to the sound, the harder it is to decide exactly where the noise is coming from. This member of the grasshopper family likes warm places and, having been ousted from houses by modern hygiene, can be found in rubbish dumps where fermentation is producing warmth. It is a harmless scavenger, but can be annoying, rubbing its wings together to produce that piercing noise. It can be eradicated with insecticide. (Fig 37).

Fig 37

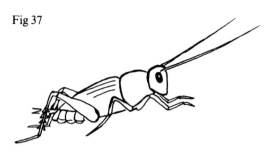

Crooks See *Walking Sticks*.

Crop Spraying See *Nuisances*.

Croquet A croquet lawn should be 28 × 35yd (26 × 32m), and the hoop and stick spacings should be 7yd (6m) in from both sides at the corners. A croquet set will have instructions with it. However, croquet can be played on a lawn of any shape, and almost any condition, just for fun. Croquet is a game which has had a revival of popularity lately, but to be played properly it does need a very good lawn, constantly tended (Fig 38).

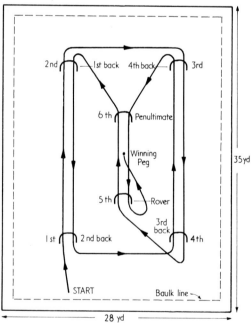

Fig 38

D

Damage by Cats and Dogs See *Nuisances* and *Sheep Worrying*.

Damp *Sources* Damp in buildings must be tackled at its source. Rising damp moves up through walls from ground level or below, because: a) there is no damp course; b) the damp course is bridged or broken; earth is heaped against the wall higher than the damp course, or rendering on the outer wall bridges the damp course, or rubble at the bottom of a cavity wall rises above the damp course; c) if the damp proof membrane in a floor is higher than that in the outside wall (Figs 39, 40, 41).

Treatment Remove the cause of the damp, replace or insert new damp courses, flue linings, etc, repair faults, and the walls will eventually dry out.

The replacement of damp coursing is usually done by specialist firms, and there are new developments in this field, although some local builders do tackle it. The Building Centre will supply names of specialist firms.

The use of silicone paints to waterproof wall surfaces is effective, but it will not of itself cure damp unless water is only entering through porous brick, stone or mortar. Silicone paints and sealers used indoors help to repel damp from outside, but do not cure it, and sooner or later the damp will get through and discolour the paper or wall.

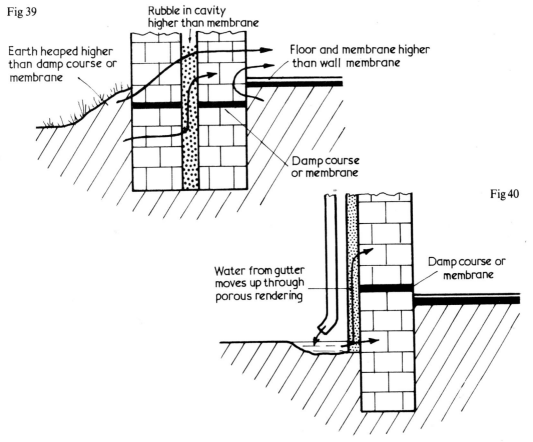

Fig 39

Rubble in cavity higher than membrane

Earth heaped higher than damp course or membrane

Floor and membrane higher than wall membrane

Damp course or membrane

Fig 40

Water from gutter moves up through porous rendering

Damp course or membrane

Damp

Fig 41

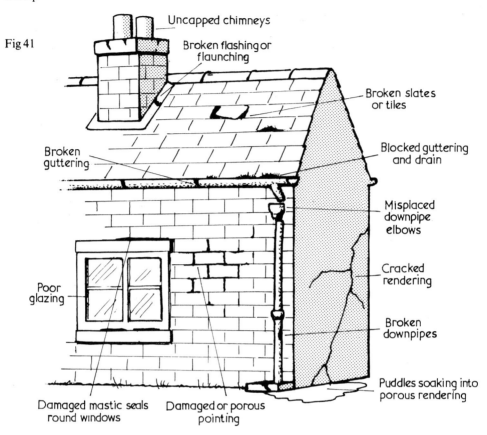

Uncapped chimneys

Broken flashing or flaunching

Broken slates or tiles

Blocked guttering and drain

Broken guttering

Misplaced downpipe elbows

Cracked rendering

Poor glazing

Broken downpipes

Puddles soaking into porous rendering

Damaged mastic seals round windows

Damaged or porous pointing

Interior walls may have to be resurfaced using either Gyproc plasterboarding, Newtonite lathing and plaster, or other types of panelling on battens. These methods create a cavity which ventilates the damp wall and allows it to dry out without discolouring the surface. They do *not* cure the damp at its source.

Useful Addresses: The Building Centre, 26 Store Street, London WC1.
Damp Proofing Contractors: Actane Services Dept, 49/51 High Street, Trumpington, Cambridge; British Knapen Gallway, 13 Elvaston Mews, London SW7; Peter Cox Group, Wandle Way, Mitcham, Surrey CR4 4NB. Dampakill, South Holmwood, Dorking, Surrey; MDC Group Services, 77 Wyle Cop, Shrewsbury; Midland Damp-coursing Co Ltd, 30 Fleet Street, London EC4; Raymond Ash & Co (Damp Proofing) 531 Hertford Road, Enfield, Middx; Rentokil, 945 London Road, Thornton Heath, Surrey CR4 6JE.

Further Reading: Beedell, S., *The Wall Book* (MacDonald & Janes); Department of the Environment Advisory leaflets, *Guides to Good Building*: No 10, *Dry Rot and Wet Rot*; No 23, *Damp Proof Courses*; No 47, *Dampness in Buildings*; No 58, *Inserting a Damp Proof Course*; No 61, *Condensation*; No 75, *Effloresence and Stains in Brickwork* (HMSO); Building Research Establishment digests: No 27, *Rising Damp in Walls*; No 54, *Damp Proofing Solid Floors*; No 77, *Damp Proof Courses*; No 110, *Condensation*.

Dams and Sluices When a stream becomes partially blocked by a jammed tree trunk, rubbish piles up behind it, the flow of water is slowed down and backs up the valley until it is level with the top of this natural dam. Unless there is a flood big enough to break down the dam, more and more rubbish collects behind it and the water deposits silt until the whole area becomes a marsh with semi-aquatic plants growing in the still water and gradually filling up the valley even more.

Use this natural sequence (as beavers do) to dam up small streams. Drive stakes across the bed of the stream and put some rocks against them in the stream bed, or attach a piece of wattle fencing on the upstream side. This allows some water through, but will gradually collect rubbish and make a natural dam which is not too much of an eyesore if it is kept tidy. Every so often the mud, which has collected at the bottom of the pond, must be cleaned out if the area is not to silt right up.

To dam a stream, make a diversion dam (Fig 42) and construct one half of the main dam (Fig 43).

Sluices may be of three types (Figs 44, 45 and 46), or consist merely of a plugged drainpipe (Fig 47) in the bottom of the dam.

Further Reading: Beedell, S., *Water in the Garden* (David & Charles).

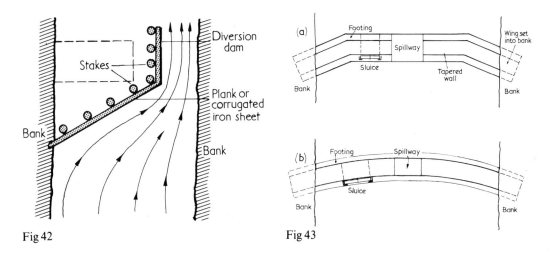

Fig 42

Fig 43

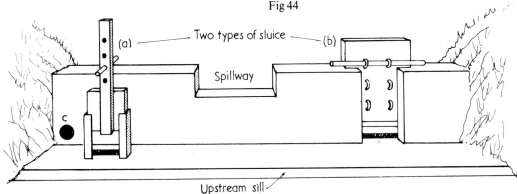

Fig 44

Gate with staples and bar
which rests on walls

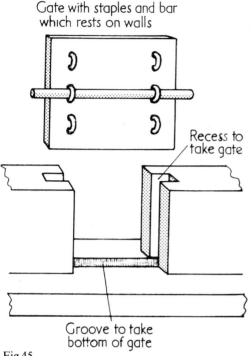

Recess to
take gate

Groove to take
bottom of gate

Fig 45

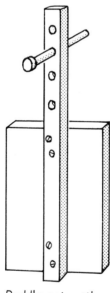

Paddle gate with
pin to rest across
wall

Fig 46

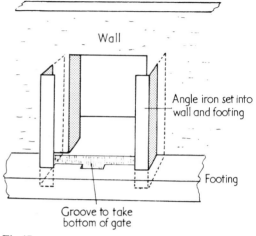

Wall

Angle iron set into
wall and footing

Footing

Groove to take
bottom of gate

Fig 47

Death Watch Beetle See *Woodworm*.

Deer *Types* Of the deer found in the UK, by far the most numerous are the two native species: the red deer and the roe deer. The fallow deer is a long-established alien, mostly on enclosed land. The sika and the tiny muntjac are Asian imports well established in the same habitats as roe deer. It is thought they originally escaped from private parks. There is a herd of reindeer in the Cairngorms. There are plenty of other deer in wildlife safari parks, established as natural herds, although not free to spread through the countryside.

The Red Deer The largest of our deer, standing 4ft (1.22m) high at the shoulder, exists in small numbers in Cumbria, Norfolk and the south west of England, where it is hunted by hounds. Its principle domain is in the mountain and moorland areas of Scotland, called 'deer forests' because many centuries ago they were thickly wooded. There are said to be 300,000 deer in Scotland where they are stalked and shot with rifles of over .22 calibre, never with shotguns. The seasons are: stags 1 July to 20 October; hinds 21 October to 15 February. The letting of stalking rights and the sale of the meat (venison),

Red deer stag

mostly to the Continent, is an important source of income to the owners of Scottish estates.

Stalking in the Highlands is so called because the hunter has to creep with the utmost stealth upwind of his prey over long distances and great heights in open country, sometimes making a circuit of several miles to approach the herd undetected. Telescopes are used to 'spy' the position of the herd and telescopic sights are mounted on rifles for greater accuracy.

The Roe Deer This is widely distributed throughout the British Isles in woodland and scrubland habitats. For obvious reasons such terrain offers a different form of stalking. Roe deer bucks in England are usually shot between 21 October and 30 April (no close season), does between 1 November and 28 February. In Scotland the seasons are bucks 1 May to 20 October, does 21 October to 28 February.

Deer Fencing Deer can be kept out of small areas by a well maintained electric fence, but this is never completely stockproof. Otherwise only very high (at least 7ft, over 2m) and expensive deer fences and gates will serve. Such fencing is always erected where they may stray into Forestry woodlands.

Culling Deer do a great deal of damage to crops and to young trees by eating shoots and rubbing their horns against the bark. Fallow deer are shot by rangers and verderers to control their numbers and if they are not being so controlled, you might be able to invoke the Agriculture Act, 1947, Section 98, which em-

Fallow deer (opposite) *Roe buck*

powers the Minister of Agriculture to serve notice in writing for the destruction of the pest, and deer do rank as pests. Deer doing damage on your own land may be shot in the close season if the shooter can prove that it was necessary in order to prevent serious damage. However, leave this culling to experts with rifles. Usually the local Forestry Commission game warden (phone book) will be only too glad to help. All those concerned are anxious to preserve our deer and, at the same time, strike a balance between preservation and damage to crops and property.

Venison Fallow deer can be farmed for venison if you have sufficient enclosed parkland pasture with well established trees. They will live and breed quite naturally and only need supplementary hay in very severe weather. This can be a very profitable business once the herd is well established. The animals become quite tame and are of course extremely decorative. An intensive study is being made on the west coast of Scotland by the Highland Development Board with a view to commer-

cializing red-deer meat on a large scale. (See also *Shooting*.)

Useful Address: The British Deer Society, Riverside House, Heytesbury, Warminster, Wiltshire, has branches all over the UK and advises its members on all aspects of management, conservation and welfare of the wild deer in Great Britain. Contact your nearest branch (Yellow Pages) if you have any problems.

Further Reading: Prior, R., *Living with Deer* (Survival Books, André Deutsch); Harris and Duff, *Wild Deer in Britain* (David & Charles); Chaplin, R., *Deer* (Blandford Press).

Dew Ponds It was on the dry chalk hills of England that our earliest human colonists survived, not down in the valleys among the lakes and rivers. They had skin-lined water cisterns, but an immediate and constant water supply for themselves and their livestock was essential. The water table was too far down to be reached by wells but they had dew ponds which remained filled during the driest sum-

Sussex dew pond

mers. Why this is so, in spite of various theories involving dew points and condensation, is still a mystery. Probably the air above the cooling surface of the water, at night, itself cools to dew point and releases its water vapour down into the pond.

Dig a hollow about 40ft (12m) across by 5ft (1.5m) deep. Twice or half as big, it doesn't matter, size is not critical. Stamp the ground hard and cover it with a thick layer of straw. Puddle clay with a little lime and water, to mud, and lay it thickly over the straw, at least 6in (150mm) and up to 2ft (0.5m) thick. Leave it until the clay has set fairly hard, but is still moist. It must not dry out and crack or be frosted. Prime it with water once and it should remain full forever until the bottom leaks or is broken.

The secret of the pond lies in the impervious and non-heat-conductive bottom which must be properly made and remain entire. The feet of drinking animals will not normally damage it, but sometimes a layer of flint is put on the clay before the pond is primed, to make the bottom harder, and a lip of chalk laid over the clay right round the edge of the pond to protect it. The lazy modern way is to use black polythene sheeting as a lining which gives excellent condensation results as long as it remains undamaged.

Difficulties of Country Living Because this book will be read mainly by people new to country life there are things which must be said, matters which are usually conveniently ignored but which can make all the difference between happiness and misery, even in this day and age when town and country seem superficially to merge more and more.

When you move into your country home, either for holidays or for good, do not expect to be welcomed with open arms by *any* section of the community. Although cottages and houses may have been derelict for years, with no local buyers, there are those who claim that they cannot get homes in their own villages because outsiders buy them up at ridiculous prices. It does no good to argue that their own homes are now a thousandfold more valuable; they cannot sell them because they must live in them. In any case the local man sees not the old place he would not buy, but the beautiful converted cottage with double glazing and all mod cons, and that is what his wife envies.

You may feel that your arrival circulates more money and perhaps provides employment. The local plumber and publican may be glad of your trade, and eventually the publican will be forced to renovate and improve to attract his new customers; then he must attract more customers to make the pub pay for its new image. The locals preferred it as it was.

Any attempt to take part in local affairs will be regarded with suspicion, except in so far as your money is concerned; and the local pays you out for having it by subtracting it from your pocket in many legal ways. You may have been lord mayor of your city, but the parish council won't want to know for several years.

Imitation is supposed to be the sincerest form of flattery, but your wish to live in a pokey thatched cottage and grow your own vegetables, fruit and flowers, to cut wood and keep stock for pleasure does not seem like flattery to those who have to do these things for a living or from necessity. They do not for one moment imagine that you feel deprived because normally you live in a plastic, metal and concrete world.

Everything you do in and around your house and garden will be watched and commented upon and it takes years of quiet achievement to impress, and years to be forgiven the images fostered by the media, not intentionally cruel or untrue, but which have made the countryman and countrywoman supersensitive. They hear that the very people who mock at their accents cannot themselves

(overleaf) *Long Melford Parish Church in Suffolk*

speak the Queen's English, they see that townspeople are amateurs at all the essential skills and crafts of the countryside, and their advice if asked for and given, is often ignored, so they remain separate and resentful.

If you are accepted in time it is a splendid tribute to your personality. Some people live happily in the countryside without being integrated, but it is hard to do this unless you have the companionship of others of your own background. To set up house in a remote district without such contacts is asking for loneliness unless it is for short periods only, or you and yours are natural-born solitaries, or interested in nothing but nature. There are many areas where two or even three levels of country society have existed side by side for a very long time without social contact; but unless you have personal contacts or family relationships already, it will be extremely difficult to become integrated into any of the levels.

These problems are, of course, not only those of town versus country. They are common to all differing groups, on a grand scale of race, colour, religion, etc, but nowhere more real than in the microcosm of village life. (See also *Village Life*.)

Dogs *Dogs and the Law* Breeding establishments must be licensed and open to inspection by a vet. The local authority issues these licences. A dog must wear a collar with its name and address on it. Exceptions are hounds, sporting dogs and terriers, and sheep or cattle dogs while working. A hound puppy 'at walk' must wear a collar on a public highway. Most dogs must be licensed but certain categories are exempt. Check at your local police station.

Guard Dogs The use of guard dogs is not normally recommended in the country, but,

Yellow Labrador

should you find it necessary, there are stringent regulations which must be obeyed. Where guard dogs are in use there must be a notice at each entrance stating the fact. At all times when they are running free a handler *must* be present, but need not be if the dog is properly secured. And, most important, you must have a licence from the local authority for the use of a guard dog.

Gun Dogs For companionship and because wounded game must never be left to suffer, and dead game must be collected for the game bag, no shooting man will for long wish to be without a gun dog. There are four main types. The choice lies between a retriever and a spaniel. Black and yellow Labradors and golden retrievers are essentially for retrieving game that has been shot. The choice is largely one of personal preference.

Spaniels, principally springers and cockers, are multi-purpose dogs combining the retrieving function with hunting and pushing unshot game from thick cover. If a companion for rough shooting is required, such a dog must be the choice. The springer is probably the easier to train, but the working cocker is a most attractive litle dog.

Bird dogs have the very specialist function of working wide areas of ground in search of game by scent alone, and then 'pointing' it by holding the classic statuesque pose until the gun arrives. They are primarily used in search of grouse in Scotland.

Multi-purpose foreign dogs, German short-haired pointers, Weimaraners, etc, can, if carefully chosen and trained, perform well and appeal to those who want to be different. They are not really for the man choosing his first gun dog.

The one absolute essential in choosing a puppy is to ensure that it comes from a working strain of proved ability, what matters is

Golden retrievers

the performance and pedigree of the parents. If they can be seen in action, so much the better, and a field trial winner may pass on the right qualities. Avoid at all costs the offspring of 'show' as opposed to working parents. Show dogs win prizes for looks arbitrarily dictated by breed societies. Field trial dogs win prizes for performance.

There are three training options. Buy a pro-

Springer spaniel

fessionally trained dog aged at least twelve months. This is quick but not cheap and involves a patient search for the right animal. Buy a puppy aged eight to ten weeks, rear it to six months, and then send it to a professional for training for the next six months. This is a good method for the busy man with no train-

74

Pointer working in a field trial

ing experience, but is expensive. You could, of course, buy a puppy and train it yourself using one of the numerous books on the subject. For the real enthusiast, who is prepared to study the subject and to accept the inevitable setbacks, there can be no greater satisfaction than producing a good working gun dog from the raw material of a tiny puppy.

Field Trials These are competitive events designed to test working gun dogs under conditions as similar as possible to those met in the shooting field. They provide an opportunity for professionals and amateurs to compete and demonstrate the high standards that can be achieved. By concentrating breeding on proved performers, the standards have been

Six-week-old retriever puppies

substantially improved in these events.

Sheepdogs These dogs are specially used by shepherds for herding and collecting sheep over considerable distances, high moorland and hill. The black and white Border collie is the breed of sheepdog commonly used today. Sheepdog trials are held during the summer months in sheep breeding areas to demonstrate the skill of both the dogs and their handlers.

Hounds Foxhounds, staghounds and harriers are used in packs in the pursuit of, respective-

76

Sheepdog trials

ly, the fox, stag and hare, with hunt followers on horseback. In the Lake District fell hounds hunt the fox with followers on foot, as do packs of beagles after the hare.

Hound-puppy walking is a scheme organized by hunt kennels whereby local people volunteer to 'lodge' and exercise (walk) one or more hound puppies during their growing period. Volunteers should get in touch with the secretary of their local hunt or hunt kennels.

Working Terriers These dogs were originally bred for digging out foxes and badgers as their name implies, '*terre*'. They are also used by farmers and gamekeepers for getting rid of rats and rabbits. There are five main working terrier breeds today: the Border terrier, brown and rough-coated, hailing from the north; the hunt terrier, known to the general public as the Jack Russell, from the famous strain bred by Parson Jack Russell from Devon; the Lakeland terrier, used with fell hounds in Cumbria; a strain of working

Jack Russell terrier

Border terriers

Norfolk terrier

Lurchers in full tilt

(opposite above) *Jack Russell puppies*, (below) *Lurcher*

Sealyham terrier, originally bred by Captain Edwardes, and maintained today by Sir Jocelyn Lucas whose kennels are near Luton, Bedfordshire; the Corgi terrier, bred in Wales for hundreds of years, is used by farmers for controlling cattle, their habit being to snap at the heels of stragglers.

Lurchers A true country dog, these were originally bred by the Romany to hunt rabbits and hares for the family pot. The name is derived from the Romany word meaning to rob or plunder. The breed is an intentional cross, usually between a greyhound (for its speed and sight) and a sheepdog (for intelligence and hardy coat), but there exist a number of other combinations of long dogs crossed with different rough-coated breeds, ie retrievers, deerhounds, etc.

Lurcher coursing is becoming increasingly popular and many clubs are being formed. A breed show is held annually at Lambourne, Berkshire.

Further Reading: Walsh, Lt Col L. G., *Lurchers and Longdogs* (The Standfast Press); Drabble, Phil, *Pedigree Unknown* (Michael Joseph); Longton and Hart, *The Sheepdog* (David & Charles); Smith, Betty, *The Jack Russell Terrier* (Witherby); Doxon, P. R. A., *Training the Rough Shooter's Dog* (Popular Dogs Ltd); Erlandson, K., *Gundog Training* (Barrie & Jenkins).

Pet Dogs There are up to 160 different types of dog recognized as pure breeds by the Kennel Club.

Choice of breed depends on your circumstances. Big dogs cost more to feed and take up more space. A good reference book on dog breeds will give you an idea of the kind of dog to suit you. The Kennel Club supplies the names of breeders in your district (send stamped addressed envelope). More important than the breed of dog is its health and temperament record, so when visiting the breeding kennels, find out the details of the parents and see and handle the dam.

Picking Your Puppy Do not hurry. Watch the pups playing and choose one which seems confident and comes towards you. Nervousness is a major fault, particularly in a family dog. A bitch is said to be more biddable but comes into season every six months, for a period of three weeks. A dog is more strong-willed and assertive, but, although he hasn't the disadvantage of coming into season, he can chase bitches that do all over the country!

Living Quarters Make sure that his outside quarters are really weatherproof and secure. His bed should be a strong wooden box just large enough for him to move about in, with one side cut away for entry, and the whole thing raised off the ground to avoid draughts. Wood shavings and layers of newspaper are the best form of bedding and unlike straw they do not collect pests. Also spread sawdust and newspapers on the kennel floor for easy cleaning. If the dog is to live indoors, find some cosy draught-free corner for his box or basket and line it with old blankets or a tear-proof polystyrene-filled bag. This type of bag is often advertised for sale in the sporting periodicals.

House Training A puppy requires constant vigilance and co-operation from the family. He must be taken outside last thing at night, first thing in the morning and immediately after meals, and always watched. Spread a thick carpet of newspapers round his bed at night.

Puppies are naturally destructive, so give him his own 'toys' ie, an ancient slipper, a big meat or rubber bone to occupy himself with, and then reprimand him if he chews anything else. Teach him the word 'No' from the start, said very firmly when he does wrong and 'growl' at him at the same time. If necessary give him a sharp tap on the nose with a rolled-up newspaper. Beating a dog, *except* for chasing sheep when he should receive a maximum deterrent for a major offence, achieves nothing and more often than not produces a cowed animal.

Training a puppy

Feeding A healthy dog is a properly fed dog. To enable a puppy to get sufficient food to keep up rapid growth, he should have several small meals a day. From 2–4 months he should have four meals per day, 4–7 months three meals, and 7 months onwards one or two meals per day.

An adult dog needs ½oz (14g) of protein per 1lb (0.5kg) body weight and good wholemeal biscuit meal according to taste. Never leave uneaten food lying about and feed him regularly. Always have a bowl of clean water available and a large marrow bone to chew. Never feed him ham, pork or poultry bones, and always consult your vet if your dog is unwell.

Exercising A puppy exercises himself by simply playing or romping, but regular disciplined exercise should be a daily routine right from the start, even if it is only a short toddle round the garden at first. An adult dog needs a proper walk every day, not just being put out in the garden.

Obedience Training Teaching him to sit and walk to heel can begin early and in small doses. Remember that his powers of concentration are limited and he will quickly tire of repetitive exercise. Between the ages of six months and a year he can graduate to obedi-

ence classes. The value of these classes lies in teaching you, the owner, the best methods of training your dog.

Parasites If you see any worms in your dog's motions, consult your vet. It is essential to get rid of these, both for the dog and the family's sake.

A country dog is prone to various skin pests however clean his bed and your house. A special shampoo can be obtained from your vet, or enquire in the veterinary department of your local chemist.

Fleas and lice picked up from other dogs or from long grass, straw, or from hens or rabbits can be removed by hand, but much the best remedy is a special shampoo. Be sure to wash all bedding and disinfect the kennel.

Harvest mites are almost invisible, tiny, red creatures which cause intense irritation and sores by burrowing into the folds of the skin, particularly in the bends of the elbows and on the stomach. The remedy is a powder or shampoo containing sulphur.

Breeding Dogs need not be an expensive hobby if you possess good outbuildings, and in fact, with some experience you might make money. Get a book on the subject from your library, or write for advice to the Kennel Club.

Bitches In Season Adult bitches should come into season every six months for a period of three weeks. The peak period is from the eighth to the fifteenth day. There are various deterrents on the market to put on or give to the bitch. (See also *Nuisances; Sheep Worrying* and *Trespass*.)

Useful Address: The Kennel Club, 1 Clarges Street, London W1. Also the International Gun Dog League at the same address.

Further Reading: *The Choice and Training of the Family Dog* (Popular Dogs Publishing Co Ltd); White, R. C., MRCVS, *The Care of the Family Puppy* (Popular Dogs Publishing Co Ltd); Bengston and Wintzell, *Dogs of the World* (David & Charles); Dangerfield, S.

and Howell, Elsworth, *International Encyclopedia of Dogs* (Pelham); Mulvany, M., *All About Obedience Training for Dogs* (Pelham); Gould, Jean, *All About Dog Breeding for Quality and Soundness* (Pelham). Periodicals: *Our Dogs; Dog World.*

Donkeys See *Horses.*

Dowsing A dowser can pinpoint by extra-sensory means (*not* by witchcraft) all kinds of things, from water and mineral supplies to the causes of physical illness and the sex of chickens. The water diviner, working on maps and in the field, can find water, tell you how far down it is, and what volume of flow

A dowser working with a forked hazel twig

to expect. Water diviners train themselves by experience and, although about 20 per cent of people have the ability to dowse, in only a few cases is it worth development. I can water divine with L-shaped wire rods, to the extent that they move across one another when I traverse a water source, but I have no further training in the art.

If you wish to try, bend a couple of lengths of coathanger wire into L-shapes and hold one lightly in each hand. The movement over water is gentle but quite unmistakable. No theory explains the power satisfactorily, but it undoubtedly has to do with electro-magnetic fields and polarity, and the receptivity and sensitivity of some people to these things.

Professional diviners are to be found throughout the country. If you cannot find one locally, contact the British Society of Dowsers, High St, Eydon, Daventry, Northants.

Drains (Domestic) *Cesspits* Where there are no sewers the usual form of drainage is a cesspit or septic tank which works by bacterial action. Its effectiveness depends largely upon siting and the soil in which it is dug; your local authority drainage officer will advise you.

Remember that a cesspit, which has been coping adequately for years with the waste

Dowsing with L-shaped metal rods

from a cottage, may be completely over-whelmed by quantities of waste, water and sewage from a 'mains-conditioned' family. The use of detergents may also have an adverse effect on bacteria and clog the drain-pipes. The local authority usually has a cesspit emptying service, which is quite expensive, but a good pit should not need emptying more than once every three or four years, some last much longer. Blocked drains can usually be cleared by rodding.

Leaking or Blocked Drains These may be a source of contamination of well-water sup-plies, or of streams, and great care should be taken to keep them in order. Drains which pass through a neighbour's land, or empty into his stream (or vice versa), may be a source of trouble, and if you have such trouble which cannot be resolved, check any deeds and covenants and consult your solici-tor. (See also *Cellars; Damp* and *Wells*.)

Further Reading: Phillips, B. G., *Building Law Illustrated* (E. & F. N. Spon Ltd).

Drains (Land) See *Dykes* and *Ditches*.

Dry Rot The *Merulius lacrymans* fungus, which causes dry rot, prefers damp soft wood so that old oak and other hardwood timbers in old houses are not usually attacked. Wood attacked by the fungus goes dry and cracks into cubes, turns brown and crumbles in the fingers. It always starts with persistent damp, so cure the damp at its source. There is only one thing to do and that is to cut the rot right out, going well back into sound timber. Treat new timber with anti-dry rot preservatives. A good coat of creosote also helps. (See also *Damp*.)

Useful Addresses: Cuprinol Preservation Centre, 5 Stag Place, London SW1; Rentokil Ltd, 16 Dover Street, London W1; Solignum Ltd, Dagenham Dock, Essex.

Ducks The more water ducks have the better,

but they will thrive on very little, even an old sinkful if the water is changed often. They do foul up and puddle small ponds and pools, and the ideal is a stream, widened and shallowed to make a pond. Lay a paved, con-creted or shingled area, which is easy to brush or rake clean beside a pond. Obviously, for a lot of birds, a big pond or lake is almost essen-tial. Equally essential is an enclosure fence, as ducks, especially when pinioned (see page 85), are easy game for predators—foxes, dogs, cats, weasles, stoats, rats and people. This should be 6–7ft (2m) high. Use 1in (25mm) chain-link fencing for the bottom 4ft (1.22m), and 3in (76mm) mesh wire netting for the top. Bend the wire outwards at the top to deter jumpers. Run the fence through bushes or tall plants to disguise its presence, but not so that it makes bridges for predators.

Fig 48

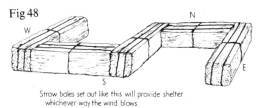

Straw bales set out like this will provide shelter whichever way the wind blows

Provide shelter in the form of wattle or straw-bale windbreaks (Fig 48), and also nest-boxes, some at ground level, some a few feet up, with planks or bits of trunks as ladders so that the birds can hop up. Wooden boxes, or small barrels with one end out, make good nests (Figs 49 and 50). If there is an island in your pond, put a sheltered nest-box on that.

Fig 49

Fig 50

Clean out the boxes annually and dust with malathion. Never put mouldy hay or straw where birds can get at it as it may carry deadly aspergillosis bacteria. Ducks need peace and quiet to incubate, breed and rear, and will not do so successfully in overcrowded enclosures. Don't let children or dogs get amongst them.

Feed young ducks with pellets and, later, cooked household scraps. Never feed with white bread. Clean up the uneaten food and droppings where possible. Provide a trough of grit or sand for eggshell formation. Give them a little cod-liver oil in winter, and alfalfa meal when grass is not available.

Domestic ducks such as Khaki Campbells, kept for egg production, should be shut up at night in a small hut where they will lay their eggs in one great heap before being let out in the morning. Otherwise the eggs will be scattered anywhere they happen to be at the time, or hidden in individual nests.

Ornamental/Domestic Some breeds of domestic duck are ornamental and useful as well, laying plenty of eggs which you can eat, are very tame, and will, unlike other breeds, rear their own young, or can be used to rear the young of other breeds. Some make good table birds,

Sheltered nest box for breeding ducks

although it seems a bit much to eat one's ornamental wildfowl or their eggs.

How to Pinion and Feather Clip Ducks, Geese, etc To stop a bird taking flight, its wings must be unbalanced; do this simply by cutting across the ten 'primary' wing feathers on one wing. This does not hurt the bird at all, but has two disadvantages. Firstly, new flight feathers soon grow so that the operation has to be repeated, and secondly, the cut area does show a little, although if you leave the last two flight feathers uncut they will almost completely disguise the fact that the bird has been wing clipped. Despite these drawbacks, no permanent damage is done to the bird, which is better than pinioning it. Pinioning is a 'once-and-for-all' job and cannot be reversed. It is best done before the birds are ten days old, the younger the better. Do it in the evening so that ducklings will immediately settle down under their mothers. The wing is spread right out and the entire end of the wing cut off with sharp scissors from just beyond the end of the 'bastard wing' which is a kind of thumb growing from the joint. No primaries can grow because the root area has been removed. Adult birds can be pinioned in the same way, but the operation should really be done by a vet as there can be a lot of bleeding. Locate the end of the bastard wing carefully before cutting off the section from which the primaries are growing. When the wing is folded back, in its normal position, the lack of primaries is hardly noticeable (Fig 51).

Fig 52

How to Catch and Hold a Duck or Goose Drop some favourite food round your feet. When the bird you want is within reach, grasp it firmly by the neck. Immediately put your other hand and arm right across the body and pick the bird up so that it is tucked firmly under your arm, like bagpipes. Don't be too rough or squeeze it, but at the same time handle it firmly (Fig 52). Birds usually respond to being gently stroked with a finger at the back of the head, and a smaller bird can be clasped right across the back under the shoulder blades with one hand, while the other holds it round the neck from the front. Small ducks can be held upside down in the palm of the hand, and bigger birds will remain still if placed upside down on a table and gently restrained.

Use a big landing net to catch difficult birds in the water. Diving birds can actually be caught under water.

A cloth hood placed over a bird's head makes it think that night has fallen, and it will relax. Transport ducks and geese in a suitable hamper or crate, or put each one into a bag or sack with its head sticking out. Tie the bag firmly, but not too tightly (Fig 53) round the bird's neck (See also *Shooting*.)

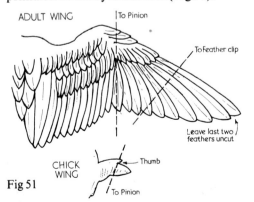

ADULT WING
To Pinion
To Feather clip
Leave last two feathers uncut

CHICK WING
Thumb
To Pinion

Fig 51

Fig 53

Duckweed

Duckweed (*Lemna minor*) This is the tiny plant which makes a bright green surface on a pond. It keeps down algae because it cuts down the amount of light getting to the water. Goldfish love it. If it bothers you, or makes a garden pond unsightly, buy some goldfish who will keep it under control. Failing that, hose the duckweed to one side of the pond and rake it out. Chemicals can be bought which will eradicate it, but their use is not advised as they may also kill other vegetation and life in the pond.

Dutch Elm Disease The first symptom of attack by the elm bark beetle, and the conse-quent growth of the elm disease fungus, is a yellowing of leaves on part of the tree in early summer. The leaves wither, and branches die back from the tip. The faster growing twigs curl down into little shepherds' crooks, which help winter diagnosis of the disease. In a severe attack, the tree dies before summer's end. But if only part of the tree dies, and the bark beetles have not begun to breed in the trunk, the tree may survive. If there are 'shot holes' in the trunk where the beetles have emerged, the tree is doomed. If a branch is cut across there will be a ring of dark brown spots; these occur in the annual ring of the

One down and four to go

year of infection. If no signs of these spots can be found after inspecting several branches or twigs, then the trouble is *not* Dutch elm disease.

Dead trees, and those so severely affected that half the crown has been killed, should be felled. Burn all branch wood on site. Deal with recently affected trees first, as they will contain the most beetles. Remove and burn all bark from any pieces of timber not burnt. The value of the timber is not affected by the disease and should offset the costs of felling.

There is a theory that the present epidemic of elm disease is due to the fact that the population of treecreepers, woodpeckers and other insectivorous birds had declined because insect pesticides killed them in turn. This allowed a population explosion among the bark beetles which cause the disease fungus to spread. In turn, there is now an increase in the numbers of woodpeckers which feed on the bark beetle. Should this be so, then maybe the woodpeckers will eventually control the beetle and the epidemic will die down.

Further Reading: Forestry Commission leaflet No 19, *Dutch Elm Disease* (HMSO); Building Research Establishment leaflet No 194, *Use of Elm Timber* (HMSO); Bridgeman, *Tree Surgery* (David & Charles).

Dyeing Wool See *Spinning*.

Dykes and Ditches Keep ditches and dykes clear and unsilted so that they can carry away excess surface and subsurface water; especi-

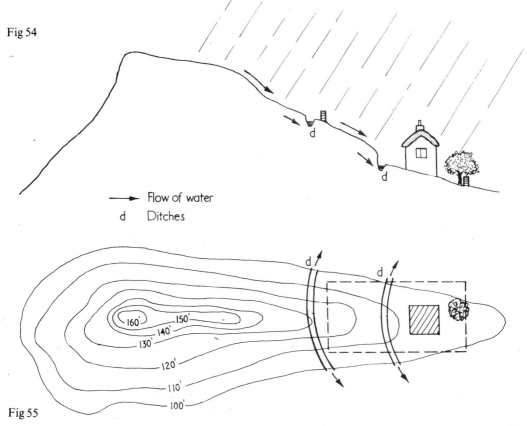

Fig 54

Flow of water

d   Ditches

Fig 55

ally those along the contour at the top of your land (Figs 54, 55). Once ditches have got into a bad condition, they are back breaking to clear by hand, and ditching machinery is expensive to hire, makes a great mess, and the resulting spoil has to be levelled and tidied. In very flat country where there is no fall, it may be necessary to install small metal wind-pumps to empty ditches into main dykes or even into streams and rivers. In most fenland areas, the river authorities maintain pumping stations which keep the dykes at their correct levels (once the job of the windmill and the 'marshman'). So maintain ditches, drains and dykes properly and you will be spared the trouble and expense which will inevitably crop up if you neglect them.

To drain marshy areas of ground, lay land drains, or 'tiles', or plastic perforated pipes. This is done by trenching down into the sub-soil at short intervals across the ground, down the fall line to a convenient ditch or stream (Fig 56). The pipes are then laid and covered over with a layer of stones and then the top-soil (Fig 57). Water runs in from the sur-rounding damp ground. Side drains may be brought in in a herringbone pattern in bad cases (Fig 58). The depth and distance apart of the drains is dictated partly by the type of soil and partly by the amount of water to be got rid of; in clay soil, 2–3ft (60–90cm) deep and $3\frac{1}{2}$–6yd (3–6m) apart; in sandy soil, up to

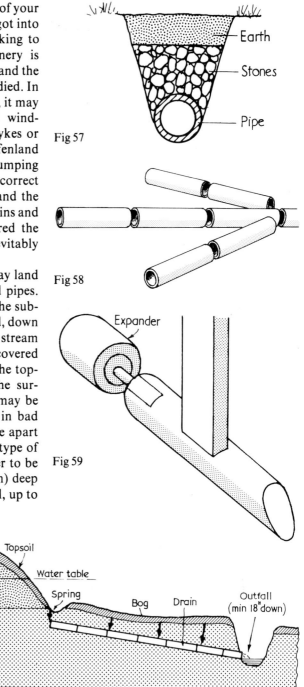

Fig 57

Fig 58

Fig 59

Fig 56

(opposite) *Restored drainage mill on the Thurne, St Benets Levels Mill, Norfolk*

4½ft (1.5m) deep and up to 12yd (12m) apart. Consult the local Agricultural and Development Advisory Services (see Ministry of Agriculture in the phone directory) or the local authority's drainage officer, or a drainage contractor.

Mole draining, which is the boring of underground drainage holes, with piping laid by a special plough, is also undertaken by contractors (Fig 59). Mole draining without pipes will last about eight years, but using modern perforated plastic pipes it is an almost permanent job.

Up to 50 per cent grants are available for drainage for registered farmers.

Further Reading: drainage leaflets; No 1, *Does Your Land Need Drainage?*; No 3, *Drainage Advice*; No 8, *Field Drainage Aftercare*, and fifteen others (HMSO).

E

Earths See *Foxes* and *Badgers*.

Earthworms Worms are the natural workers of the soil without whom the land is a desert. They are also the food of moles who collect them, bite off their heads and store them for later consumption. If you wish to breed earthworms, put a layer of onion skins on an area of bare earth and cover it with grass cuttings, leaves, a few twigs and kitchen waste to make a compost heap (but do not add any activators). Cover the heap with earth and leave it for six months when there should be hundreds of worms in the bottom layer. Remove the worms required and rebuild the compost heap.

Earwigs *(Forficula auricularia)* Many people hate this small insect and believe that it will crawl into their ears. This is utter nonsense. It would never do any such thing and feeds on carrion, waste leaves, rubbish and roots. It does damage in gardens by nibbling at the roots of seedlings, but the presence of a lot of them in outbuildings probably means that they are doing a good job of cleaning up the place. Should you need to get rid of them, leave about the place some inverted flower pots or small boxes full of hay, moss or crumpled paper. The earwigs will congregate in these and can then be destroyed.

Eels Eels abound in all rivers and still waters, even to quite small ditches. They make excellent eating and are easy to catch. Perhaps it is their snake-like looks and tendency to wriggle and die slowly which put people off them. Eels can be caught in 'hives', torpedo-shaped withy baskets which are baited with such things as fresh chicken guts, shrimp heads, or almost any fresh meaty or fishy waste. Fine-mesh wire cages do the same job perfectly well. These are sunk below the water surface and left overnight. Alternatively, bait a long line, with hooks at short intervals, with earthworms and leave it in the water overnight. Eels can be caught by 'babbing', that is by tying a bunch of worms, each threaded onto knitting wool, on the end of a piece of string on a stick. Lower this to the bottom of the stream or in a shallow estuary and after a few minutes bring it up and shake off the eels that are clinging to it.

Mature eels return to the sea after seven or eight years to swim off to the Sargasso Sea to mate, and it is these big fish (the best for smoking) which can be trapped on weirs which they have to negotiate to reach the sea.

To Smoke Eels Gut, but do not skin them. Clean and lay them in dry salt for twelve hours. Hang them on a stick and dip into boiling water for a few seconds, to open the fish out. Smoke at 140°F (60°C) for two to four hours, according to size.

Further Reading: Moriarty, C., *Eels* (David & Charles).

Eggs See *Birds*; *Ducks* and *Poultry*.

Elderberries See *Fruit* and *Wine-making*.

Electricity *Way Leave* The Electricity Board can use privately owned land either to put in underground cables, to erect pylons or to cross with overhead cables, and there is nothing you can do about it if it is the only practicable route. The Electricity Act, 1947, gives them these powers. They will negotiate with you on a standard form of agreement and pay you a small sum annually in respect of a licence for a way leave and of incidental right of access for repair. This way-leave payment acknowledges your ownership, and your proprietary rights are properly protected. If the cables obstruct your views, cause damage, or reduce the value of your property, it may be that you can claim compensation. The Electricity Board's valuer will, with your co-operation, decide upon this, but should no agreement between you be possible, then the Lands Tribunal will have to decide the compensation. In any such case, consult your solicitor.

Damage caused to your property at a later date is covered in the way-leave agreement, and should there be damage to your property caused by cables, etc, erected before your time, then check the way-leave licence obtained by your predecessor in title; it will certainly cover indemnity against your loss.

Generators If you have no mains supplies, then a diesel oil generator is the only complete answer. This provides all light and power requirements. A windmill running a small generator can supply lighting and some power, but is dependent upon the wind for the amount. Storage batteries hold enough power to carry you over calm spells for lighting requirements in most areas of Great Britain which is a windy country. If you can install a hydro-electric system on a constantly running stream which it is possible to dam up, you may be able to get what electricity you need,

but this could be an expensive installation. (See also *Solar Heating* and *Windmills*).

Useful Addresses: Department of Energy, Energy Technology Division, Thames House South, Millbank, London SW1P 4QJ; Low-Impact Technology Ltd, 73 Molesworth Street, Wadebridge, Cornwall (make aero-generators—battery-charging windmills); New-age Engineers Ltd, Barnack Road, Stamford, Lincs; Industrial Instruments, 1a Stanley Road, Bromley, Kent (make aero-generators).

Further Reading: Survival Scrapbook No 5, *Energy* (Unicorn Bookshop, Brighton); McLaughlin, *Make Your Own Electricity* (David & Charles).

Estate Agents To be found in every town, these tend to specialize in different types of property. The agent will inspect your property for sale, advise on likely prices, draw up particulars and circulate them, and will charge you commission if and when the property is sold; this commission is on a sliding scale according to value, and you should ascertain this from the start.

For the prospective buyer the estate agent provides particulars of properties and makes appointments to view.

There is nothing whatsoever to prevent you selling your property directly and dispensing with the services of an agent, but he may claim commission if he has advertised the property or has a 'For Sale' notice upon it, and you might be hard put to it to prove that the buyer had contacted you directly and had seen neither advertisement nor board.

Some estate agents will make greater efforts on your behalf if they are made the sole agents, spending more on advertising, etc. Estate agents who are also auctioneers conduct property auctions and do all the necessary advertising.

If a deposit is paid on a property the estate agent holds the money until the deal is completed. But of course solicitors are involved in deed searching and conveyancing generally and also extract payment on a sliding scale for their services. (See also *Auctioneers*.)

F

Falconry Because all hawks and falcons are protected, it is illegal to take a young hawk from a nest, and the only way to get a hawk is to buy it from overseas. Falconry demands a lot of time and attention to your birds and is not to be recommended for any but the totally dedicated. Demonstrations of falconry are given at game fairs and, if you live in the south east, at Chilham Castle, near Canterbury in Kent. If you are seriously interested in fal-

conry, contact the British Falconers Club for further information.

Useful Addresses: The British Falconers Club, Hon Sec C. J. Morley Esq, Hereford Stock Farm, Smarden, Ashford, Kent; Falconry Centre, Newent, Glos.

Further Reading: Woodford, M. H., *A Manual of Falconry* (A. & C. Black).

Fantails See *Pigeons*.

Farmhorses Until recently farmhorses had almost disappeared as working animals except in some hilly areas, although some breweries kept working teams and breeders kept the stocks going. Now the farmhorse is again an economic proposition as fuel costs soar and, for some jobs on some soils, beats tractors out of sight.

Percheron stallion

First recorded about 1506 the Suffolk punch was developed on the East Suffolk coast. Standing 15–16 hands, this bright chestnut horse, with clean legs bearing no hair or 'feathers', was the first type to replace draught oxen for agricultural work.

Heavy horses had aways been bred in England for military use, and during the fifteenth century the breed began to get smaller and smaller. Henry VIII enacted a statute to reverse this trend and imported some good Flemish mares. This interest in breeding eventually produced the 'great horse of England' that we now know as the shire horse, bred mainly in Lincoln, Cambridge and Huntingdon. Slow moving but tough, shire horses can be a variety of colours, from grey to bay and black, with white markings. They have long hair or feathers on their legs, and stand up to 17 hands.

The Percheron, a breed developed in Le Perche district of France, south and west of Chartres, stands about 16 hands, is always

(opposite) *Grey Shire horses—usually bay, brown or black*

grey or black with dapples, and has clean legs. They are docile and very powerful horses, easy to break. Percherons are distributed worldwide, more so than any other breed of heavy horses.

Clydesdales were developed as commercial draught horses in the eighteenth century in Lanarkshire in Scotland. They may be bay, brown, or black with white faces and feathered legs. Not so bulky as the other breeds of heavy horse, they are active and tough. (See also *Horses*).

Useful Address: The Heavy Horse Preservation Society, The Old Rectory, Claypit Street, Whitchurch, Shropshire.

Further Reading: Hart, E., *The Golden Guinea Book of Heavy Horses* (David & Charles); Whitlock, R., *Gentle Giants* (Lutterworth Press).

Farriers See *Wrought Iron* and *Horses*.

Feathers Although it may seem a shame, there is little use for feathers, except for fly tying, when the feathers of mallard, woodcock, pheasant and teal can be used in very small quantities. The best way to get rid of feathers is to burn them. They can be put on compost heaps. If you wish to use them for stuffing cushions, they must be dried right out or they will smell terrible after a little while. Pile the feathers loosely in a big shallow dish in a very slow oven (not a gas oven or any oven with an open flame). The moment the feathers get too hot they will singe and burn, so the heat really must be very low. Only when the feathers are thoroughly dry (check specially the ends of the quills), can they be used. If anyone in the household suffers from allergies, don't use feathers to stuff cushions or pillows.

Felling Trees See *Trees*.

Fencing It depends on what you want to keep in or what you want to keep out. Post and

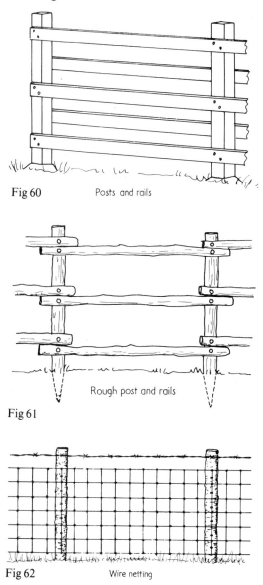

Fig 60   Posts and rails

Fig 61   Rough post and rails

Fig 62   Wire netting

stockproof, but provide no windbreak, and are also quite expensive (Fig 62). Wooden fence posts are needed for corners and as straining posts (see page 95), but, even if creosoted or dipped in preservative before being put in, will rot and break off at ground level eventually. Concrete-filled holes do keep the posts more rigid, but merely postpone eventual breakage. Build up the concrete a little round the posts, to run away surface water and prolong life (see Fig 60). Metal and concrete posts have to be set firmly in concrete, but last indefinitely. Or use short concrete posts set in the ground to which wooden posts may be attached.

Panel fencing, made of thin wide strips of wood woven together in a framework of battens, is cheap and very popular for gardens, but does not have a very long life, even if creosoted regularly or painted with preservative. The tighter the weave or the set of the strips, the more windproof the fence, but this can be a disadvantage if the fence is in an exposed place, as it offers so much resistance to the wind, while not being intrinsically very strong, that it is easily wrecked by winter gales. The pressure of wind on too close a fence causes continual movement and strain on the fence posts, which eventually succumb.

Split chestnut fencing (Fig 63), made from split chestnut stakes held together with twisted wire, makes an excellent and quickly erected stockproof fence, but does not look

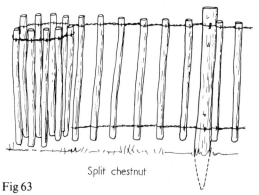

Split chestnut

Fig 63

barbed wire fences must be at least 3ft 9in (1m) to contain cattle and horses, but will not prevent them from reaching over to eat your roses. An extra strand of wire at 4ft (1.22m) should do this. Post and rail fences of different types are much nicer to look at (Figs 60 and 61), form windbreaks and are stockproof, but they cost much more to install and to keep up. Wire-mesh and chain-link fences are

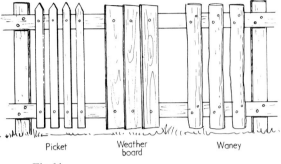

Picket   Weather   Waney
          board

Fig 64

very beautiful. Its main advantage is that the whole fence can be removed and used elsewhere just by removing the staples which hold it to the posts. It can then be rolled up all of a piece.

Sheep hurdles and wattles made of split hazel, coppiced and cut when seven years old, are sometimes used for fencing, but these are now expensive and less and less coppicing is done. These hurdles last for years and make attractive country garden fences and windbreaks. They must, of course, be attached to posts for permanency.

If you live near a sawmill, you may be able to get 'waney' planks cheaply. These are flattened half-moon in section with the bark still on them. Nailed to posts and rails they make excellent fences (Fig 64).

Barbed Wire It is not illegal to erect barbed wire by a public highway (and this includes a footpath), but if the local authority thinks it has been placed where it may be dangerous to people or animals using the highway, they may serve an abatement of nuisance notice under the Barbed Wire Act, 1893. This requires that something must be done about that nuisance within a certain period (never less than a month). A case could be brought for damages caused by barbed wire put up along a public highway.

To Erect a Barbed Wire Fence Barbed wire is really the cheapest way to make a stockproof fence where none exists. The wire must be strung tightly. Loose wire is highly dangerous

and useless. The run must start either on a convenient tree, or, failing that, a stout post set into a hole at least 2ft (600mm) deep, and tamped well down with stones, or even with coarse concrete poured in. It must have supports on the side, against which the pull will be exerted, or make a colonial box anchor (Fig 65). Such posts or anchors are essential at corners and bends (Figs 66 and 67) and at 21–32yd (20–30m) intervals. Intermediate

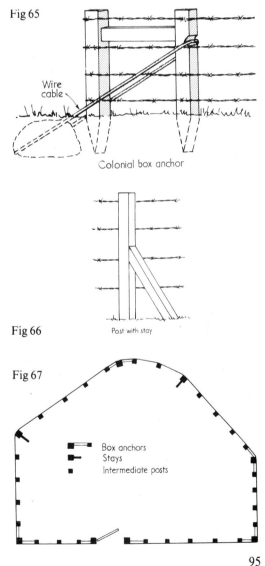

Fig 65

Wire cable

Colonial box anchor

Fig 66   Post with stay

Fig 67

■—   Box anchors
■—   Stays
■   Intermediate posts

posts or 'droppers' should be driven into the ground at about 10ft (3m) intervals. Peeled and pointed chestnut stakes make excellent posts and should be stood in a tub of creosote for forty-eight hours before use. The wire is firmly stapled to the straining post at one end and taken along to the next big post where it is pulled tight by levering it with a pair of pliers. (Use special fencing pliers or wire strainers, or a big pair of ordinary pliers.) Then get an assistant to hammer in a staple on each side of a barb to hold the wire firmly. The top strand should be at about 3ft (1m), or a little higher, to contain stock, but at about 1½yd (1.5m) to prevent cattle or horses reaching over to nibble at tall plants. Put on at least two more strands below the first, at about 1ft (300mm) intervals, or three or four equally spaced strands. Strain all strands between the main posts before stapling the wire back to the droppers, otherwise you will get in an awful muddle and the tensions will be very uneven. (See also *Boundaries*).

Ferrets Small creamy-white animals of the weasel family with pink, almost sightless, eyes, ferrets are kept to drive rabbits from their burrows. Ferrets do well in hutches, if allowed plenty of straw to make warm nests, as they hate the cold. They should be housed in sheds in winter. Ferrets breed prolifically and if they escape will crossbreed with their wild cousins, polecats. The results of this crossbreeding are larger and better sighted, and are prized by some.

The 'jill' or female is smaller than the 'hob' or male, and less aggressive. Ferrets can give careless handlers a nasty nip. They hunt by scent and sound when underground and grip their prey hard, but can be made to release by applying pressure just above the eyes.

Ferrets can be fed on bread and milk, or biscuits and suitable scraps, but are by nature carnivores and do best on a meat diet of lights

Ferrets crossbred with polecat

or any fresh offal. Ferrets kept for rabbiting hunt better if fed on a meat diet.

Ferreting for rabbits is usually done by pegging nets over the warren exit holes, and then putting in a muzzled ferret, either free running if he is known to come out without trouble, or on a line if he tends to stay down. Occasionally a ferret refuses to come out and has to be dug out. Special ferret collars, with a small transmitter, can be bought and, with the appropriate small receiver, you can pick up a signal and know exactly where to dig for him. Such are the wonders of modern science! (See also *Rabbits*.)

Further Reading: Lloyd, Samuel and Ivesster, *Rabbiting and Ferreting* (British Field Sports Society); Marchington, J., *Pugs and Drummers* (Faber).

Fertilizers Artifical fertilizers are made up from different proportions of the chemicals nitrogen, phosphates and potash, according to the job they have to do. Their use in conjunction with lime and farmyard manure is essential for all kinds of production of crops and grass, from garden to farm. Take advice from garden shops and agricultural merchants, or from the Ministry of Agriculture Advisory Service, as to their use and suitability. It is much too big a subject to be covered here.

Whereas lime and farmyard manure provide long-term fertility, artifical fertilizers provide a quick boost for growing plants. (See also *Compost*; *Lime* and *Manure*).

Field Sports See *Hunting*; *Shooting* and *Fishing*.

Fire Fire is always a danger in the countryside; the nearest fire engine is usually several miles away, and old buildings are dry and highly inflammable. Local fire prevention officers from the fire brigade will always advise if asked as to ways and means of reducing risks and siting extinguishers. If your house has high bedroom windows, keep a long enough ladder handy outside, or ropes inside the bedrooms which will reach the ground, with some solid point of attachment in the bedrooms. A bed itself will do as it can be pulled across to, and jammed against, a window. Install fire extinguishers at accessible points in the house both upstairs and down. For really tall buildings, special fire escape ropes and harnesses can be installed.

In case of fire, keep doors shut, and only open windows in order to escape through them. Smoke kills just as often as fire, but there is usually a clear layer of air right down at ground level. The old specific of wet towels wrapped around head and face can help a lot if you have to escape through smoke.

One of the commonest causes of fires in old buildings is antique electrical wiring, and when moving into a new home it is always wise to have the wiring checked. Rewiring may be expensive, but not as expensive as a disastrous fire. Wiring installed many years ago was not intended to carry such things as washing machines, dishwashers, television sets, deep freezes, fridges, etc, usually all at once.

Check the pointing in chimneys, especially up in the loft. If smoke is escaping, it should be renewed, as a chimney fire might prove really disastrous, especially if the roof is thatched. Chimneys should be swept regularly.

Use fireguards in front of all open fires. Be very careful with any kind of open flame, with oil heaters, oil lamps or candles. Never set lamps or candles anywhere near curtains or soft furnishings as they may blow onto the flame or the flame may waver in a draught and set them alight, or the heat from the lamp glass may singe and eventually light a curtain. Do not put water on paraffin fires, as it spreads them. Try to smother flames or use a powder fire extinguisher. Buckets of sand, kept in handy places, are another sensible fire precaution.

If a fire is discovered before it has really taken hold, determined action will usually put it out. First make sure that everyone is out of the building or helping with the fire fighting, and then dial 999. Of course, use fire extinguishers, pull down blazing curtains and beat out the flames, or throw water or sand on them.

If your property is in the middle of woodland or heathland and at risk from bush fires in dry weather, then consider making firebreaks round it. Bush fires can jump across remarkable distances, and you should take advice from local forestry officers or fire officers about firebreaks. Keep brushwood, grass and bushes well cut back.

Fireproofing Thatch To do this, make up enough of the following mixture to spray the thatch thoroughly. The job should be done when the thatch is dry as it will then be at its maximum absorbency: 50gal (227 l) water, 28lb (12kg) ammonium sulphate, 14lb (6kg) ammonium carbonate, 7lb (3kg) boracic acid, 7lb (3kg) borax, 7lb (3kg) alum. Mix everything together. Repeat this treatment every three years.

Fireback basket and hood made by a smith skilled in wrought iron

Fireproofing Wood Wood can be made fire resistant by painting it with proprietary silica-based compounds, most containing mon-ammonium phosphate, or borax and boracic acid. No treatment prevents timber or thatch from catching if the fire is hot enough, but fireproofing does help to prevent ignition from sparks, cigarette ends, etc.

Certain building materials are more fireproof than others. Polystyrene foam and certain plastics are extremely inflammable and give off choking and lethal fumes as well. Polystyrene foam should never be used when there is any risk of it catching fire from cookers, fires or heaters.

Fireplaces So often fireplaces in old houses have been filled in and replaced by very ugly grates. The presence of a big lintel beam, or the ridge of the old fireplace edge, or a wide chimney breast going through the room above proves the existence of a big open fireplace. If the brickwork is encrusted with soot

98

then it must be chiselled off and this can be a monumental job as wood soot is very sticky. Clean brickwork with a heavy wire brush or by rubbing it with other pieces of brick. Pointing should be made good with fireproof cement.

Chimneys Huge open chimneys merely serve to suck all the warmth out of a house and create draughts, and really the only way to use them is to install a grate with a hood and flue which passes up through a register—a sheet of metal fitted horizontally just above the lintel beam. This prevents air rushing up the chimney and rain coming down, and usually ensures that the grate burns without smoking. The hood over the fire also controls the smoke and cuts down smoking. If a fireplace with register, hood and flue still smokes, you may have to install a cowl on the chimney pot or an extra flap on the lintel (Fig 68).

Fireplace converted into deep cupboard

Fireplaces which are not to be used for fires make attractive alcoves for any purpose and, if filled in with shelves and sliding doors, make excellent kitchen cupboards for the storing of preserves, wine or large utensils, because of their great depth. A fireplace could be a very good place for setting up hi-fi equipment. Always completely seal off a chimney that is not being used, both just above the fireplace and at the chimney pot, so that no draughts go up through it, and no rain comes down.

Modern fuels are so efficient that little heat goes up the chimney which remains cold and causes condensation which must be prevented, so, when installing gas fires or central heating boilers, it will be necessary for the chimney to be lined with a special flue liner. This prevents the condensation carrying chemicals from the exhaust gases into the brickwork.

Open fireplaces frequently have a brick oven in the side, once used for making bread.

Fig 68

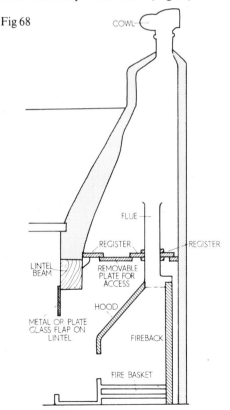

COWL

FLUE

REGISTER

REGISTER

LINTEL BEAM

REMOVABLE PLATE FOR ACCESS

HOOD

METAL OR PLATE GLASS FLAP ON LINTEL

FIREBACK

FIRE BASKET

Elizabethan lintel beam—salt cupboard on right

A faggot would be burned in it, the ashes raked out, and the bread put in to cook in the residual heat left in the bricks. Some fireplaces have small cupboards in them, formerly used for keeping the household supply of salt dry. This was especially important near the sea where rock salt, without modern chemical additives, would deliquesce very quickly if not kept dry.

Birds in Chimneys Some species of birds will nest in chimneys if they can find a suitable ledge near the top. Jackdaws, starlings and pigeons are the main culprits. The best way to get rid of them is to light a fire and create masses of smoke. Temporary summer capping of chimneys may sometimes be necessary if the birds are really persistent. Birds occasionally fall down chimneys. Usually this is because they are enjoying the warm air coming up from rooms below (even when the fire is not lit), and perhaps try to get right inside for shelter. They are unable to fly directly upwards, specially bigger birds, and end up in the room below or scrabbling about on the register. Just open every window to its widest and hope the bird will fly out. Do this *before* removing a register, so that the sooty bird will, hopefully, fly straight out, and neither dirty up the room nor bash itself to death on a shut window in the attempt.

Sweeping Chimneys The old way to sweep a wide chimney over a wood fire was to drop one end of rope down it and tie a large bundle of holly twigs halfway along it. This should be big enough to be compressed by the chimney so that it will give it a good scrape as it is pulled through. Someone remains at the lower end of the rope to pull the bundle down again, and it should be worked up and down until the chimney is good and clean. (See also *Solid-fuel Stoves*.)

Further Reading: Department of the Environment Guides to Good Building No 44, *Smoky Chimneys;* No 30, *Installing Solid Fuel Appliances, Open Fires and Convectors* (HMSO); West, *Fireplace in the Home* (David & Charles).

Firewood Ash undoubtedly makes the best firewood of all, and pine the worst. Pine is also dangerous as it sends out showers of sparks. Wood for fires should always be cut in the autumn when the sap is not running. It then dries out well and neither sparks nor smokes too much when burnt. Always use a fireguard and make sure that it is properly in place whenever the room is empty, day or night.

If you have a big open hearth, bind up clippings or pollardings into bundles or faggots, using wire or a thin twisted twig to tie the bundle, not string because it burns away immediately and allows the faggot to disintegrate. A faggot thrown on a fire which has died right down, or even on hot overnight ash, will light easily and burn up quickly to restart the fire.

Wood-burning stoves take long logs (see page 209) and will burn almost any kind of wood efficiently and effectively.

Firewood should always be kept under cover, but if it must be out of doors, stack it neatly and put some kind of roof over it; a sheet of corrugated iron or polythene will do. (See also *Solid-fuel Stoves* and *Trees*.)

Fishing More people go fishing each weekend than watch professional football. This includes sea anglers, coarse fishermen and game fishermen.

Sea Angling Done from beach (free), pier, jetty or promenade (pier tickets), or from boats (boat hire, or parking, running and maintenance of your own boat), sea angling can be as cheap or expensive a sport as you make it. The novice should find a helpful sea-angling friend or a good boatman. In some cases boatmen will supply rod, tackle and bait as well as know-how. In all seaside towns there are tackle dealers who will advise on equipment.

Clothes Always wear at least one more layer of woolly clothes than you think you will need. Take good wet-weather clothing and insist on having a lifejacket with you in the boat. Take plenty of food and hot drinks. One gets very cold boat fishing because no exercise is involved. Seasickness pills are almost essential for the beginner.

Coarse Fishing All inland water belongs to someone, and therefore fishing licences and permits are necessary. First, River Board licences, which do not cost much but are essential for most rivers and lakes, although there are some exceptions. Additionally, day licences, permits or club membership will probably be required. Local tackle shops can advise you on what is necessary and often sell permits themselves for local water. The one thing not to do is to assume that you can just start fishing wherever you like. Many ponds, lakes, reservoirs and stretches of river are the preserve of clubs without whose permission you must not fish. Notices are usually clearly posted by such waters.

There are dozens of types of rods, reels, lines, hooks, etc, for different species of fish and ways of fishing, and the best advice I can give is to buy a medium-priced rod on the advice of an angling friend or tackle dealer. There is no such thing as a general purpose rod, but do not buy expensive specialist gear

A 35lb (15.8kg) tope

to begin with. Fishing is not just a matter of dropping a baited hook in the water. You must learn the habits and habitat of your quarry at different times of the year, in different weather conditions, by experience and from experienced anglers, and from the many good books on the subject.

Close Season Although river boards make their own variations to suit local conditions, the close season is from 15 March to 15 June. Each river board has its byelaws designed to prevent overfishing, damage and commercialization. Study them, or sooner or later you will run into trouble.

Clothes Good warm clothes, especially underclothes, waterproofs and wellingtons, big umbrellas or fishing shelters, all in sober camouflaging greens and browns (fish have sharp, if limited, vision) are essential.

Game Fishing This is the sport of fishing for salmon and sea trout which spend part of each year of adult life at sea, returning to our rivers to spawn. Although found in still

waters, particularly the Scottish lochs, these fish are caught primarily in the rivers which debouch clockwise round our coast from Hampshire via Cornwall, Wales and the Irish Sea around Scotland and south to Yorkshire. They are rare in the rivers running into the sea from Lincolnshire south and then west to Sussex.

Freshwater trout also come into this category, the two principal species being brown trout and rainbow trout, which spend their entire lives in rivers and other inland waters throughout the British Isles. Provided the water is pure and unpolluted and contains plenty of food for the fish, trout will thrive. In recent years the availability of trout fishing has been greatly increased by the stocking of manmade inland waters, such as reservoirs and worked-out gravel pits.

How to Obtain Fishing Rights The right to fish is normally the property of the owner of the water or of its banks, who may sell, lease or otherwise dispose of those rights. Ownership may, therefore, be with an individual, a club or syndicate, or even a property company or

102

Tailing a salmon

hotel, and it is necessary to find out which before an approach can be made for fishing in a particular water. A wide variety of general fishing is on offer through advertisements in the sporting and angling press and through agents specializing in sporting property.

Fishing Methods There are two types of game fishing—fly fishing and bait fishing—each with sub-divisions. The first involves presenting the fish with a concoction of feathers tied to a small hook, designed to imitate a natural fly, insect or small fish, or to satisfy the whim of the angler as to what will appeal to the fish at that particular moment in that particular water. Fly fishing may be either 'dry-fly' in which the fly floats on top of the water, or 'wet-fly' in which it sinks below the surface. Dry-fly is essentially for trout in water where it is known to be effective, mainly the chalk streams of Hampshire and Wiltshire and some inland lakes. Wet-fly is used almost exclusively for salmon and sea trout. Dusk-to-midnight fishing for sea trout with wet-fly is particularly effective and exciting.

Bait fishing or spinning involves the use of an artificial lure designed to imitate a small fish. To the purist it is a poor substitute for fly fishing, but it has many adherents and in certain conditions and at certain times of year there is no alternative. The bait itself may be of metal, wood or plastic, round, tapered, spiralled or flat, gold, silver or coloured, large, medium or small. Choice is a matter of knowing the water and the varying conditions.

Rods and Equipment These may be bought from any reputable tackle dealer who will advise you. Cane and carbon-fibre rods are the most expensive and glass-fibre rods are in most general use. Length and flexibility vary according to the type of fishing, fly or spinning, and according to the target fish.

Seasons The close seasons for salmon, sea trout and brown trout vary from place to place and are made by local water authorities, based on legally specified lengths of time during which the fish must be protected. Only in December is game fishing of all kinds totally prohibited throughout the UK. In

103

Spinning for salmon

practice the best of the salmon fishing on most rivers is from March to September, the best of the sea trout from June to September, and the best of the brown trout from April to June and again in September. As a guide only the open seasons are:

England and Wales

Salmon	February – 31 October
Brown trout and sea trout.	1 March – 30 September
Rainbow trout	No close season

Scotland

Salmon	November – January
Brown trout	15 March – 6 October
Rainbow trout	No close season

Fish caught late in the season do not make such good eating.

Fly fishing for salmon

105

Fishponds

Useful Addresses: Salmon and Trout Association, Fishmongers Hall, London Bridge EC4R 9EL; Anglers' Cooperative Association (protection against polluted fishing water) Westgate, Grantham, Lincolnshire NG31 6LE.

Further Reading: Wiggin, Maurice, *Fishing for Beginners* (J. M. Dent & Sons); Harris, Brian, *Pursuit of Still Water Trout* (A. & C. Black); Plunkett-Greene, Harry, *Where the Bright Waters Meet* (Witherby); Hill, *Coarse Fishing for New Anglers* (David & Charles); Willock, C., *The ABC of Fishing* (André Deutsch).

Fishponds A fishpond, whatever its size, should have a deep area in which the fish can shelter from excess heat or cold. This provides a large bulk of water which has to be heated or cooled before the pool becomes uninhabitable. Shallow pools are death to fish.

A formal pool which has a deep central area and a shallow edge for plants

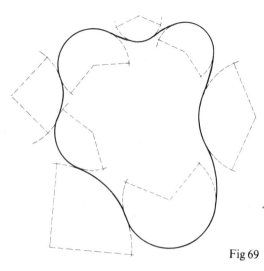

Fig 69

Making Artificial Fishponds Informal pools can be of any shape, but the inside and outside curves should be based on the radii of imaginary circles to produce pleasing shapes. Define outlines with pegs and string before starting to dig (Fig 69). To measure the surface area of a pool, square it off as shown in Fig 70. Site

Informal pool with header pond and small cascade and fountain

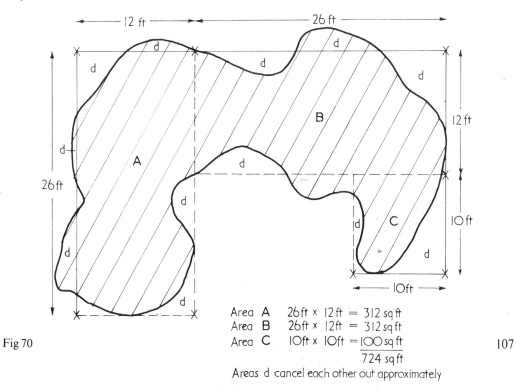

Area **A**   26ft x 12ft = 312 sq ft
Area **B**   26ft x 12ft = 312 sq ft
Area **C**   10ft x 10ft = 100 sq ft
                          724 sq ft

Areas d cancel each other out approximately

Fig 70

Fishponds

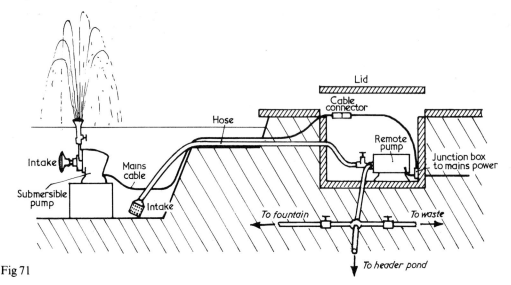

Fig 71

remote control pumps as near as possible to all intake and output points. A small submersible pump (Fig 71) is fine for a fountain, but a larger remote pump is needed to pump up water for header ponds and cascades. Formal pools should be shaped as shown in Fig 72 and the concrete poured behind shuttering made from hardboard and battens or planks

Fig 72

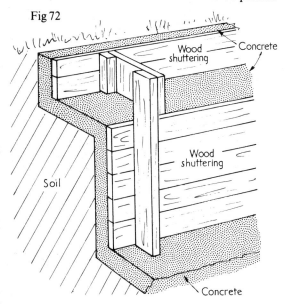

(Fig 73). Provision must be made for the drainage of pools if possible, so that they can be cleaned out occasionally, and this is usually combined with overflow. The alternative layouts for drainage and overflow installations, shown in Fig 74, can be adapted for informal ponds.

Be sure, when installing electrically run pumps, that the wiring is heavy-duty cable suitable for such work and that all plugs, connections, etc, are properly made with special rubber parts and are, wherever possible, protected from weather and surface water.

Natural Ponds These can be cleaned up and stocked, but a deep area must be made as they tend to be uniformly shallow and the contents fluctuate with the weather. If you are lucky enough to have a spring-fed pond then there should be no trouble. A weir or dam with a lower section for overflow will regulate the outflow of water at the lower end of the pond, although an extra barrier of very fine wire-mesh netting across the pond, well inside the weir, may be necessary to prevent fish from escaping downstream. It rather depends on the amount of water likely to be flowing over the spillway. Unfortunately, pollution can get into natural ponds all too easily from ditches or road drains, and dissolved fertilizer draining off the local farms causes masses of extra plant and algae growth, too much for healthy fish. Many other aquatic creatures inhabit ponds, from frogs (see page 117) and newts to moorhens, reed warblers, swallows and martins after mud for nests, and small animals for drinking water. Beware the wandering heron if you have a shallow pond, for he will systematically fish it out. Put up a strand of thin wire round the pond on posts 18in (450mm) high. A heron cannot step over this to reach the pond.

General Although a pool may freeze over, water more than a couple of feet deep is unlikely to freeze solid and, provided a hole is kept open to allow noxious gases to escape and oxygen to get in, the fish will survive below the ice. Keep a large plastic football in the pool at night and remove it during the day, leaving a hole. Bail out a little water to

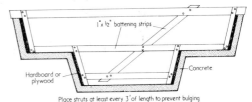

Fig 73

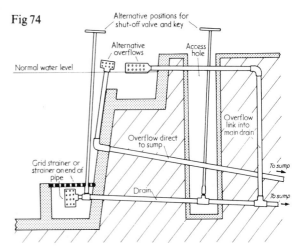

Fig 74

Natural pool

create an air space between ice and water where gas exchange may take place, but do not reduce the water level so that fresh ice layers keep forming. Electric pond heaters with insulated wiring are obtainable, and even an aquarium heater will keep a small hole open. Sweep snow off fishponds as it cuts out light.

Put a net over the pool in autumn to catch leaves or they will rot and choke the fish. A well set-up pond with plenty of growing plants should not become foul. Some green duckweek on the surface provides edible shade for the fish. If a pool becomes stagnant and smelly, remove the fish to a large container with some of their pond water and some fresh water, and give the new water in the pond a day at least to settle and mature. If the fish in the container show signs of distress, gasping at the surface or rolling, run in a trickle of water or put in an aerator, if you have one, until they can be returned to the pool.

Pond Fish The best species for garden fishponds are golden orf which grow up to 18in (450mm) long and live for many years. They need plenty of room in a well-established pond and will breed if there is a fountain or cascade. Carp thrive in big natural ponds, but do not show up at all so are not very rewarding, except when kept for food, in which case they should be fed regularly with oatmeal or barley. Golden or common tench are nice quiet greeny-gold fish, bottom feeders which scavenge away and keep the pool clean. Their presence in a pool is reputed to keep the other fish healthy and they are sometimes called 'doctor fish'. They need a medium-sized pool as do rudd (not roach which look very like them), silver fish with red fins. Both species are surface feeders, and may breed and thrive in ponds. Minnows do well but like a pond with fountains and cascades. Avoid the aggressive stickleback. Gudgeon are excellent scavengers, but you will not see much of them. Stone loach also scavenge and like some shallow, rocky, well-planted water in

which to lurk. They get very active before a storm hence their nickname 'weatherfish'.

None of the other native species of freshwater fish do well in garden pools; they get too big, cannot be seen, or just do not thrive.

Fish thrive on the natural contents of the pool but need extra dry food in warm weather. Like other creatures, they will swim near the surface and ask for it if they want it. Just feed them as much as they clear up. Unwanted food sinks, rots and fouls the water. Feed fish well in October and November before the water gets cold, as they can build up good flesh for the winter when they eat little and become very sluggish. Fish may look for food on sunny days in winter and should be given what they can eat.

Goldfish They grow well in outdoor pools if fed. If there is plenty of plant cover in the pool, where fry can hide, they may breed. Goldfish will spawn, but other fish and pool inhabitants usually eat up most of the fry as they hatch. (See also *Algae*; *Duckweed*, and *Trout Farming*).

Further Reading: Beedell, S., *Water in the Garden* (David & Charles); Harvey and Hems, *The Book of the Garden Pond* (Faber); Burton, R., *Ponds* (David & Charles).

Flagstones See *Algae*.

Fleas and Ticks There are forty-seven British species, all parasites of mammals or birds. On the whole fleas stay with their chosen hosts; the chicken flea, the rabbit flea, the cat flea, the dog flea, even if they land on you, will not usually bite, and will return as soon as possible to their own species of host. Domestic animals get flea and tick infestations very easily in the country, and the best way to treat them is with the appropriate flea shampoo, from your vet, and to burn all bedding, disinfect beds, etc, and start again. Fleas lay their eggs on the hosts or in their dens, nests or beds, and the eggs fall into the hosts' beds and the larvae live on nest debris, eventually returning to the host animal. (See also *Pests* and *Dogs*).

Flies The unwanted ones, use insecticides or fly repellants, but never in rooms with either tropical fish or goldfish, or caged birds. The best way to get rid of flies is to eradicate and clean their breeding grounds—rubbish dumps and dustbins—but in the countryside there always seem to be plenty about. A modern electric flycatcher is horrid but effective, and quite safe unless someone pokes a finger or a wire into it. Install well out of the reach of small children. The insects are attracted by the heat and light and fly in onto live wires.

If you are really plagued, then insect screens as used in the USA and tropical countries are the only answer. Make simple wooden frames to fit each opening window frame and cover them with fibreglass or fine nylon-mesh screening net, stapled or tacked into place. The edges and tacks are then covered with half-moon-shaped moulding mitred at the corners which can be prised off easily enough if the screening needs renewing. Hold the frames in place on the outsides of sash windows with turnbuckles, or on the insides of opening windows. They will have to be put up, in the latter case, after the windows have been opened, or hinged on the same side as the window, but opening inwards.

The Building Centre (see *Association Addresses* on page 12) will give you details of any manufacturers of screening operating in this country. (See also *Pests*.)

Further Reading: Ministry of Agriculture leaflet AL 365, *Houseflies, Blowflies, Cluster-flies* (HMSO).

Flooding See *Natural Disasters*.

Floors There are so many different types of modern flooring that it is impossible to describe them here. Check floors in old houses very carefully and remove any rotten or worm-eaten boards, and replace joists showing signs of rot. Have the house properly treated for woodworm. If you wish to cover up a rough old wooden floor in order to lay a carpet or other modern flooring material upon it, surface it with hardboard, butted tightly together and tacked firmly into place. To make a solid sub-floor, use chipboard, upon which wood blocks, vinyl or carpet can be successfully laid.

Slate (quarry tile) floors should not be touched with polish. Just clean with detergent and water. A little milk added to the last wipe over with a cloth will darken and shine the surface a bit. (See also *Woodworm*.)

Useful Address: Rentokil Laboratories Ltd, Felcourt, East Grinstead, Sussex.

Flowers (Wild) In spite of the depredations of chemical sprayers, indiscriminate pickers and uprooters, our countryside abounds in wonderful wild flowers. It is illegal to uproot any plant without the permission of the owner of the land. Only those flowers which grow in the utmost profusion, such as bluebells, should ever be picked in bunches. There was a time when meadows almost everywhere were full of cowslips and orchids, now rare in most areas because of over-picking. Some species of flowers have become jealously protected rarities. As a child in Norfolk, I could pick bunches of primroses from the hedgebanks of every field, and in every wood; now they have to be sought after.

Listed below are several good flower-identification books. For the beginner Collins Pocket Guide is the best as it avoids technical botanical words as far as possible, and is well keyed and illustrated. Visually, Keble Martin's book is one of the easiest from which to identify.

Dry Flowers Place them carefully between folded sheets of blotting paper, and weight with books. After drying, the flowers can be attached carefully to sheets of drawing paper with little strips of Sellotape, and annotations

It won't hurt to pick a few catkins

such as name, and place of discovery etc, written in. In this way, families, species and subspecies may be kept together.

A Photographic Collection Use colour slides for these, although without special equipment for microphotography it is difficult to record really small detail. However, anyone with a good camera might find it worthwhile to buy the necessary bellows extension and study the techniques. They are really not at all difficult and are most rewarding.

Design Pictures Make these from dried flower petals and leaves. Use diluted wallpaper adhesive, applied with a fine watercolour brush, to stick them to the paper backing, having first laid out your design and marked very lightly in pencil the position of each

Primroses

Jack in the Pulpit (wild arum)

separate piece. Frame the picture behind non-reflective glass, with a proper backing board, so that the flowers are pressed tight against the glass. Cover the back with a well-stuck-down piece of brown paper so that no moisture or insects can enter.

There are various ways of drying or preserving flowers for indoor arrangements.

Dangerous Plants About one hundred wild flowers and berries are poisonous, and it is as well to know at least the most common of these such as deadly nightshade, laburnum, yew, aconite, Jack in the pulpit, hemlock, monkshood and the rarer thorn apples. As a general rule don't eat the berries of wild or garden plants, except for blackberries, raspberries and elderberries, without proper identification.

Further Reading: Keble Martin, W., *The Concise British Flora, in Colour* (Michael Joseph); Fitch and Smith, *Illustrations of British Flora* (L. Reeve & Co Ltd); McClintock, D. and Fitter, R., *Collins Pocket Guide to Wild Flowers* (Collins); *The Observer's Book of Wild Flowers* (Warne); Polunin, Oleg, *Flowers of Europe* (Oxford University Press); Reverend Johns, *Flowers of the Field* (Routledge & Kegan Paul); Hutchinson, *British Wild Flowers* (David & Charles); Stevenson, *Dried Flowers for Decoration* (David & Charles); Tampion, Dr J., *Dangerous Plants* (David & Charles); Phillips, Roger, *Wild Flowers of Britain* (Pan).

Foot and Mouth Disease Should you be unfortunate enough to be in an area where restrictions on movement have been imposed due to an outbreak of foot and mouth disease,

113

you will be left in no doubt at all by the authorities as to what you can and cannot do. If your own stock is affected then your premises will be subject to Ministry of Agriculture control until the outbreak is over. All necessary slaughtering and disinfecting is done by the Ministry. When foot and mouth strikes an area no visitors or visiting are welcome. All domestic animals and pets must be kept shut up and totally under control, and all entrances to your property provided with disinfectant footbaths. Even car traffic is halted at the gates of clean areas so that the virus shall not be carried in on car tyres.

In other words you should, with your neighbours, do everything you possibly can to help to contain the outbreak and you will be most unpopular, and perhaps be breaking the law, if you don't co-operate. There is no vaccine available in this country against the disease, although research is continually going on, and our attitudes towards vaccination may in due course be altered by our involvement with our European Common Market partners, some of whom do have vaccination schemes. (See also *Notifiable Diseases*.)

Footpaths A footpath is exactly what it implies, a right of way for the walker. If he is carrying a gun and has a dog, then he may be using it for sporting purposes and could be trespassing. Dogs may be taken on footpaths for passage only. Horses and ponies must be led, *not* ridden, and if this is a regular occurrence, then the permission of the parish council should be sought. Anyone who uses a footpath across your land and strays from it, or uses it for any purpose other than passage, could be trespassing.

Footpaths have been dedicated by the original owner of the land, either in the form of a deed or else by implication, and any landowner can still do this if he wishes to create a footpath for use by the general public. If a footpath is really never used at all, then a landowner can apply to the local highway authority for an extinguishment or diversion order under Section 110 of the Highways Act, 1959. This would mean that the local authority would have to be satisfied that a shorter or better path was being provided or that the need for the footpath had completely disappeared.

Failing a width specified in writing in a deed of dedication, an inclosure award, or a statutory order, the generally accepted rule for the width of a footpath is that required for two people to pass, usually about 3ft (1m). In some cases, when the footpath runs between two hedges or some other physical boundary, the law assumes that the whole of the area is a footpath.

To find out if a footpath on your land is explicitly defined, consult the map and statement prepared by the county council in the course of the survey of public rights of way.

The local highway authority should pay for at least 25 per cent of the upkeep of stiles and gates, 100 per cent on long distance routes, and is responsible for the maintenance of the footpath. The owner must maintain the stiles and gates or the local authority may take care of them and send the occupier the bill. Normally agreement can be reached with your local authority over problems of this kind.

Public footpaths are marked with signposts where they leave a metalled road. These may be put up by the local authority without the landowner's permission, and often point straight across ploughed fields, or fields with crops in them. Anyone ploughing across a footpath for the sake of working convenience is only allowed to create a transitory barrier to progress, must give seven days' notice of his intention to do this, and should make good the surface within six weeks after ploughing. This is, in practical fact, frequently not done. The National Parks and Access to the Countryside Act makes it an offence, penalized by a fine, to plough up and not restore a path. Although you are not committing a trespass if you trample a path through standing crops, on the line of the footpath marked by signposts and on an ordnance survey map, be careful to keep exactly on the right line; you could be committing a trespass if you stray. You may remove an obstruction enough to allow you to get through.

I know of a case where a footpath had not been used for many years. The ground was regularly ploughed and cropped. Suddenly, because the owner of the land wished to turn his estate into a wildlife park, a gang of footpath walkers turned up and marched twelve abreast through standing corn. Many other footpaths on the same estate were regularly used and were maintained by the landowner who would have restored the ploughed one had he been asked. This kind of behaviour on the part of so called 'conservationists' is not calculated to win them many friends.

Land usage has changed, hedges are being torn down, woods grubbed out, etc, and footpaths do disappear. It is really a matter of all those concerned getting together and considering each others' interests as well as their own.

Various people make it their business to walk footpaths to keep them marked and open, and any local society interested in preservation or protection will certainly know who you should contact in your area.

The local authority may give fourteen days' notice, enter and restore the surface of a footpath. (See also *Bridleways*; *Rights of Way* and *Trespass*.)

Useful Addresses: The Council for the Protection of Rural England, 4 Hobart Place, London SW1; Commons, Open Spaces, and Footpaths Preservation Society, Suite 4, 166 Shaftesbury Avenue, London WC2H 8JH; Ramblers Association, 1/4 Crawford Mews, London W1H 1PT; Scottish Rights of Way Society, 32 Rutland Square, Edinburgh 1.

Further Reading: Campbell, A., *A Practical Guide to the Law of Footpaths*, and McArevey, M., *A Guide to Definitive Maps*, both obtainable from Commons, Open Spaces, and Footpaths Preservation Society.

Foreshore Rights The shore below high water mark is Crown Property unless the Crown has assigned it to someone else. This can be a local authority, a river board, the National or some other trust, a lord of the manor, or a private individual. No one has a right to cross an assigned foreshore or to park cars or boats or tents upon it. Foreshore controlled by local authorities is subject to their byelaws in such respects. That controlled by private individuals or others is protected by the laws of trespass in exactly the same way as any other property, and you cannot do anything without the express permission of the owners.

The ground above high water mark, mistakenly referred to as the foreshore, belongs to whoever owns the land adjoining it. In most cases, unless it is in the hands of owners of private houses, no one worries much about pedestrians using the area, but the moment cars or boats are parked, tents put up, and beaten tracks made, then farmers, golf clubs, and other owners are perfectly entitled to enforce their rights and can take action against trespassers if any damage has been done. Rights of way frequently do exist to allow access to beaches, but should not be assumed as a matter of course. (See also *Boundaries*; *Beachcombing*; *Rights of Way* and *Shooting*.)

Forestry See *Trees* and *Dutch Elm Disease*.

Fossils There are two basic types of fossils. First, those made by the alteration of the hard parts of shells and bones. Circulation of water has dissolved and replaced those parts by silica, lime and iron. The second types are moulds and casts. A plant or animal lies in soft mud which hardens into stone, then rots away leaving a perfect impression behind and thus making a mould, stone solidifying in this mould then makes a cast of the original (Figs 75 and 76).

Fossils

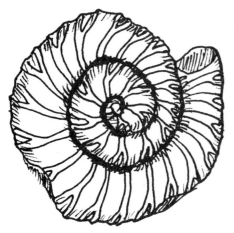

Fig 75 *Ammonite*

Fig 76 *Sea urchin*

Red fox

Ammonites are of the first type; whorled fossils by replacement of the ammonite by pyrites. In the second group are sea urchin fossils—flint casts of the creatures.

Look for fossils along the foot of chalk, sand, clay or limestone cliffs, slag or shale heaps from coalmines, and quarries. Do not climb up or down cliffs or rocks unless you know exactly what you are doing; these places can be very dangerous, even slag heaps can slide under your weight.

There are plenty of books and museum exhibits on the subject.

Further Reading: Rhodes, F. and Zim, H., *Fossils* (Hamlyn).

Foxes(*Vulpes vulpes*) The native red fox thrives in Britain and in recent years has become a surburbanite as well as a country dweller, taking rich pickings from dustbins and catching unwary cats. Some authorities believe that the urban fox is evolving into an unmistakably different type, much finer in bone structure than his rural brother and with a sandier coat. Some differences have been noted in the set of the teeth of the urban fox, evolving to make it easier to get lids off dustbins perhaps! It is only the fact that the fox is mainly nocturnal which leads many people to believe that he is fairly rare. Yet there is an estimated population of at least 200,000, reaching nuisance proportions in some areas.

Foxes eat all other small mammals and birds that they can catch, plus, in hard times, rats and even insects. Unfortunately they like domestic poultry and no such birds are safe at night unless carefully shut in. Foxes will even dig under doorways to get into pens, and can easily climb and jump over quite high walls and fences. They seem to become wildly excited by running birds and will kill indiscriminately, wiping out a whole flock of squawking hens when one would be enough.

Hunting is probably the most humane way to exterminate foxes and, although it may seem unpleasant, cubbing (or cub hunting), in the early autumn, is designed to control and cull the young foxes reared during the summer. Unfortunately the business of sending down terriers and digging out foxes is often necessary. You should notify your local hunt of a litter of cubs if they are likely to become a problem. Pest control officers will try to get rid of foxes for you, but may resort to gassing or poisoning. Neither method should be attempted by anyone without experience, and either can be terrible in execution. Shooting foxes is also a matter for the expert, as a shotgun will only kill a fox at very close range, and a non-fatal shot with a rifle, easy to inflict on such a large and quickly moving animal, can also lead to dreadful suffering. Gin traps are illegal. Snares which tighten inexorably each time the animal struggles will also inflict much agony before death. Ordinary snares which hold but do not tighten will keep the animal captive for some time and he can then be shot in the snare. Again, these should only be set by the experienced and will also catch cats, dogs and badgers unlucky enough to get into them. All in all, fox control is a problem.

The fox is a beautiful vicious killer. Were he an ugly creature one might feel less disposed to give him the benefit of the doubt when he has just wiped out one's harmless and useful poultry.

Orphan fox cubs are easy enough to rear, but unfortunately never become totally tame and must be released on maturity, so think twice before taking one on especially as foxes have a rank and lingering smell! (See also *Hunting* and *Traps*.)

Further Reading: Burrows, R., *Wild Fox* (David & Charles); Fitzgerald, B. Vesey, *Town Fox, Country Fox* (Survival Books, André Deutsch).

Frogs and Toads There are three species of frog and two of toad in this country. All are totally harmless and, as adults, eat nothing

(above) *Common toad*   (below) *Common frog*

but insects, slugs, snails and earthworms. They are themselves the food of many species; grass snakes, rats, pike, otters and herons. Tadpoles are a major food supply for fish, newts and other pond creatures. Only their phenomenal reproduction rate ensures the survival of the species, which have declined of late, so please do encourage frogs and toads to breed. For all their coldness they are pleasant creatures and we humans use them badly for many laboratory purposes, from dissection to pregnancy testing.

Fruit Wild fruits include blackberries, blueberries, crab apples, cranberries, elderberries, haws, medlars, rosehips, rowan berries, sloes, whortleberries.

Of the 500 subspecies of bramble, there are always some ready to pick from August to October, although they do say the Devil spits on them on 30 September. Use blackberries for wine, bramble jelly, blackberry and apple jam, for making purée to eat as a sauce with milk-puddings, making into mousses and whips with evaporated milk, white of egg, etc. Any recipe for raspberry desserts will probably be just as good with blackberries.

Blueberries (whortleberries) well sweetened, make lovely tarts and pies with shortcrust pastry, and can also be used for jelly to eat on bread or with meat and poultry.

Crab apples (see page 121) will make wine, puddings, pickles and jelly, but need more sugar and more cooking than ordinary apples as they are hard and very sour. They contain a lot of pectin and so their products set well. In fact they can be added to other fruit to provide pectin. They mix well with blackberries.

Cranberries, lightly stewed with sugar, make cranberry sauce to eat with turkey, or blend a pint (0.5 l) of cranberries and a tablespoonful of grated horseradish, the juice of half a lemon, and 3oz (85g) of white sugar in a liquidizer and serve as a relish with beef.

Haws make good wine and an unusual jelly.

Haws

Medlars can be used for jelly and wine.

Rosehips make good wine, and excellent syrup, although, for the latter, they must be de-pipped which is tedious. Put through a mincer, put in $1\frac{1}{2}$ pints (0.75 l) of boiling water to each 1lb (453g) of prepared hips. Leave for fifteen minutes, strain through a jelly bag, and then put the hips back in a saucepan, add $\frac{1}{2}$ pint (0.25 l) of boiling water and reboil. Stand for another twenty minutes and strain into the first lot of juice, reboil and reduce to 1 pint (0.5 l) of liquid. Add $\frac{1}{4}$lb (198g) of white sugar and reboil for five minutes. Use on milk puddings, or just by the spoonful, diluted to taste, as a drink.

Rowan, the red berries of the mountain ash tree, make good jelly and wine. The jelly is especially good with grouse.

Sloes make excellent wine, and even better

Rosehips

sloe gin (see *Liqueurs*) but are too sharp for other uses.

For jam and jelly recipes consult any good specialist book.

Fruit (Garden) This includes blackcurrants, redcurrants, strawberries, raspberries, loganberries, gooseberries, rhubarb (not a fruit but used as one), peaches, plums, greengages, damsons, cherries, apples, pears.

All fruit is expensive to buy these days, so if you have your own ground it is well worth growing it. Then there is the extra pleasure of eating really fresh fruit, and of preserving or freezing what cannot be used at the time. Strawberries, raspberries, loganberries and any of the hybrid berries of this type produce enormous crops in relation to the space they take up and are ridiculously easy to grow. Late fruiting types of raspberry, such as 'Zeva', do well and produce fruit up to the end of October. A couple each of well-established gooseberry, blackcurrant and redcurrant bushes, will provide pounds of fruit. All can be established in two seasons.

The others mentioned above all grow on trees and so take considerably longer to establish to the point where they produce a crop, but in the long term are worth it.

Bird Damage to Fruit Most birds love soft fruit, and unless this is grown in proper wire cages it may be necessary to net it using fine-mesh nylon net on stakes. Open the netting in winter so birds may get in to kill pests. Black cotton strung backwards and forwards over strawberry beds, in and out of raspberry canes, both high and low, will deter birds who only need to bump into it once to be frightened away. Cats are the ultimate deterrent! Blackbirds and others go for cherries. It is a matter of beating them to it, unless you install an automatic bird scarer, which is effective, but usually creates bad feeling among neighbours without fruit, who prefer peace and quiet (see *Nuisances* page 168). Bits of aluminium foil and other patent scarers do a little good, but birds get used to them very quickly. Some people pull old nylon stockings over branches of cherries to preserve at least a few for themselves. It looks most odd. Of course a blast or two with a shotgun is more effective than anything else, but again local bird lovers may get upset. Bullfinches and other finches can wreak absolute havoc among the buds of fruit bushes and apple trees, just picking them off and eating them. There is really no sure fire way to get rid of them (except cats). Special sprays will keep the birds off, but are likely to do too much damage to the fruit and other plants.

Children as bird scarers come a bit pricey these days. Pigeons are devils for picking away at vegetable seedlings, especially peas, and netting may be the only answer until the plants are really well grown up. Pigeons will also attack winter vegetables especially in hard weather. I do not know how else to get rid of them except by shooting. If you don't like cats, train a dog to chase birds, he will get rid of them without killing them, but of course may himself do damage to plants.

Blewits. Growing in the autumn among fallen leaves in meadows by trees. Bun brown on top, pale mauve beneath

Hawk-shaped kites keep away birds, but cannot be flown for long without attention, except in very steady weather.

Crab Apples This is the original wild apple on which all cultivated apple stocks are based. Hard, small and green, ripening to scarlet, they will give anyone bad stomach ache if eaten raw. Crab apples contain much pectin so are favourites for jelly.

Medlars These are not really very common but can be found in old cottage orchards and wild in hedgerows. The medlar has gnarled grey bark on a crooked trunk, usually thorny, and large, pale green, oblong leaves with almost no stalks and slightly downy. The five-petalled solitary white flowers of May turn into pear-shaped yellowish-brown fruit in little cups. Gather them in October and store them until they soften, then use the fruit. Cook it with plenty of white sugar and a few drops of vanilla, then put it through a sieve or liquidizer and serve with dollops of cream for a dessert.

Medlars also make good wine. Use 6–8lb (2¼–3¼kg) of ripe soft fruit, crush it and pour boiling water over it and then, after two days, strain this into a demijohn, add 2lb (1kg) sugar made into syrup, and a teaspoonful of pectozyme, 1 teaspoonful of yeast nutrient, and 1 dessertspoonful of yeast started in some of the juice, when the liquid is at blood heat. (See *Wine-making*, page 249, and *Liqueurs*).

121

Giant puffball

Further Reading: Beedell, S., *Pick, Cook and Brew* (Pelham); David, Elizabeth, *Summer Cooking* (Penguin); *Farmhouse Fare* (Hulton Press Ltd); Wright, Macer, *Countryman Gardening Book* (David & Charles); Hills, L. D., *Grow Your Own Fruit and Vegetables* (Faber); Oldale, A. and P., *Growing Fruit, 1001 Questions Answered* (David & Charles).

Fungi Apart from the well known field mushrooms (*Agaricus campestris*) there are many varieties of edible fungi, several of which usually get kicked over as 'toadstools'. These include the puffball, the parasol mushroom, field and wood blewits, fairy ring mushrooms or champignons, chanterelles, morels, horse mushrooms of several varieties, and St George's mushrooms.

There are no rules of thumb whatsoever which divide the edible from the deadly. Only a positive identification against a well-illustrated text book is safe, and even then you must be very certain. No identification chart is included here because colour is essential for safe identification. However, once having properly identified any of the species mentioned above, you will never mistake them for anything else, nor will you mistake anything else for them.

Keep away from what look like field mushrooms, but are pale olive-yellow on top and white underneath, or only very pale pink, and have a white sheath, or vulva, at the base of the stem, as they are the deadliest of all, the 'death cap'—*Amanita phalloides* (Fig 77). They grow in or near deciduous woods, particularly beech and oak, in the late summer and early autumn.

It is as well to study your book and get the picture of the several deadly species firmly in your mind before looking for edible fungi. An expert friend can be a great help to resolve doubts, but once again be sure he really is an expert.

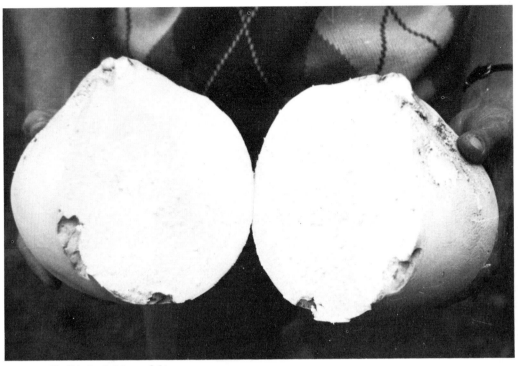

Giant puffball halved. Most of this one was eaten at once, the rest was deep frozen

Incidentally it is no offence to take mushrooms of any kind or to trespass to find them. Wild mushrooms and other fungi become the property of the picker the moment they are picked. Action could only be taken for trespass for which only a nominal award would be made in the absence of malicious damage. Only if the owner could prove that mushroom spawn had actually been put down would he keep you from picking them, as he could claim they were cultivated. Equally, the only way to prevent others from picking fungi on your property is to get there first.

Further Reading: Forestry Commission leaflets No 106, *Mushrooms and Toadstools of Broadleaved Forests*, and No 107, *Mushrooms and Toadstools of Coniferous Forests* (HMSO); Wakefield, *The Observer's Book of Common Fungi* (Warne); Svrcek, Dr, *Mushrooms* (Octopus Books).

Fig 77

123

Furniture Country furniture is so popular that the days of cheap 'finds' at sales and in junk shops are long past. One can pay £60 for an ugly kitchen table which would not have fetched a fiver twenty years ago. Any antique chests, cupboards, tables and chairs, eg, beechwood chairs with elmwood seats, fetch fantastic prices. Even painted or varnished softwood cupboards and dressers which can be stripped down command high prices and become harder and harder to find.

There are firms who specialize in making new furniture to traditional designs using old wood, not exactly 'reproduction' as it does not pretend to be what it is not. Pine furniture made from old and therefore well seasoned, once used wood, can be made to your own requirements and looks much nicer than the same things made from new wood.

Such furniture is not cheap, but certainly costs less than antiques, and can be just as beautiful.

Useful Address: The Collins Brothers, 2 Bedford Road, Southborough, Tunbridge Wells, Kent (make country furniture from antique pine).

Further Reading: Toller, *Country Furniture* (David & Charles); Woodforde, J., *Furnishing a Country Cottage* (David & Charles); Lloyd, G., Ed *Polish and Shine*, WI leaflet; Filbee, M., *Dictionary of Country Furniture* (Ebury).

G

Game This term is applied to those wild animals, birds and fish which are hunted for sport or food, and to the flesh thereof.

Game birds which may be shot in Great Britain at permitted times of the year are the pheasant, partridge, grouse, blackgame, capercaillie, ptarmigan, woodcock, snipe, wildfowl and wild goose. The open seasons for shooting these birds are:

pheasant	1 Oct–31 Jan
partridge	1 Sept–31 Jan
grouse	12 Aug–10 Dec
blackgame	20 Aug–10 Dec
capercaillie	1 Oct–31 Jan
ptarmigan	12 Aug–10 Dec
woodcock (England and Wales)	1 Oct–31 Jan
woodcock (Scotland)	1 Sept–31 Jan
snipe	12 Aug–31 Jan
wildfowl (inland)	1 Sept–31 Jan
wildfowl (foreshore)	1 Sept–20 Feb
wild goose	1 Sept–20 Feb

Game animals are the hare, rabbit, red deer, roe deer, sika deer and fallow deer. Game fish are salmon, sea trout and brown trout. Close seasons for deer and fishing may be found under those headings

Useful Address: The Game Conservancy, Fordingbridge, Hants, issues a leaflet on how to tell the age and condition of game birds.

Further Reading: Drysdale, Julia, *The Game Cookery Book* (Collins). Hargreaves, Barbara, *The Sporting Wife* (Witherby).

Gardens 'All England is a garden, such gardens are not made by saying "Oh how beautiful" and sitting in the shade.' My mother's favourite quote about gardens, if a little trite, rather sums it up, and a country garden can be an enormous pleasure, or a life sentence to hard labour. A small country garden is little different from a town garden of the same size, but a big country garden contains trees of all sizes, areas of wilderness and weeds, perhaps marshy or shaded areas, running or still water, and is exposed to cutting winds or blazing sunshine, to frost running downhill into sheltered pockets. All these problems need a different approach and the garden must be planned to take these factors into account and, more than anything, to take into account the amount of time and work you are prepared to put into it. Nowadays big lawns are no problem, various types of mechanical cutters see to that; but the edges must still be trimmed! So it may be only a partial solution to put it all down to grass. (See also *Motor Mowers*.)

Further Reading: Wright, Macer, *Countryman's Gardening Book* (David & Charles); Beedell, S., *Water in the Garden* (David & Charles); Fish, M., *Cottage Garden Flowers* (David & Charles).

Gates Maintain your gates well. Gates which will not swing and shut properly are much more likely to be left open than good gates, and wear out much sooner. Gate posts must be strong and set in a hole at least 2ft (600mm) down with plenty of stones tamped down hard round the base, or with strong box anchors (see page 95). Good properly hung gates do much to improve the look of a place, and are stockproof and safe.

An effective, stockproof but untidy looking gate can be made with four or five fence posts (according to width) and barbed wire and staples. The two outer posts should be about a foot (300mm) longer than the inner ones. Make the gate about a foot (300mm) narrower than the gap to be filled. Attach one end of it firmly with loops of wire to the hanging post, and staple a loop of wire at the top and bottom of the shutting post. Place the bottom of the outside post in the bottom loop on the shutting post, pull the gate across at the top and slip the top loop over the outside post. This should shut the gate with enough tension to make it stockproof (Fig 78).

Gates of split chestnut or ash, or oak pales, can be made simply, without mortice and tenon joints, provided they are tightly bolted (Fig 79). (See also *Access* and *Fencing*.)

Geese (Ornamental) Ornamental geese are easier to keep than ducks as they need little

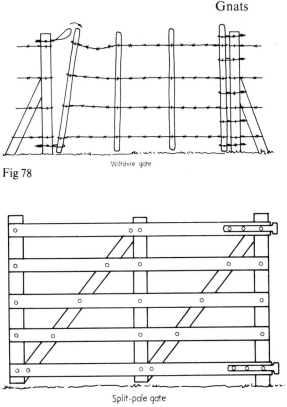

Fig 78

Wiltshire gate

Fig 79

Split-pale gate

water, just enough for an occasional splash, although they will appreciate a pond. Being big they are less vulnerable to predators and so do not necessarily need enslosure, although a fox may take a goose occasionally. They need only one feed a day of a little grain and household vegetable scraps, and otherwise act as very efficient lawn mowers, especially useful in orchards and areas difficult to mow by machine. If they breed they will rear their own young. Breeders of ornamental ducks will also supply geese. Goose eggs make very good omelettes! (See also *Poultry, Ducks* and *Shooting*.)

Generators See *Electricity*.

Gnats See *Mosquitoes*.

125

(opposite) *Ornamental geese with raft shelter*

Goats A good goat will provide milk for two years between kiddings. Goats must be milked twice a day and are therefore a definite tie. The milk has a stronger taste than cows' milk and not everyone likes it. It is often medically recommended in cases of asthma and eczema, to replace all bovine products to which sufferers are allergic. Goats do not suffer from bovine TB or brucellosis so the

Milking

milk can be drunk unpasteurized. It makes very good yoghurt and soft curd cheese. Any surplus can be used for rearing calves, lambs or pigs destined for the freezer, or for weaning kittens and puppies. Siamese cats may take goats' milk but reject cows' milk.

Goats must be kept in enclosures of pig or sheep netting 4ft (1.2m) high fixed to posts at 6ft (1·8m) centres, or, for short periods they can be tethered on a running tether—a line staked firmly at each end, with a shorter line to the goat's collar attached to a ring sliding along the tether. If tethered, water must be far enough from the tether so it cannot be knocked over and a shelter of some kind also at full tether length. If you have no grazing and are prepared to carry all food in, then goats can be kept successfully in a yard with some dry shelter.

Goats will thrive in summer on grass, branches and various kinds of weeds, but when growing, pregnant, or in milk, need concentrates to provide extra protein—up to 4lb (1¾kg) a day—and will need hay, and kale if available, in winter.

Go to your next county show and visit the goat tent for advice and information and a chance to see the different breeds.

Useful Address: The British Goat Society, Mrs May, Lion House, Rougham, Bury St Edmunds, Suffolk (for full information and address of your nearest goat club).

Further Reading: *Goat Feeding* (British Goat Society); *Dairy Work for Goatkeepers* (British Goat Society); Jeffery, H. E., *Goats* (Cassell); Downing, E., *Keeping Goats* (Pelham), MacKenzie, D., *Goat Husbandry* (Faber); Shields, J., *The Modern Dairy Goat* (Pearson); Salmon, J., *The Goatkeeper's Guide* (David & Charles); Ministry of Agriculture leaflet No AL 118, *Dairy Goatkeeping* (HMSO).

Grants Grants are available from many sources for all kinds of things, and these are intended to preserve our countryside and its buildings, to establish amenities, to help with the high costs of such things as tree planting and to bring old properties up to modern standards of living.

In fact, in these days of enlightened planning, every effort is being made to preserve and improve, whether property is privately or publicly owned.

There is a horticulture development scheme which provides capital grant aid over a very wide range of projects. But these grants are not easily come by and there are a number of qualifying tests. For example, there is a minimum income test which seeks to make sure that all applicants can make at least £2,900 per annum from their land once the improvement is completed. Similarly, accommodation for pigs is grant aidable, but only if the applicant intends to spend between £5,000 and £25,000 and has a farm big enough to supply at least a third of the pigs' feeding stuffs.

Capital grants are available for buildings, silos, yards, farm waste disposal, gas and electricity, water supply and storage, purchase of livestock, roads, bridges, field drainage, pens, land improvement items, orchard grubbing, freshwater fish farming for food, plant and machinery. Should you wish to know the possibilities, contact your nearest office of the Ministry's Agricultural Development and Advisory Services, whose officers are there to help. The main thing is not to assume that grants are available automatically, or to start work on any project for which a grant is available before plans have been approved by the Ministry of Agriculture. (See also *Ancient Monuments*; *Historic Buildings*; *Nature Conservancy*; *Trees* and *Home Improvement Grants*.)

Further Reading: Ministry of Agriculture leaflets, FH1, HCGS 1, and FCG 1; books nos 23–77 (HMSO).

Grass To get the best out of an orchard or paddock for ponies, donkeys, house cows or goats, it should be farmed. Invest in an electric fence and allow the stock access to only one-third at a time. When that has been eaten down (but not too closely or nothing will re-grow but weeds and ploughing up and reseeding is the only cure), close it off and move on to the next place, and so on. This allows the grass to grow again in the first pieces. All stock prefer short freshly grown grass. Cut weeds and remove and burn them, particularly yellow ragwort (which is poisonous to stock, growing or cut and dead) also thistles, docks and nettles. Take out and spread droppings. Stock will not feed on grass growing strongly around their own dunged areas. A dressing of basic slag in autumn sweetens the ground and a little nitrogenous fertilizer in the spring promotes growth. It really does depend on the type of ground and its basic fertility. A long established meadow which has been well looked after will produce any amount of grazing if given occasional dressings of fertilizers, and if it is rested and trimmed properly. Grazing land may also need a dressing of lime every three or four years.

Haymaking If you wish to make a little hay for the winter, and have not enough to justify machinery or getting a farmer to do it for you, wait until the grass has grown tall and is just in flower, but is still green with a thick bottom to it. Do not leave it too long or it will become yellow, dried out and seedy.

Wait for a spell of good weather and cut it and spread it around loosely. Next day, provided there has been no rain, turn the hay again, and again on the morning of the third day. If the weather is really hot, then by afternoon the hay should feel dry and crackly when a handful is taken up and twisted, and it can then be raked (see *Hayrake*) into rows, collected and stacked in an open shed.

Haymaking is largely a matter of experience, so take advice from someone who knows until you have gained that experience.

To reseed an area, best done in May, it must be ploughed and cultivated until a very fine seed bed has been made. Scatter a suitable small-paddock grass-seed mixture (take advice from agricultural merchants or seedsmen) over the area and rake it in. If possible roll the surface so that the soil is consolidated round the seeds. Once a good growth has been established the grass can be lightly grazed or mown and then laid up again for a few weeks. This will do it nothing but good as it causes the roots to grow and spread. Reseeding can also be done in early September if the soil is not dry, but must not be grazed until the following spring.

Burning Grass and Heather The burning of rough grass (and heather) is prohibited in England and Wales from 31 March to 15 November, except in Northumberland and Durham where the period is 15 April to 31 October. Landowners must get a licence if they wish to burn during this period. Get application forms from divisional offices of the Ministry of Agriculture. Twenty-eight days' notice is required. Take precautions, don't burn at night between sunset and sunrise, and give at least forty-eight hours' notice in writing to anyone having an interest in the land and to neighbours. Adequate supervision and safety equipment must be available. (See also *Motor Mowers* and *Horses*.)

Further Reading: Hubbard, C. E., *Grasses* (Pelican Books).

Grass Snakes See *Snakes*.

Greenhouses Modern greenhouses are very easy to put up and come with complete instructions. The smallest, 6 × 6ft (1.75 × 1.75m) greenhouse, provides a surprising amount of room for growing bedding plants, etc, and a few pot plants and tomatoes. A 'cool' greenhouse, unheated except perhaps with a portable oil stove in the worst frosts, is adequate for this work, but must be heated (and this is expensive) if it is to house non-winter-hardy plants of any kind. Before deciding on

the size, remember that a big greenhouse will cost a lot to heat, and will take up a great deal of time if it is to be properly used. For most garden purposes a greenhouse about 8 × 10ft (2 × 3m) is adequate. In any case it can always be extended and can be sited with that in view.

Planning permission is necessary.

Grouse There are four species: the red grouse of the heather hills; the black grouse in the grassy woodlands; the capercaillie in coniferous woodlands, and the ptarmigan in the high bare mountains—all inhabit Scotland. The capercaillie is found in the north of England and north and central Wales, and the red grouse can also be found in all the moorland areas of the British Isles. Red grouse are the sportsman's target and although thousands

Controlling heather burning

The results of good heather burning

130

are shot, the population is not endangered as there is always a surplus which, if not culled, would probably die of starvation during their first winter. As it is, the owners of shooting moors burn large areas of heather in rotation to ensure the growth of new young plants on which the grouse can feed, thereby maintaining the population at as high a level as possible. (See also *Game*.)

Guard Dogs See *Dogs*.

Guinea Fowl See *Poultry*.

Guns See *Shooting*.

Gun Dogs See *Dogs*.

H

Ha-Ha A ha-ha is a kind of small dry moat designed to exclude unwanted animals from a garden, without obstruction of the view. It is usually built where house and garden are at a higher level than the ground in front (Fig 80).

First excavate a ditch (on your own land if it is a boundary). This should be 5ft (1.5m) deep at the garden side, 4ft (1.22m) across the bottom, and about 9ft (2.75m) across the top, and should have a slight fall to carry away water. There will be a lot of spoil which will have to be transported elsewhere or spread around. Then build a brick or stone supporting wall on the garden side. This should be on a concrete base about 2ft (610mm) wide and 9in (230mm) thick, and should come right up to garden level and be topped with coping stones. Set small land drains in the wall so that backed up moisture can escape. The wall must be strongly built or pressure of water and soil behind it will cause it to collapse in time. On the field side the slope should be at about 45 degrees and need not be stone-faced

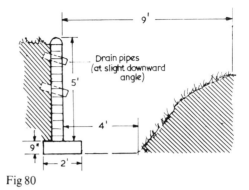

Fig 80

Brown hare

but seeded or turfed so that it does not slip.

The odd name is supposed to be the exclamation made by someone coming unexpectedly upon the ditch, in which case it would be more likely to be pronounced 'ha HAAAAAAAh!' as in *Winnie the Pooh*.

Ham See *Preserving Food.*

Hares (*Lepus capensis*) Hares are much bigger than rabbits, with longer ears and longer hind legs. The brown hare lives in open country, downlands, sand-dunes and lowlands generally. It spends the day in shallow depressions under cover, known as forms, and feeds mainly at twilight and just after dark. Hares are unaffected by myxomatosis and, since rabbit populations were reduced, have taken over some woodland areas. Mountain or blue

Mountain hare in its white winter coat

hares, *Lepus timidus*, are a little smaller than brown hares and live in rocky terrain mostly in the Scottish mountains. In winter their coats turn white for snow camouflage, but their ear tips always remain black.

Hares make good eating, but are unpleasantly bloody to skin and prepare for the pot. (See also *Game* and *Hunting*.)

Further Reading: Ewart Evans, G., and Thompson, D., *The Leaping Hare* (Faber).

Harriers See *Hunting.*

Haymaking See *Grass.*

Hay Rake Essential tool for haymaking without machinery and always useful around the garden, a hayrake is easy to make. For the handle use a freshly cut ash pole which fits your hand and height comfortably, and split it at one end to about 18in (450mm) back. A

Fig 81

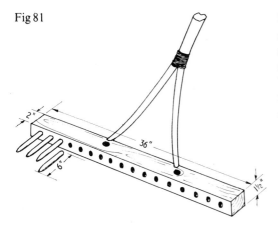

bar on its long side, about a foot (300mm) apart, slightly slanting, big enough to take the split ends of the ash pole. Drill holes 2in (50mm) apart through the other plane of the bar to take the tines, which should be a tight fit and need to be tapped home. Such a rake can be knocked up in no time, and costs nothing. A good dollop of woodglue in the holes will help to keep the tines in place, and a couple of wedges tapped in alongside the split ash in the bar will tighten up the handle assembly. Bind just above the split with wire (Fig 81).

piece of wood about a yard (915mm) long makes the bar, with sixteen or seventeen 6in (150mm) pegs or tines of oak, about ½in (10mm) in diameter, whittled to a rounded point at one end. Drill a couple of holes in the

Hazel Nuts See *Nuts*.

Heating See *Calor Gas; Solar Heating* and *Solid Fuel Stoves).*

Hedgehog and young

Heavy Horses See *Farmhorses*.

Hectare This is the metric unit of area measurement which has replaced the acre. To be exact: 1 hectare, 1 are and 17 square metres equals exactly 2¼ acres. If you must translate acres into hectares accurately then buy a ready reckoner!

Agricultural returns must be made in hectares, but the Ministry has to employ people to reconvert the hectares to acres before it can make up its analysis!

Hedgehog (*Erinaceus europaeus*) the nocturnal hedgehog lives in fields, hedgerows, open woodland and gardens. At dusk and dawn he comes out to feed on insects, worms, fallen fruit and any small creatures he can find. Hedgehogs can be trained to come to a saucer of milk put out regularly. They catch adders by biting them and then rolling up until the snake has attacked so often that its venom is exhausted and it becomes easy prey for the hedgehog. Foxes kill hedgehogs by forcing them towards water where they must swim to escape and then catching them while swimming unrolled. Badgers have some trick which forces hedgehogs to unroll, whereupon they disembowel them.

Mating hedgehogs chase round in tight circles nose to tail letting out the most fearful banshee wails imaginable, a sound which even many country people have never heard.

So many hedgehogs are killed by cars because their protective reaction to everything, including an approaching motor, is to curl up into a ball. One wonders when some extra bright beast will decide to run instead and by surviving and breeding produce an evolved hedgehog which does not always curl up!

Further Reading: Forestry Commission leaflet No 77, *Hedgehogs* (HMSO); Burton, M., *The Hedgehog* (André Deutsch).

Hedges Hedges provide the ideal fence. They are stockproof without being dangerous, they

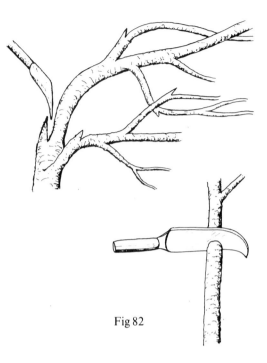

Fig 82

break up strong winds, they provide shelter and shade. They also provide a habitat for many species of flora and fauna. Thousands of miles of hedges have been removed for agricultural convenience, but some 600,000 miles remain, an area twice that of our nature reserves. In the old days hedges were maintained by handwork. Every five years or so the tall saplings were thinned out, with enough left to be split, laid over at an angle (Fig 82) and interwoven, so that the following year's growth would form a thick and even barrier (Fig 83). To make the symmetrical perfectly interwoven hedge of the expert takes years of practice, but to make a good stockproof barrier is really very easy. Split saplings can be held in place by stakes with an angled shoot at the top, if they cannot be interwoven, and extra pieces threaded in to finish off and firm up (Fig 84). Nowadays mechanical hedge cutters have transformed the art of hedging. Once the hedge has been established, annual clipping causes it to thicken and bush

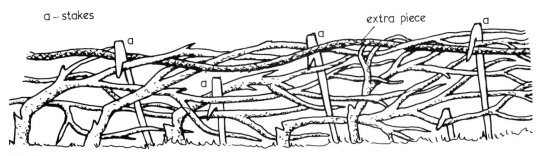

a – stakes   extra piece   a

Fig 83

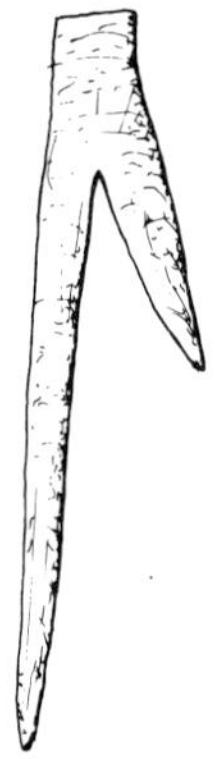

Fig 84

out into a stockproof and very neat fence, never needing to be cut and laid.

Hawthorn, hazel and blackthorn make excellent and quick growing hedges, laid once and then kept clipped. In some areas beech is used and, although slower growing, it makes very solid and wind-resistant barriers, retaining its leaves until late in the year.

For garden hedges there are many flowering and evergreen shrubs from rhododendrons to tamarisk, and conifers of the cypress family. Take advice from a local nurseryman as to what is suitable for your soil and locality. Some species do better near the sea than others, and some will only thrive on acid soils.

There is no legal maximum height for a hedge, but if it overhangs a public highway or footpath, or obscures light from a street lamp, you must cut it back if the local authority serves you with a notice, or they will do it and send you the bill. (See also *Boundaries*.)

Hens See *Poultry*.

Herbs Dried herbs from a shop are a good substitute for fresh herbs, and it is well worth drying or deep freezing your surplus crop of summer herbs for winter use, but nothing beats fresh herbs.

Most herbs can be raised from seed, either planted direct or started in a cold frame or greenhouse, others do best propagated from cuttings.

Mint There are many varieties. *Mentha spicata* is best for mint sauce; broad-leaved mint is fine for cooking with vegetables (peas, new potatoes, etc), and variegated apple mint is delicately flavoured for chopping into salads. All are best grown from runners taken from established plants (in your friends' gardens) and need only to be set in damp soil to take root and thrive.

Marjoram This will also grow from runners.

Dill, *Parsley*, *Chervil* and *Borage* Sow a pinch of seed directly into the garden.

Fennel, *Hyssop*, *Chives* and *Lovage* Sow a pinch in March, April and May.

Pot Marjoram, *Rosemary*, *Sage* and *Thyme* Make cuttings and grow in sand until established, then plant out.

Basil Sow seed in March in fine seed compost in a cool greenhouse, and put plants into individual pots when well established. Will thrive in conservatories out of doors in summer, but must be kept indoors in the winter.

Spread lemon-scented *Balm* by division, and also *Chives*. Do this in late March.

Angelica The seeds should be sown in September–October in a cold greenhouse. They do not remain fertile for long so must be

135

got going early. The plants should be put out in early spring.

Garlic Plant cloves of garlic in the garden in midwinter and they will produce giant-sized bulbs the following year.

To Dry Herbs Pick them when leaves and stems are young and tender, flowers when fully open, seeds when ripe, according to type. Always pick dry, but not in the heat of the day. Tie in small bunches and hang in an airy place, or lay out on sheets of paper. When dry, put the herbs into glass jars with airtight tops and store in a dark place. Check on the first morning after putting in the jars; if the herbs are not dry there will be mist inside the jar, and the herbs must be tipped out and dried again.

Growing Herbs A herb garden should be sheltered from the north, yet not too shady, and the different species should be set out so that they can easily be reached for picking. A chessboard design of stones or concrete slabs and earth makes separate plots for each herb, limits their spread and keeps your feet from the mud.

Soil should be well-drained and of medium texture, not too light or heavy. Dig in well rotted compost or manure, and some bonfire ashes before planting. Do not use artificial fertilizers as herbs do not usually need them.

Many herbs can be found wild; garlic grows in sandy soil near the sea. Fennel grows particularly well near the sea but can be found in many habitats. Wild mint, wild marjoram and wild thyme are common. Many other wild herbs can be used for cooking, for herb teas, etc.

Further Reading: Beedell, S., *Herbs for Health and Beauty* (Sphere Books); Loewenfeld, C., *Herb Gardening* (Faber).

Historic Buildings If you own or live in a building of outstanding architectural or historic interest, it may be eligible for repair or conservation grants from the Historic Buildings Council. If it is already listed permission must be sought for any proposed alterations.

The Civic Trust also administers grants from this council for purposes not covered by existing exchequer or local authority grants.

Local authorities have powers to make grants and loans for the repair or maintenance of buildings.

Grants are available for historic gardens.

The Architectural Heritage Fund will in some cases provide short term loan capital for buildings preservation trusts.

House renovation grants through local authorities may in some cases be obtained. (See also *Ancient Monuments* and *Grants*.)

Useful Addresses: Historic Buildings Council for England, 25 Savile Row, London W1X 2HE, Architectural Heritage Fund, Civic Trust, 17 Carlton House Terrace, London SW1Y 5AW; Ancient Monuments Secretariat, Department of the Environment, Fortress House, 25 Savile Row, London W1X 2HE; Department of the Environment, 2 Marsham Street, London SW1P 3EB; The Society for the Protection of Ancient Buildings, 55 Great Ormond Street, London WC1N 3JA; Local Authorities, County Councils' Amenities and Countryside Committee, County Hall.

Further Reading: booklets Nos 23/77, *Grants for Listed Buildings* (HMSO).

HMSO Her Majesty's Stationery Office produces an enormous range of publications many of which are very useful indeed. The agricultural section alone contains hundreds of leaflets on agricultural and horticultural subjects.

No 1, Agriculture and Food
No 5, Department of the Environment
No 27, Ancient Monuments and Historic Buildings
No 31, Forestry Commission
No 37, Meteorological Office
No 50, Miscellaneous
No 61, Building

The AL series of leaflets are free, or cost just a few pence. The digests cost a few pence.

Addresses of Government bookshops: 49, High Holborn, London SE1 9NH (callers only); PO Box 569, London SE1 9NH (post); 13a Castle Street, Edinburgh EH2 3AR; 41 The Hayes, Cardiff CF1 1JW; 80, Chichester Street, Belfast BT1 4JY; Brazenose Street, Manchester M60 8AS; 258 Broad Street, Birmingham B1 2HE; Southey House, Wine Street, Bristol BS1 2BQ.

Home Curing See *Preserving Food.*

Home Improvement Grants The following grants are available under the Housing Act, 1947. Apply to your local authority *before* starting any work at all.

Improvement Grants These are given at the discretion of local authorities towards the cost of modernizing old houses to a good standard. After improvement the dwelling must meet a prescribed standard and have a useful life of thirty years. The maximum eligible expense is £3,200, but the local authority may be prepared to approve a higher amount (which varies according to grade) if the dwelling is listed and the improvements involve special works or the use of materials necessary to maintain its character. Grants cannot, however, be approved for the improvement of owner-occupied dwellings with a rateable value above £300 in Greater London and £175 elsewhere in England. Where a property is being converted, with the help of a grant, to form two or more dwellings, in one of which the owner will continue to reside while the rest are made available for letting, the rateable value limits are doubled.

Intermediate Grants These are available as of right for the provision of standard amenities which a dwelling lacks, but may also assist with the cost of any repairs necessary to bring it up to a reasonable standard and give it a life of fifteen years. Grant is based on an eligible expense of up to £700 for standard amenities

and up to an additional £800 for repairs. These grants are given subject to conditions which require that the dwelling be kept in owner-occupation, or available for letting for a period of five years. The amount of grant is determined as a percentage of the expense eligible for grant. This is normally 50 per cent.

Honey Honey is just about the most natural food there is, and is most health giving; it can be used as a substitute for sugar for every purpose, and gives a pleasant and distinctive flavour to such things as tea, coffee or fruit. It is excellent with baked apples, or on cereal or porridge.

Use honey to make wines; mead (honey wine), metheglin (honey and herb wine), or melomel (honey and fruit juice wine). Use $2\frac{1}{2}$lbs (1kg) honey per gallon of water.

Take a spoonful of honey to glaze roast meat, ham and pork.

Straight or mixed with a little rum it makes a delicious sauce for ice cream.

For cake and biscuit making, substitute three quarters of the weight in honey for the stated amount of sugar and reduce the amount of liquid used by one tablespoonful for every four tablespoons of honey. Add a small pinch of baking soda to neutralize the acids in the honey.

When using honey for jams or sweets, a higher degree of heat will be needed.

Cakes and biscuits made with honey are brown and a little chewy. They absorb atmospheric moisture and so keep well. For the same reason, sweets made with honey must be stored in airtight tins so that moisture is not absorbed.

All books on beekeeping devote chapters to honey extraction and storage. (See also *Bees.*)

Hornets See *Wasps.*

Horses To buy and keep a horse can be expensive. It must have proper shelter, and a good horse must be fed hay, nuts and oats all year round if it is to be ridden constantly,

Useful cob type of pony for both children and adults. Rough, tough and good fun, if not elegant. Here being ridden by boys from the Junior Leaders Regiment

138

grazing being purely supplementary, particularly for hunters in summer, and for brood mares, mares and foals. Unless you have two or three acres for the horse to stretch his legs in and graze (and this should be divided into thirds—see *Grass*—animals kept grazing in the same area for more than six weeks may have to be wormed, so the horse must be moved regularly), he must be exercised every single day, even in snow, when he must be led. This really meant that to contemplate keeping a horse without some grazing ground is letting yourself in for a lot of time-consuming work. In addition the horse must be shod every six to eight weeks according to use, and

his feet checked and cleaned every day. Tack—saddlery, bridles, etc—must be fitted to each animal and kept in perfect condition, and the horse will require grooming and brushing over once a day, and mane and tail pulled occasionally. If he is in a stable, food and water must be taken in twice or three times a day, and the stable mucked out morning and night.

If the horse is to be used for hunting he must be at least partially clipped during the winter and kept rugged up (rugs are another

Small girl and small Shetland pony. Oversize stirrups and wellingtons, hat on the back of the head and no chinstrap. (Compare with picture, top right p. 141.)

expensive item). Unless you live right in the middle of hunting country and are prepared to hack home miles after hunting, you will need a car capable of pulling a Rice trailer or horse box.

Veterinary costs, if incurred, are very high. It goes without saying that your fences and gates must be in good order to keep a horse in; and that in addition to shelter there must be dry storage for feed, hay and tack, and somewhere to stack up dung.

It is often possible to rent grazing from a farmer or to share a field with other horse owners. Horses get bored on their own and love to have company.

It is difficult to give advice about the best horse to buy, for needs vary so much. Beware the ex-racehorse or blood horse, it is much more delicate than the sturdier hunters, hacks and cobs which abound. The best way to buy a horse is to go to a reputable dealer living near you, recommended by someone you trust. The dealer at a distance is far more likely to sell you a pig in a poke! Have your choice looked at by a local vet before making a final decision, and ask for a warranty if you buy.

Ponies Many of the above comments apply except that they can be kept rougher. They will do well on a couple of acres of grazing with a little hay and pony cubes in winter, and none in summer. A well-coated pony, bred from one or other of our extremely hardy native moorland or forest breeds, will live happily in a field in winter with a good dry shed to keep him out of the wind and his feed dry. A less hardy pony, trace or blanket clipped, especially in a restrictive small paddock, may need a New Zealand rug to keep him warm and dry. One advantage of rugging a pony or horse is that he can be saddled and ridden direct from the field in damp weather. Riding ponies range from the tiny wide-backed Shetlands to the very beautiful Welsh mountain ponies used for showing and the better young rider.

Driving Ponies A general-purpose riding pony can be schooled to pull a trap, but it is a pity to use a good riding pony for this purpose as different muscles and action develop. Ponies are normally schooled for driving as well as riding, if required, when they are being broken.

Donkeys Contrary to common belief, a donkey takes quite a bit of looking after and needs good food and at least an acre of ground split into thirds. Supplement feeding with pony cubes and hay in winter. Donkeys do not need to be shod, but must have their hooves trimmed by a farrier every six to eight weeks. They are not as hardy as moorland ponies and need shelter all year round, and stabling in the winter.

Choose a lively donkey, as an old or stolid one will never perk up if it has got set in its ways. Excellent for teaching small children the rudiments of animal care and the feeling of being on an animal's back (but not for learning to ride) and very good for harness work in small carts, although it may be difficult to find a cheap donkey harness. Your local saddler will advise on harness, saddles, etc.

General It is important when buying an animal, that it has been properly broken and schooled. Donkeys and children's ponies, particularly the small ones, get handed from owner to owner as children outgrow them, and can develop bad habits due to a succession of beginner riders. However, they are often very kind, being family pets as much as anything and are very safe for small children. Beware of the notoriously jumpy or difficult pony, however well he looks or performs in the hands of an expert. Also be sure that the animal is not in the least traffic shy. Nowadays few drivers slow down for horses and, even in the heart of the country, enormous agricultural machines can appear round any corner.

Riding Clothes A good riding hat, securely fastened, is absolutely essential for riders of

Prize-winning turnout

New Forest pony. Note how the girl's trousers have ridden up allowing the stirrup leathers to rub

Boy on a donkey. Hat well forward and chinstrap fastened

all ages. Walking shoes with a good heel are all right for the absolute beginner, but jodphur boots are really the best for everyday use. For winter use, and if your horse is kept in a wet field, riding wellingtons are good dual purpose footwear and need no maintenance! Children can wear jodphurs and jodphur boots for gymkhanas, etc, but adults should wear breeches and top boots for every kind of showing and hunting. Always buy footwear one size too big so that warm socks can be worn, for feet get very cold when riding. Also, if boots are the slightest bit too tight, the foot and calf may swell and it becomes next to impossible to get the boot off. Many people ride in jeans for exercising and hacking around, but they are a little thin and not at all waterproof, and legs get rubbed against stirrup leathers. For those who cannot wear tight breeches or jodphurs there are excellent narrow trousers with a foot strap especially for riding. Wear shirts and ties or roll neck sweaters for everyday. Anoraks for hacking are effective but look awful. Hacking jackets are fine for all occasions except for showing

141

or hunting, when navy blue or black riding jackets are *de rigueur*. A stock is worn instead of a tie, for hunting. This gives good support to neck and head in case of a fall, and can be used as a sling or bandage for horse or rider in case of accident.

Learning to Ride Always get instruction from a qualified teacher. Branches of the Pony Club, usually affiliated to local hunts, take children on after the preliminary riding-school stage and give schooling in all aspects of the sport. They run gymkhanas, hunter trials and competitions designed to improve standards. There is a graduated series of tests in riding, horse management, etc, right up to expert level.

All children, even those without their own ponies, should belong to the Pony Club. Its official instructors are always knowledgeable about horses and riding, and can help parents as well as children over any problems especially where parents themselves know nothing about horses!

For adult beginners, after basic riding school, instruction can be had from British Horse Society Instructors. To find out which schools with good instructors are available near you, contact the British Horse Society, or check in the Yellow Pages under 'Riding Schools'.

Riding schools, and their horses and instructors vary enormously in quality, and local advice may help you to choose a good one. It does rather depend on the depth of your pocket! (See also *Farmhorses* and *Hunting*.)

Useful Addresses: The British Horse Society, National Equestrian Centre, Kenilworth, Warwickshire CV8 2LR; The Donkey Breed Society, White Shutters, Exlade, Nr Woodcote, Reading; The Donkey Society, Mrs W. Greenway (Hon Sec), Prouts Farm, Hawkley, near Liss, Hants; Morgan Davies (Carriages) Ltd, Newton House, Ravenglass, Cumbria (makers of beautiful small carts).

Further Reading: *Riding Magazine*, *Horse and Hound* weekly paper; *The Manual of Horsemanship of the British Horse Society and the Pony Club* (The British Horse Society)—this is an excellent book and there are many others on riding, training, etc; *The Observer's Book of Horses and Ponies* (Warne); Rossdale and Wreford, *Horse's Health from A to Z* (David & Charles); Hinton and Nestle, *Show Horses and Ponies* (David & Charles); Baker, J., *Horses and Ponies* (Ward Lock); Barwich, Robin, *Donkeys* (Cassell); St Clair, Jane and Melinda, *Keeping a Pony* (Sphere).

House Dating It is possible to tell the age and type of your cottage by applying a few simple rules. This island was once very well wooded, and timber was used for the basic frame construction of all small houses. It was infilled with wattle and daub, and then plastered, and stone was used only for rough footings, except in areas where large lumps of more or less rectangular stone lay around. Stonemasons were few and far between and were all busy building our wonderful cathedrals, castles and monasteries. (Only when Henry VIII stopped a lot of that did the stonemasons turn to domestic architecture, and the ruined monasteries and abbeys became sources of ready-dressed stone.) Bricks were not used for village work until the end of the sixteenth century, when chimneys were added to old cottages and built into the new ones.

The very earliest stone cottages were made of slabs of roughly dressed stone, and mortar was used more as a draught-proofer than a binder. Sometimes a double wall was built and infilled with loose random rubble. Stone building is very regional, so dating these cottages is a matter for the local expert. The earliest were only one room wide because it took some centuries for carpenters to learn to make wider roofs.

Flint was commonly used in the chalk country of southern England. In Sussex the

SUSSEX

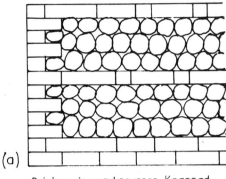

(a)

Brick quoins and courses. Knapped
flints in courses

NORFOLK

Fig 85

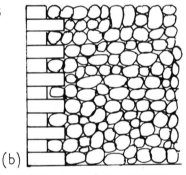

(b)

Brick quoins but no courses.
Flints usually unknapped and
haphazard.

flints were knapped or split, so that the flat
shiny surface was exposed, laid in courses,
and often used in groupings with brick
courses and quoins (corners). In Norfolk,
another area where flint was extremely common, they were left unknapped (kidney flints)
and laid in mortar in much rougher courses,
with brick quoins only (Fig 85a and b).

From this it follows that any cottage containing brick or dressed stone must be post
sixteenth century. An enormous rebuilding of
cottages took place during the fourteenth and
fifteenth centuries which swept away almost
everything which predated that time. In the
sixteenth and seventeeth centuries there was
another period of rebuilding which covered

up and extended the old, rather than destroyed it.

From Jacobean times onwards timber
framing died out gradually as brick and stone
took over and has only returned in our own
times. It follows that if a cottage has timber
framing it must be fairly old. But there has
been so much superimposing, and adding and
strengthening, and so many old timbers from
ruined houses have been reused, that it is easy
to make mistakes.

All kinds of detail, types of roof timbers,
shapes of mouldings and arches, methods of
jointing, types of windows and patterns of
framing, help dating.

In the fourteenth- and fifteenth-century
cottages a series of bays were built according
to the size of the house. Each bay consisted of
a pair of large posts, whole trees placed upside
down with the thicker root end at the top, to
allow more room for the necessary mortice
and tenon joints. Each pair of posts was
joined across the house by a tie beam, massive
and often curved slightly upwards to take
stress. Each set was joined at ground level by
another beam called a ground sill, which
rested on a wall of stones or rubble (making
an effective damp course). At ceiling level the
pairs of posts were joined by another beam or
wall plate on which the rafters rested. Normally there was no ceiling.

Later, when a top floor was put in, usually
at one end of the 'open hall', another beam
would cross the bay to take the weight of the
floor joists. The walls themselves contained
curved beams, or braces, which crossed the
angles and strengthened the whole structure.
Later walls have vertical timbers set between
the main framing, and the later the work the
closer this 'studding'. Studding began around
1430 and persisted until the end of the sixteenth century. Around 1600, both bracing
and studding went in to make the panels with
which we are so familiar.

The roof reveals most. Even if it has been
reframed, the original traces will be there. The

143

Half a 'Kentish Wealden' house which originally continued symmetrically to the right of the picture. Notice the sill resting on a rough brick foundation; the wall plates, close studding, and jettying, and the wooden glazing bars set into the wall plates and sills. There would have been no glass in these windows, only shutters which ran in grooves behind the glazing bars

These old rafters have only a collar joining them, no longitudinal purlins. They rest on the wall plates

A crownpost supporting the purlin which in turn supports the collars linking the sets of rafters

Wooden mullions once held glass in what is now a party wall. Note the big tie beam on which the joists rest

earliest, late thirteenth-century roofs were just pairs of rafters joined at the peaks resting on the wall plates. So the whole thing could, and did, collapse sideways in a gale, like a pack of cards. Next came crownpost roofs. Each pair of rafters was linked just below the ridge with crosspieces, or collar, and then a long purlin was placed longitudinally underneath to join all these. The weight of the purlin was taken on the crown post, a vertical beam with curving braces top and bottom which rested on the middle of the tie beams in each bay.

This method persisted until the sixteenth century when it was superseded by methods which left the attic space less cluttered. Heavier principal rafters were placed above the main posts in each bay, linked by purlins resting on smaller individual rafters; and between purlins and principals were curved wind

Early Tudor doorframe

145

braces. Then, about 1600, the wind braces were left out and the rafters framed closely into the purlins, making butt purlin roofs.

The earliest door frames, from 1220 to 1300, had pointed Gothic arches. Round arches followed until 1400, and then more flattened arches. Last came the very flattened Tudor arch with a point in the middle, almost ogee-shaped. The spaces in the arch corners—the spandrels—were left solid, but after 1470 the Tudors hollowed out spandrels and carved them (Fig 86).

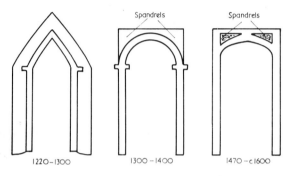

Fig 86

Early doors do not have frames, but one large timber or hanging stile on the hinge side only. The door planks overlap slightly and cross battens from the stile hold them rigid.

Early windows were unglazed, with just a series of vertical posts set close together to keep out intruders, and solid shutters inside running along grooving in the sill, to keep out weather and light. In Tudor times, small glass windows were made with wooden framings, or mullions, to hold diamond-shaped panes set in lead frames.

In the late fourteenth century the method of construction known as jettying, whereby the second floor overhangs the gound floor, appeared. Our ancestors took a long time to tumble to the fact that the strength of a joist is in relation to its depth, and laid their joists flat, which made the floor springy. To counterbalance this, and gain space outwards, the ends of the joists were carried out beyond the

A dragon beam set diagonally across a room to take the ends of the joists which protrude beyond the wall to form jettying. Notice the wall plates on which the outer ends of the joists rest, and the diagonal braces in the walls

wall plate. But if the jettying had to extend at the sides, as well as fronts and backs, then the builder had to fit a 'dragon beam' running diagonally (resting on a 'teazel post') from the outside corner of the house across the ceiling so that longer and longer joists could be set in it, projecting out beyond the walls.

Walls were originally infilled with wattle and daub, or clay lump, or various mixtures of clay, earth, cow dung, horse hair, straw; anything which would make a waterproof and fast-setting fill. As brick infilling became practicable, in Tudor times, the spaces were filled with bricks, often set in diagonal patterns, and sometimes, to gain space, walls were built right up to the jettying, and the inner studs and braces and old infilling were removed.

In some areas, the timber framing and/or wattle and daub were clad with wooden planks, and in other areas houses were built using 'cob' without timber framing. In the West Country, the local mud pie or adobe was clay, straw, a little chalk, cow dung and horse hair, and, after a stone footing had been made, wooden shuttering was put up a couple of feet high and the mixture puddled in. When it was set, the shuttering was raised and the process repeated tapering off until rafter level was reached. Window lintel cross beams, to hold ceiling rafters, etc, were set in where necessary as building proceeded, until the final roof timbers were added and the whole lot thatched. Provided that cob is kept dry, it lasts for centuries.

There are small details which will help to date your cottage. Where brick chimneys were added, in Tudor times, the staircase to the top floor often went up alongside, as a break had already been made in the ceiling and this was a good place to build the stairway. Fireplaces, big and beautiful, are always found below where you can see traces of wide chimney breasts, either in bedroom or living room.

Cottage architecture was so local, so much a matter for the village craftsmen, that hard and fast rules do not exist. Styles were imposed more by the local materials available and the skill of the builders, than by fashion, and architects, for cottages at any rate, just did not exist. Which is perhaps why we love them so now; the natural proportions dictated by the eye of the builders remain, no matter how many mod cons are superimposed.

Hunting Deer, foxes, and hares are hunted with packs of specially bred hounds. Deer and foxes, and in some cases hares, from horseback, and hares (and foxes in some mountainous areas) on foot. In addition there are drag hunts which are set up purely for riding across country without the final kill, especially in the semi-urban areas where motorways and other works of man make it impossible for normal hunting. Hunting thrives in most parts of Britain and without the control of the fox inherent in foxhunting the animal would become such a pest that it would soon have to

The Old Berkshire Hunt

be virtually exterminated. Except in areas such as Norfolk, where shooting interests predominate, the country is divided into districts which are the preserve of one particular hunt which will meet at least twice a week, always in different parts of its 'country', so that control of the animal is as even as possible. Cub hunting begins when the harvest is in, and the main season follows on until March. In hunting country, he who shoots a fox which is being a nuisance may be very unpopular, but there is no law which says that you cannot do this. If you do not wish the hunt to come on your land, you are entitled to prevent it by notifying the master through the secretary, with a map of your land. It is obviously impossible to prevent hounds from following animals across your property, but hunt servants will try hard to keep them away if you do not want them. Anybody, including hunt servants and foot followers, who enters onto land where the occupier has warned off the hunt could be guilty of trespass. The master is responsible for his own trespass and that of the hunt servants only, and not for the trespass of followers if he has warned them not to go on to the land.

To keep a pack of hounds nowadays is expensive, so those who wish to hunt must pay a subscription. Should you be a newcomer to the sport, contact the local hunt secretary who will provide all the information you need. There is so much to learn about etiquette and technique that no beginner should attempt to go it alone. Find some helpful and experienced person to take you under his wing. The Pony Club runs special hunts for its young members. (See also *Foxes*; *Hares* and *Deer*.)

Further Reading: Summerhayes, R. S., *The Elements of Hunting* (Country Life); Sassoon, Siegfried, *Memoirs of a Fox Hunting Man* (Faber); Page, Robin, *The Hunter and the Hunted* (Davis-Poynter); Ivester Lloyd, J., *Beagling* (Herbert Jenkins).

Improvement Grants See *Grants* and *Home Improvement Grants*.

Insects See individual headings and *Pests*.
Further Reading: Tweedie, *Pleasure from Insects* (David & Charles); Burton, John, *The Oxford Book of Insects* (Oxford University Press); Ford, R. E. L., *Studying Insects* (Warne).

Insurance Normal household policies should give adequate cover, but if you intend to carry out any unusual work, such as tree felling or crop spraying, or if your house or buildings are thatched, do check the cover. Insurance may be required for special stock. Check also that contractors who come onto your farm are fully covered by their own policies against accident while on your property.

Useful Address: The National Farmers Union Mutual Insurance Society Ltd, through either its local secretaries, or Head Office at Stratford upon Avon, Warwickshire (they specialize in country insurance and will advise you).

Ivy An ivy-covered wall may look attractive, and provides a nesting habitat for several species of bird, but it will also house hundreds of snails. The hairy surface roots cling to the mortar and draw moisture from it after rain, so the mortar tends to become soft and crumbly and if the ivy is pulled off too roughly, the mortar will come with it and the wall may collapse or become so weakened that it must be repointed or even rebuilt. Therefore work carefully when removing ivy. Any kind of creeper on walls is not really very good for them, and should not be encouraged.

If ivy is growing on your wall on your neighbour's side, you have no right of entry, without his permission, to cut it back or to uproot it. But should the ivy damage your wall, then you might be able to claim for the damages. Consult a solicitor.

Contrary to popular belief, ivy on trees is not parasitic and does not strangle its host. It uses the tree solely for support, and draws its sustenance from its own roots in the earth beneath. The amount it takes is minimal compared with that taken by the roots of the host tree. The only damage it does is to grow so well that it covers the host tree, keeps out light and weighs down branches. Ivy is a habitat for nesting birds and many kinds of insects, and provides food for both, the birds feeding on the insects and on ivy berries.

(above and below) *Jacob's sheep*

J

Jacob's Sheep This is a breed whose popularity is increasing rapidly, especially among those who wish to keep just a few animals. They are large white sheep with big brown spots, and two, four, or six wonderful horns. They are alert, intelligent and friendly, which is saying a lot for sheep. They are excellent mothers, lambing rate being about 180 per cent. The end products are small joints of

149

sweet lean meat from the lambs, and wool. The fleece is neither bleached nor dyed before use, and is most popular with hand spinners and weavers, being soft and springy. Jacob's sheep do well on limited grazing with some supplementary feeding, but there are some problems; the sheep must be sheared, their feet need attention about every six weeks, and they will have to be dipped or sprayed to keep off flies and the consequent maggots which are unpleasant to deal with. As with all sheep, there may be lambing problems.

There are exhibits and classes at all important agricultural shows, where full information can be obtained.

If you keep more than four sheep for their wool, you must register with the British Wool Marketing Board. (See also *Sheep*.)

Useful Addresses: The British Wool Marketing Board, Kew Bridge House, Brentford, Middx. Mrs John Thorley, Hon Sec Jacob's Sheep Society, St Leonards, Tring, Herts.

Kennel Clubs See *Dogs*.

Kennels See *Dogs*.

Lakes At what point does a pond become a lake? Lakes are larger than ponds and usually formed naturally by geological action. A lake takes the drainage of a large area and discharges it through a single stream, often being the source of a major river.

All rivers are controlled by river boards

and, if you acquire a lake, check with your river board if you wish to use any of the water for domestic or agricultural purposes, or if you intend to run drains of any kind into it, or to dam it in any way. Swimming-pool drains containing chemicals might be a problem, as those living downstream have a right to clean water.

In the natural course of things, lowland lakes eventually disappear as they silt up, and the smaller the lake the more likely this is to happen. Artificial lakes made during the last century, when labour was cheap, are by now becoming silted up and to dredge them out costs a fortune and any fish may have to be moved temporarily. However, it can be done, and plant growth should be kept under control. Make sure the outlets are clear, because the scouring effect of fast moving water after heavy rain does carry away some silt.

The stocking of lakes with fish and ornamental wildfowl can do nothing but good as they help to keep the natural ecological cycles going, clearing a lot of small weed and controlling other pond life. (See also *Fish*; *Ponds* and *Riparian Rights*.)

Law The reference section of your local library has copies of legal reference books in which you can look up for yourself all the laws regarding rights of way and property. In this book I have included brief notes for guidance as it is not possible to quote whole acts, etc, here. However, new acts and statutes are made constantly and these do not find their way into the law books until new editions are published. Therefore, the notes in this book, while correct at the time of writing, are subject to alteration, and in any important matters you should always consult a solicitor.

Further Reading: Stones, *Justices Manual*, 1976; *Megarry's Manual of the Law of Real Property*; Evans, *Law for Gardens and Small Estates* (David & Charles); Fox, *Countryside and the Law* (David & Charles).

Leathercare *Tack* This is the general term for

Loch Duntelchaig, source of the river Nairn

all saddles, bridles and harness. It must be kept soft and supple, or it cannot be trusted not to break at a vital moment. Leather is an organic material and if it dries out it cracks and dies, and may be impossible to restore. To keep it in good order, it should have saddle or special glycerine soap rubbed well in before use when it is new. Tack should always be wiped off with a damp cloth after use, and then more saddle soap rubbed well into it with a dry sponge and plenty of spit. This is hard work but there is no short cut. Glycerine saddle soap is less sticky than ordinary saddle soap and does not dirty riding clothes quite so much. Tack not in everyday use should be liberally coated with neatsfoot oil and hung in a dry place where it will not get mouldy. Check it every so often.

Other Leather Items Any other articles made of leather may also be kept supple with saddle

151

soap and neatsfoot oil. Leather which has dried out and begun to go rotten and powdery can be treated with alcohol and castor oil; a mixture of 3 parts oil, to 2 parts alcohol, should be painted on liberally. Follow this with a dressing of neat castor oil the next day. Continue with the oil until some suppleness has come back into the leather. Then change to neatsfoot oil, or a proprietory hide food.

Stitching Renew stitching with waxed thread which can be bought from a saddler. If the stitch holes have broken right out, it becomes a saddler's job. He will probably insert a new piece, and has the equipment to do the skilled work. New patches can be made to match older parts of a harness by rubbing in coach-aline oil which is dark and thick. (See also *Boots*.)

Useful Address: The Leather Institute, 82 Borough High Street, London SE1.

Leatherjackets Leatherjackets are the larvae of the cranefly or daddy longlegs, which live in moist soil and attack the roots of plants. They do a great deal of damage, even to the point of causing bare patches to appear in grassland or lawns. Rooks seen picking away at the ground are eating these larvae and are thereby doing a useful job and should be allowed to get on with it. The holes they make can be raked in later if necessary. To eradicate leatherjackets where rooks would be a nuisance, water the lawn with Murphy-chlordane worm killer. (See also *Pests*.)

Leaves Many kinds of leaves can be preserved for use in flower arrangements in winter. The leaves keep shape and become smooth and glossy, but colour usually deepens and turns brown or golden, rather than green. Laurel and other evergreens, beech, both green and copper, preserve well. It is worth trying almost any leaves, provided they can be picked well before they are going to fall off the tree naturally, and are still in good condition. Unfortunately, many leaves get tatty at the

end of the summer and are just not worth bothering with. Make up a mixture of 1 part of glycerine to 2 parts of boiling water, enough to half fill a big jam-jar. Stand the branches in this, until the solution has been absorbed into the tiny veins on the leaves, and they have become silky. Left too long the leaves will get sticky and drop glycerine all over the furniture.

Eucalyptus preserves well, and it is even worth trying the leaves of some other plants provided they are healthy.

Once leaves have been preserved, provided they are dried off, they can be stored in plastic bags and kept indefinitely.

Licences See *Fishing* and *Shooting*.

Lighting If your property is not on the electricity mains supply, and you have no generator, then bottled gas is an excellent alternative. This is run from large cylinders of gas through small-bore copper piping to light fittings with globes and mantles. There are also paraffin lamps of various kinds. Pressure lanterns, working on the 'primus' principle, run for up to eight hours on a filling and must be pumped every hour or so to keep the pressure up as the fuel is used. They provide a bright and safe light, but hiss loudly while burning. A paraffin lamp, with a wick which lights up a mantle and gives an excellent light, does not hiss, but cannot be left unattended as it tends to flare up and smoke badly.

For portable lighting paraffin pressure lamps are excellent as they burn in all weathers and provide a brilliant light. The ordinary hurricane lamp provides a dim light at very low cost for use in outbuildings, etc. A good torch lantern with fresh batteries should always be kept handy for emergencies. The old fashioned candle has its uses, but is not a safe light (see also *Electricity*; *Calor Gas* and *Paraffin*.)

Lightning Lightning takes the shortest path it can find from cloud to earth, using the best

152

Cause

Effect

available conductor of electricity. Therefore anything, a human, a tractor, a tall tree, or a building, sticking up from ground level, makes a target. Because flesh is a better conductor than wood, lightning will pass from a tree to a human (or animal) sheltering beneath it. Someone carrying a metal object, such as a gun, a hayfork or a golf club is more likely to be struck than his companion carrying no metal.

Therefore, take the obvious precautions; do not carry or touch anything metal, or ride on a tractor or other machine. Do not shelter under trees, or near a wire fence, as lightning earths more easily through you than through a wooden fencepost. The middle of a wood is safe enough because there are many trees, not just odd ones sticking up. In open country or bare hills, get as low down as possible, in a hollow in the ground, and spread out, do not remain in a group. Do not shelter in buildings with corrugated iron roofs, especially if they stand alone. If you are swimming, get out of the water. Water is an excellent conductor,

and a strike will travel considerable distances through it to a body. When riding, dismount and take shelter. If in a tent, don't touch the tent poles. In a car, don't touch the metal skin. You will be perfectly safe as the lightning will jump the rubber tyres to earth itself. If in a boat with a metal mast sticking up, get ashore if possible. A piece of wire tied to a shroud and trailed in the water acts as an effective 'earth'.

Indoors, disconnect television and radio aerials, and keep away from fireplaces. Shut windows, as lightning likes draughts.

Electric shocks kills by paralyzing the nervous system. So treat a victim for electric shock like drowning—with the kiss of life and cardiac massage—if you know how. Keep him warm and get medical help as quickly as possible.

Watch an approaching storm to see if it is coming directly towards you. A heavy storm is usually preceded by a strong gust of wind, so if one suddenly comes, then you are right in the storm path. Thunder can be heard ap-

153

proaching from between fifteen and twenty miles, and five seconds between flash and thunder means the discharge was one mile away. The thunder from a passing storm, obviously going downwind by now, can only be heard for five or six miles.

Lime Lime in soil acts as a sweetener and a reagent without which the full value cannot be obtained from other fertilizers, be they 'artificials' or farmyard manure. Soil testing will prove what the Ph or acidity level of the soil is. Only some soils with a great deal of natural chalk in them have sufficient lime never to need extra applications if fertilizers are being used. Powdered lime should be put on and raked into garden soil, but coarser lime or basic slag can be used on grassland in the autumn. By the end of the winter it will have been absorbed into the soil.

Soil-testing kits can be bought from some garden shops and agricultural merchants. The Agricultural Development and Advisory Service (see telephone book) will also arrange to carry out soil testing for you. Before planting crops, grass or making new orchards, it can be very useful indeed to know the actual chemical balance of your soil. (See also *Manure* and *Fertilizers*.)

Further Reading: Ministry of Agriculture leaflet AL 270, *Soil Analysis for Advisory Purposes* (HMSO); Maddox, *Your Garden Soil* (David & Charles)

Liqueurs Liqueurs are simpler to make than wine and absolutely foolproof; nothing can go wrong. They can be made from sloes, morello cherries or any soft fruit, and some combinations of herbs. Use a large screwtop jar, put 3oz (85g) of sugar in it and fill with fruit. Then add half a bottle of gin for sloes, or brandy for other fruit, enough to cover the fruit. Close the jar and turn it every day for three weeks, by which time the alcohol will have soaked up the colour and flavour of the fruit. Strain off the liquid into a nice bottle,

and use the fruit up in a summer pudding, or beat it with a large tin of evaporated milk and a packet of gelatine to make a most unusual fruit jelly.

Further Reading: For other recipes, Beedell, S., *Home Wine Making and Brewing* (Sphere).

Listed Buildings See *Conservation*.

Lizards We have three native species, the common lizard, *Lacerta vivipara*, the sand lizard, *Lacerta agilis*, and the slow worm, *Anguis fragilis*. The slow worm looks like a snake as it is legless, grows to about 18in (460mm) long, is smooth, grey-bronze, with a darker back stripe on females, and occasional blue spots. The other two four-legged types are grey-brown with spots. The common lizard is yellow or orange beneath, the male sand lizard is bright green beneath in summer. All three types can shed their tails if picked up by them. A new but stumpy tail will grow again in due course. All are quite harmless and do no damage at all.

Lords of the Manor
Manors were lands granted to tenants known as lords of the manor before the Statute Quia Emptores, 1290.

A manor was the lord's demesne with his residence and any waste lands and lands held by him or by his freehold tenants. There are many customs and some laws relating to manorial rights which are residual of the old order of society, but are still operative in our modern society. They mostly concern the use and preservation of the waste and common land, and sporting rights of various kinds. In many cases the rights of the lords of the manor have been vested in other bodies. The writer knows of an area of dunes adjoining river and sea where the rights have been vested in the local river board who keep up the sea defences in this case. (See also *Commonland*.)

Useful Address: The Manorial Register, Historical Manuscripts Commission, Quality House, Quality Court, Chancery Lane, London WC2 (provides information about lords of the manor).

M

Manure Farmyard manure (FYM) from cows, horses and pigs is extremely useful for the vegetable garden as it provides, in addition to the natural organic fertilizers, phosphates, potash and nitrogen, the 'humus' or decaying vegetable matter which is absolutely essential for the maintenance of proper soil structure and the bacterial action which is continually taking place in it. Soil containing plenty of humus retains moisture well, and FYM also provides a complete fertilizer when spread on grassland to be laid up for hay.

Manure removed from stock sheds should be neatly stacked. There will be some effluent which is full of nutrients, but may, nevertheless, have to drain away, so site your heap where this can happen without making a mess. Provided the stack is neatly made, rain will not leach away too much nutrient. The straw, etc, in the manure will continue to break down and after a couple of months should be friable enough to be spread on grassland, or dug into vegetable ground by trenching. The longer the heap is left the more the straw breaks down.

All fertilizers, including FYM, work better on sweet soil, which has been limed some months beforehand. Never apply FYM and lime at the same time.

Do not use FYM on ground in which you intend to grow root crops—carrots, parsnips, etc. They hate it. Potatoes, on the other hand, like plenty of FYM in their soil.

Horse manure may carry leatherjacket larvae, so should be used with care. Chicken and pig manure are very strong and should only be used sparingly.

If you have no manure of your own, a local farmer or stable will usually sell bags of the stuff quite cheaply. (See also *Lime*; *Fertilizers* and *Compost*.)

Medlars See *Fruit*.

Meteorology Recorded weather forecasts are available by telephone in many areas, brought up to date every few hours. Look in your telephone code book under 'Special Services' for the number. These forecasts are regional in character and much more useful than the national forecasts. The met office of a local RAF station, or the coastguards, may also be prepared to give advice about weather. They don't mind a bit if you ring in fact they enjoy being helpful to the general public!

The science of weather forecasting never seems to be very exact, although radio and television forecasts are based on satellite photographs and reports from weather ships and ground weather stations continuously collecting data. The trouble is that there are so many regional variations which are not dealt with by the national forecasts.

So it is useful to be able to forecast local weather conditions and, because the rules remain the same, there is usually much truth in the old saying such as 'rain before seven, sun before eleven'. Rainy fronts are usually travelling pretty fast in this country and will cross a given area in under six hours.

Weather is made by changes in atmospheric pressure which basically consist of circular movements of air separated by troughs or ridges of low or high pressure made up of air masses of different temperatures—hot or cold fronts—which push each other around. To be a successful forecaster you do need an accurate barometer with a needle and dial which records present pressure (Fig 87), or a

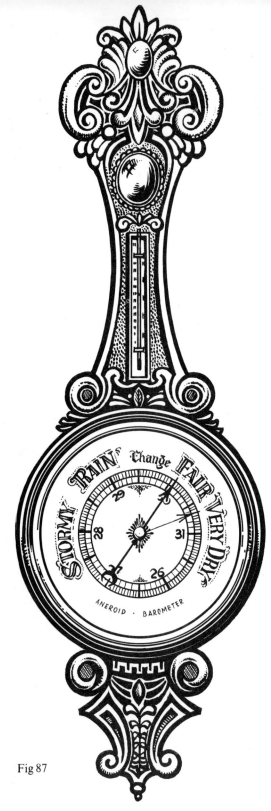

Fig 87

barograph which records pressure by making a trace on a drum. There are various rules of thumb, the most important of which is that rising pressure denotes better weather approaching, and falling pressure worsening weather, although other factors must be taken into account to judge how soon, and how windy, or wet. Wind direction is also very indicative of local weather.

The weather during the first few hours of each day usually gives a good indication of what is to follow. In summer the early dew soaks the grass, and in winter the ground is white with frost. If frost fades quickly, or the dew is missing, there is a change on the way. Following dew or frost, a fine but not too sharply defined sky and horizon indicates continuing fine weather, especially if the sun sinks in an even red glow.

The clouds give excellent indication of approaching weather. Generally speaking, hard-edged clouds, very clean hard blue skies, vivid broken dawns and sunsets mean bad weather. Dusky heavy skies mean thunder; soft hazy mists and skies and soft colours mean fine weather.

Animals, plants, birds and insects know well what weather is coming. Pheasants 'clock' at distant thunder, and bees rush home; rooks congregate in trees for shelter. Many insects hatch in warm humid weather which usually means thunder coming, and cattle running with their tails up are scared by the warble flies which hatch under these conditions. Swallows fly low to eat other hatching insects. Owls hoot at night and cocks crow much more frequently when there is rain about. Seagulls make for the land if wind is coming, and ducks fly low. Pigs get very upset when heavy rain is on the way. Before bad weather there is a sense of general restlessness among birds and animals, including humans whose rheumaticky joints ache.

The collection of records, especially in certain

A barograph. Cover off, and two weeks' trace superimposed on one sheet

Early morning dew on Deal pier

Mares' tails, fine weather, but it is windy high up and there is a change coming

(opposite) Wet and windy, full gale blowing, more to come

Mackerel sky, rain coming soon

areas, is of value to the Meteorological Office. The taking of daily recordings of rainfall, temperature, etc, is essential and there must be no break. Contact the Meteorological Office if you are interested. They will supply the necessary help, registers and instructions.

Useful Address: The Meteorological Office, Met 08B, London Road, Bracknell, Berks; 26 Palmerston Place, Edinburgh 12; Tyrone House, Ormeau, Belfast.

Further Reading: Lester, *The Observer's Book of Weather* (Warne); Bowen, *Britain's Weather and Its Workings* (David & Charles).

Mice, Shrews and Voles *Mice* These can be a great nuisance in houses, and a good cat is the best mousetrap. Where there are no house mice the timid wood mouse or long-tailed field mouse, browner than the grey house mouse, may take up residence. Mice are dirty and destructive, and definitely not wanted indoors. In the garden field mice nibble at bulbs and seeds and are equally unwelcome.

Backbreaking traps baited with melon seeds, cheese and bits of bread, are most effective, if rather unpleasant.

The various species of small mice and shrews are all the prey of cats, foxes, hawks, owls and snakes, so are usually under natural control. Should there be a bad infestation for any reason, and it can happen, call in the pest control officer from your local council.

Shrews Small insectivorous mammals, mouse-like but with long noses, they do no damage and keep some insect pests under control. Pigmy shrews are the commonest, up to twenty-five per acre, according to the time of year. The common shrew lives mainly in woodlands, and the watershrew inhabits riverbanks.

Cats catch them, but never eat them, as they have a very unpleasant smell.

Voles These are small mouse-like mammals with blunt noses and tiny ears and short tails. Extremely common, the short-tailed field

160

vole is about 4in (100mm) long. Voles feed mainly on grass and do little appreciable damage, except in young forestry plantations where they can become a plague and produce sufficient numbers to do a lot of harm by eating young shoots and seeds.

The population of field voles and water voles is kept under control by their natural predators.

Further Reading: Forestry Commission leaflet No 90, *Voles and Field Mice*; Ministry of Agriculture leaflet No AL 516, *Control of Farm Rats and Mice with Anticoagulant Poisons*; AL 490, *Water Voles* (HMSO).

Midges See *Mosquitoes*.

Milling If you are fortunate enough to have a working windmill or watermill in your area, then you may be able to buy fresh-ground grain for home baking. Only a few mills work these days and most of their produce goes to health food shops. Some grind for animal feedstuffs.

Miniature stone mills, either hand or elec-

(opposite) *The fat dormouse* (Glis glis)

Pakenham Mill, Suffolk, one of the few working windmills left in Britain

trically driven, can be bought, and hand-driven plate mills also produce good flour for bread making. Keep one in an outhouse and you can have a fresh supply of home-ground flour whenever it is needed. (See also *Watermills* and *Windmills*.)

Mink Unfortunately for wild duck and ground-living game birds, for coot, moorhens and fish, escaped mink have colonized waterside and woodland habitats in many parts of Britain. Although beautiful they are vicious killers and as, in this country, there are no wild predators to control them, they present a real threat to native wildlife.

Under the Mink Keeping Order, 1972, and the Destructive Imported Animals Act, 1932, occupiers *must* notify the Ministry of Agriculture of any mink at large on their land. They should trap and destroy them, and advice and cage traps on loan can be obtained from the Ministry. These Orders provide that mink may only be kept under licence, and the keeping is subject to various regulations. Before setting up a mink farm you must apply to the Ministry of Agriculture divisional office.

Mink farming is a specialized and difficult business. (See also *Traps*.)

Further Reading: Ministry of Agriculture leaflet UL *Wild Mink at Large* (HMSO); Hodgson, R. D., *The Mink Book* (Fur Trade Journal of Canada).

Mistletoe Mistletoe is a parasitic plant which grows high in the branches of broad-leaved trees in the southern half of England. It favours apples, sometimes poplars, and oaks. It does no real harm to the tree as its needs are slight. It is propagated by birds depositing the seeds into crevices on the bark of the tree. It is possible to plant seeds by making a slit in the bark of a tree in a suitable place, such as the angle between twig and branch, and placing the seed underneath. With luck one may eventually germinate (Fig 88).

Fig 88

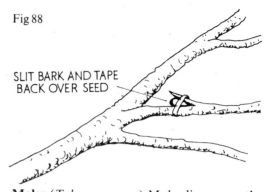

SLIT BARK AND TAPE BACK OVER SEED

Moles (*Talpa europaea*) Moles live on earthworms and do considerable damage to lawns as they search for them. They like soft soil to work in, and the more worms the better, conditions which are often fulfilled by gardens. Every village once had its mole trapper, but the profession is hardly lucrative enough by today's standards. Poison is probably the best way to get rid of them, but its use is not recommended except in expert hands. Mole traps set in tunnels are commonly used and do catch a few. Your local district council will send along their pest officer to do this job. Exhaust gases from motor mowers, cultivators, or cars, piped into mole runs, may account for some.

Given time and patience, watch until you see the ground moving as a mole works, walk up quietly, and, using a ·410 shotgun at point blank range, shoot him through the ground. This is a rather dangerous proceeding, as any solid object in the ground might cause a ricochet into your legs.

There are various ways of discouraging moles. Whether or not they work is almost unprovable, and no guarantees can be given. Moles are said to hate the plant *Euphorbia lathyrus*, or caper spurge, so plant it round your lawn. Pieces of lemon pushed down the holes drive them away. Bottles, stood upright in an excavated run so that the wind sings across their tops, make a humming noise which moles hate, as does everyone else in the neighbourhood. Any pressure maintained over the surface may discourage them—from stamping, to using a lawn mower, such as a flymo which exerts downward air pressure. Some cats hunt moles, waiting till they come right to the surface before pouncing. I had a Siamese who did this for sport—she never ate her catch.

Application forms for the purchase of strychnine to destroy moles may be obtained on application from the Ministry of Agriculture Divisonal Offices. Because of the dangers, permits are only given in approved cases. (See also *Pests*.)

Further Reading; Ministry of Agriculture leaflet AL 318, *Moles* (HMSO).

Mosquitoes, Midges and Gnats Fortunately mosquitoes found in our islands do not carry malaria, but, nevertheless, inflict nasty bites

when they suck our blood. Mosquitoes breed in water, usually in small stagnant pools, water butts, etc. A spoonful of petrol on the top of a water butt will make a film on the surface and kill the larvae. Spray crude kerosene (paraffin oil) on water at the rate of $\frac{1}{4}$ pint (142ml) per 100 square feet (9.3sq m) to kill larvae in ponds or pools. This will also cope with gnats.

Although, unfortunately, it is impossible to eradicate midges without using DDT, take comfort from the fact that the enormous clouds one sometimes sees are probably non-biters. The biters can be most unpleasant in their effects. Insect repellent cream smeared on exposed skin helps, but must be renewed frequently to give full protection. The larvae of biting midges live in water and this can be even a very small puddle.

Emperor moth, with wings spread in repose

A common blue butterfly, with wings folded in repose

Moths To tell the difference between moths and butterflies, check the posture of the insect at rest. Butterflies hold their wings erect, moths fold them along their backs and sides. The antennae of moths are thick and feathery, and their bodies are plump. There are 2,000 species of moths as opposed to sixty-eight of butterflies. Moths tend to be nocturnal but are not exclusively so.

To attract moths, grow nectar-bearing plants: honeysuckle, valerian, buddleia, jasmine, tobacco plants. A patch of sugar syrup painted on a tree trunk (½lb (226g) to ¼ pint (142 ml) water, heated till it has dissolved) will attract moths by the score.

Look for moths in the daytime in long grass

and on brick walls where they are well camouflaged.

Clothes moths were originally inhabitants of nests and dens where they lived on bits of hair, feathers, and wool, but have happily adapted to the man-made products of these things hanging conveniently and safely in dark cupboards, well away from the moth's natural enemies.

Anti-moth sprays are the surest way of keeping them in check, and synthetic fibres do not interest them. Carpets, curtains, etc, especially in dark corners and dusty old houses, should have regular anti-moth treatments. Moths do not like cedar wood and

164

boxes lined with this were once commonly used for storing clothes and linen. It is the larva, not the moth, that eats its way through the woollens, but anti-moth spray discourages the moth from laying its eggs in the first place. (See also *Butterflies*.)

Further Reading: South, R., *Moths of the British Isles* (Warne); *The Observer's Book of Moths* and *Larger Moths* (Warne).

Motor Mowers There are several types of mower on the market and choice really depends on the work to be done. A smooth easy lawn without steep banks or awkward corners is best cut by an electric or petrol driven mower with traditional cylinder blades (these will need sharpening regularly) with a fairly heavy roller attached. Nothing makes a nicer looking, or shorter, cut. One word of warning here; petrol mowers are fairly noisy, and the pull start can be heavy work for the elderly. Of course care must be taken when using a long cable on an electric mower, not to run over it, but one quickly gets the knack of flicking it out of the way. Electric mowers need little maintenance and are quiet. The new style of two-bladed rotary mower leaves a lawn without stripes, cuts off all the spiky bits, can be used when the grass is damp, and needs only occasional attention to the blades. It cuts long weedy grass very well, but does not cut low enough for those who like very short cropped lawns.

A hover mower is wonderful for banks and undulating ground, but must be used with care as it is very easy to swing it across one's own foot—it moves almost too lightly.

All these mowers come in a progression of sizes (and prices to match) from small models for small lawns to self-propelled mowers with seats for huge gardens and orchards. Remember that the more often the grass is mowed, the easier it becomes to cut, so do not buy a massive machine which will only cut rough grass, for, after half a season, a much lighter machine can do the job.

A self-propelled mower does not have to be licensed if it is *never* driven on a public road. (See also *Grass*.)

Mushrooms To grow mushrooms on anything but a very small scale—in the top of a special bag of compost which can be bought complete with spawn already growing—you will need an outbuilding which can be darkened, or a good cellar. Special compost must be made up from horse manure, or from straw with an activator, and carefully maintained at a correct heat and dampness (it heats naturally by decomposition). The compost is put into boxes, such as fish boxes, and the spawn is sown into it. The two spawn suppliers below will provide technical information.

If you have a suitable old pasture or long-established lawn (either of which should have a high level of humus or organic matter in the soil) then it is possible to plant mushroom spawn and grow your own in natural conditions. Cut a turf sod lsq foot (30sq cm) and 1½in (4cm) thick, then take out 4 more inches (10cm) of soil. Put a piece of spawn into the hole with a spadeful of horse manure. Put back the turf and tread it down firmly. Wait and see what happens. Of course, when using commercial spawn, the mushrooms will be of that species, which is not exactly the same as *Agaricus campestris*, the wild field mushroom. Unless you can dig up some spawn of these wild mushrooms, and replant it, the mushrooms will not have the true wild flavour. (See also *Fungi*.)

Useful Address: Mushroom Growers Association, Agriculture House, 23 Knightsbridge, London SW1.

Further Reading; Alkins, F., *Mushroom Growing Today* (Faber); *How Mushrooms Should be Grown*, W. Darlington & Sons Ltd, Rustington, Sussex (also supply spawn, etc); *Growing Your Own Mushrooms*, Samuel Dobie & Sons, Llangollen, Clwyd, North Wales (also supply spawn).

N

National Trust The National Trust for Places of Historic Interest or Natural Beauty was set up in 1895 to act as trustees for the nation in the acquisition and ownership of land and buildings worthy of preservation. This it has done and is doing with outstanding success. For all queries and information contact:

The National Trust, 42 Queen Annes Gate, London SW1H 9AS; or for Scotland, the Scottish National Trust, 5 Charlotte Square, Edinburgh EH2 4DU.

Natural Disasters From the safety of town houses, the dangerous realities of floods, gales and blizzards seem far away. If you live in the country, especially in remote places or among the high hills, they can be all too near. Telephone and electricity supplies are the first to go, making it difficult to summon help. Rescue helicopters, mountain rescue services, police, army, etc, soon get on the job and the display of any unusual sign such as sheets laid out in a cross, or a cross trampled in snow and marked with anything dark, will bring investigation.

The rules are commonsense. Don't take your car out in bad conditions, but if caught out in them, don't try to battle on. Conditions are going to get worse before they get better. Seek shelter in the nearest building unless it is more than a hundred yards away—then stay put in your car. The exception to this is flood conditions which are obviously going to swamp the car. Get out quickly and make for higher ground, even if it is the roof of a house or up a tree. If caught in snow, stay in the car, having made sure the exhaust pipe is clear from the outside. Keep a leeward window slightly open, or, as your breath freezes them up, you will asphyxiate. Poke a hole up through the

Village flood

Who started the windscreen wipers?

snow if possible. Don't take alcohol, it makes you lose heat. Tuck anything available, such as road maps, seat upholstery, floor mats, inside your clothes for extra insulation. Don't go to sleep. In winter, carry a survival kit in your car boot—sleeping bag, small solid fuel or camping stove, a thick jumper and some long johns, a shovel, a stick, a slab of Kendal Mint Cake and some chocolate, a small saucepan, some powdered soup and half a gallon of water. Transfer it into the car immediately you get stuck.

At home, always keep a stock of food, potatoes, dried and tinned food, flour and dried yeast, and drinking water if your supply is electrically pumped. Deep-frozen food will last a few days if the electricity goes, and, in snow, could be taken out and buried in a convenient drift which would keep it frozen for quite a long time. Also have a stock of fire-wood or other solid fuel. Keep reserve supplies of any medicines (such as insulin for the diabetic) which might run out, with dangerous results.

It is best to let a gale blow itself out before attempting repairs. A flying tile or branch can be lethal.
Sit tight and keep your head down is the rule.

Nature Conservancy Section 3 of the Nature Conservancy Act, 1973, enables grants to be given to individuals and organizations, private or public, for the establishment, maintenance and management of nature reserves.

Nature conservation plays a very important part in our lives nowadays, and if you wish to become involved in it, contact the Nature Conservancy Council who will refer you back to what is going on in your area.

Useful Address: Nature Conservancy Council, 19 Belgrave Square, London SW1.

Nettles Nettles are a sign of good soil, they tend to grow round old buildings and rubbish dumps where there is plenty of organic fertilizer present. Once you have got rid of them, the ground can be used for more productive crops, although some birds love nettle seeds and some moths and butterflies find them a habitat much to their liking.

Picked when they first appear, nettle tops cooked in salted water with a knob of butter taste a little like spinach. If they are too old they have the texture of (one imagines) gritty, furry caterpillars. Nettle wine has an unusual flavour, but this must not be too strong, so use about half a bucketful of leaves to each gallon. Be sure that they are picked from an absolutely clean place and use young nettle tops to make wine. Nettles can be eradicated by weed killer, but, if continually cut as soon as they sprout, will disappear from grassy places as the grass gains strength and smothers them. Dig them out of flower and vegetable beds, roots, runners and all.

Rubbing dock leaves on nettle stings is supposed to alleviate them, but I have not found that it actually helps at all. In fact nothing helps nettle stings, they just fade away after a time.

Newts Three closely related species of newts or salamanders are found in the British Isles: the smooth newt, the palmate newt, and the great crested newt. They breed in water and are amphibious, spending much time on land.

Noises See *Nuisances*.

Norfolk Reed See *Thatch*.

Notifiable Diseases The following diseases are notifiable, and if your vet suspects them the local office of the Ministry of Agriculture must be told immediately. They will decide what action must be taken, and will themselves supervise that action.

Any domestic animal found dead in a pad-

dock or shed should not be moved at all until your vet has seen it, unless you are absolutely certain of the cause of death. Anthrax in four-footed animals; brucellosis melitensis in ruminating and equine animals and swine; cattle plague in ruminating animals and swine; epizootic lymphangitis in equine animals; foot and mouth disease in ruminating animals and swine; fowl pest in poultry; glanders or farcy in equine animals, parasitic mange in equine animals; pleuropneumonia in cattle; rabies in ruminating animals, equine animals, swine, dogs and cats; sheep pox in sheep; sheep scab in sheep; swine fever in swine; swine vesicular disease; teschen disease; tuberculosis (certain forms only) in cattle.

The following diseases are now very rare and have not occured in this country for some years: cattle plague, epizootic lymphangitis, glanders or farcy, pleuropneumonia and sheep pox. (See also *Foot and Mouth Disease*.)

Further Reading: West, *Rabies in Animals and Man* (David & Charles).

Nuisances If any type of nuisance is really taken too far you may well have legal redress or protection. But, on the whole it is difficult to prove that a nuisance is really so bad, and also, if it happens as a result of someone else going about his business, the law will not want to know! Our society is based on tolerance, and the law expects tolerance and only acts when demands on that tolerance become quite unreasonable. So the first thing to do is to ask the person responsible for the nuisance, in the politest possible way, to do something about it. If he does not, or will not, co-operate, then you must consult your solicitor. He alone can tell you exactly what the legal position might be.

Crop Spraying One of the most common forms of nuisance these days is the damage done by crop sprays drifting across gardens, orchards, etc. Normally the farmer does not do it deliberately, so you should tell him what has happened. Usually he will make good the damage, although it may be necessary to get an arbitrator (see page 11) to decide on the amount. If he refuses to be friendly about it, then you can sue him for whatever loss you have sustained, and ask for an injunction ordering that there shall be a cessation of nuisance. Farmers who do a lot of crop spraying are almost certain to be insured against damage by their sprays.

Barking Dogs Interference for a substantial length of time with the enjoyment of a neighbouring property constitutes a nuisance and the sufferer can ask the county court or the high court to issue an injunction forbidding its continuance. However, you would have to prove that the barking kept you or your family awake every night to have much chance of a successful action.

Noise The Noise Abatement Act, 1960, gives protection to residents against noise from agricultural implements, tractors, bird scarers, and the like, but only if you and at least two other residents can satisfy the local authority that the noise amounts to a nuisance. Unsilenced engines working continually, bird scarers going all night—that kind of thing—could be dealt with, but normal usage of engines, etc, does not usually constitute a nuisance. Most local authorities have a byelaw prohibiting the use of noisy bird scarers during the hours of darkness.

Smells Smells from battery chickens, pigs or goats may be very bad, but courts are reluctant to call them nuisances if they are caused by someone lawfully earning a living. Mutual tolerance comes into it again, and you can do little but ask for every effort to be made for the smell to be lessened. The same applies if it is your stock that is causing the smell.

Quarry Blasting Anything of this kind which causes damage to your property does constitute a nuisance and those who cause it will usually be prepared to put things right and are probably insured anyway.

Limestone quarry blasting sends clouds of dust out over the countryside, and large scale work can create problems for both local residents and agriculturists of one sort or another. Such matters are rarely taken up by individuals. Groups are formed by affected people to fight it out with those who cause the nuisance, but it is very difficult to stop something once it has got started, and also if it is the livelihood of those who run and work the quarry, or if its product is badly needed by industry. This is why it is so important to be eternally vigilant, to pick up these things in the planning stage and put forceful objections before it has become a *fait accompli*.

Damage by Wandering Cats and Dogs You have no redress against the owners of the animals, unless they have actually sent a dog on to your land, or allowed it to trespass knowing that it is a chaser of stock or game, which would be hard to prove. However, the owner of a dog which kills or injures livestock is liable for the damage. The law accepts that cats wander freely and there is little that anyone can do about it.

Nuisance to Water Supply If a stream entering your property is being polluted from above, you may be able to take action to have it stopped. (See also *Sheep Worrying* and *Riparian Rights*.)

Useful Address: Noise Abatement Society, 6 Old Bond Street, London W1.

Nuts *Chestnuts* Only the sweet chestnut is edible. The trees are to be found in deciduous woods and the nuts ripen in October, and, in a good year, can be picked up by the bagful. If gathered dry and stored, spread out, in a dry place, they will keep till Christmas. Chesnuts are full of goodness, and can be eaten roasted or boiled, used in stuffing, or candied to make 'marrons glacés'. There are many recipes using chestnuts. Polenta, which is chestnut flour, has always been a staple food in Mediterranean countries where the chestnut grows to its very best.

Cob or Hazel Nuts These grow mostly in

169

hedgerows, usually cut back and allowed to re-grow. The nuts ripen in September and October.

Walnuts These are now few and far between wild, as so many walnut trees have been cut for their valuable timber. Walnut trees are usually found in gardens and parks, not in woodlands where the nuts can be taken. The nuts look like large green plums by September and at this stage are soft and can be used for pickling. Test by piercing the nut with a darning needle. By October the inner shell has hardened with the kernel inside it, and the green husk goes brown and falls away. Walnuts keep well if gathered and stored dry.

Nuts are the most nutritious and tasty of natural foods.

Further Reading: Beedell, S., *Pick, Cook and Brew* (Pelhams).

O

Oil Lamps See *Lighting*.

Orchards When planning a new orchard, choose the ground carefully. A slight slope is best, or land drains will have to be installed to carry water away to a ditch or dump. There must not be a hedge, solid fence or wall at the downhill side of the orchard, or it will act as a frost barrier. Spring frosts literally drain downhill, as the air just above the ground becomes very cold and slips below warmer layers above it (Fig 89). If a barrier exists, the frost and cold air build up against it to the detriment of trees not above the hedge level. Gaps should be made in any barrier already there to allow frost to drain away. Windbreaks of quick-growing willow and alders help to protect the trees. Orchards should be

170

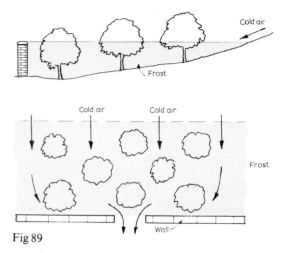

Fig 89

below 400ft (121m), and not too near the sea.

If a site has previously been used for fruit trees or bushes and is used again within seven years, certain fungi may attack the newly planted trees unless the ground has been chemically sterilized.

Keep the bases of young trees free from grass and weeds so that they get all available nourishment, but once trees are coming into production, allow grass to grow as this reduces nitrogen uptake by the trees which then use up their energies on flowers and fruit. Grass also conserves the fertility in the soil, protects it from direct sunlight and frost, and provides a habitat for useful predator insects. It can be grazed by horses, ponies, goats and poultry, although the dung from all types of poultry is a little rich for eating apples. If possible, concentrate poultry under the cooking-apple trees.

Cut ungrazed grass once a month in summer and leave the cuttings to rot into the ground.

Orchard trees are subject to many pests and diseases, and may have to be sprayed regularly to control these. Consult specialist books for information.

Pruning methods are fully described in gardening books, but a practical lesson or two from an expert is the best way to learn.

Cutting out branches to keep the middle of the tree open

Only small branches are left to bear fruit—these bend in the wind and the apples do not fall off. Apples blow off rigid thick branches which do not move to the wind

Pear trees need more shelter than apples so should be put in the most sheltered part of the orchard, well away from any chance of frost damage, as they blossom before apples.

Plum trees do not grow well in grass and need much nitrogen. A heavy layer of garden compost round the base of plum trees helps them to fruit well. For this reason they need a separate part of the orchard to themselves.

Old Orchards In spite of the fact that the trees may have dead branches, and that the apples they bear may be maggoty, much can be done to reclaim old orchards. They may contain varieties of apples long gone out of favour which are none the less delicious for domestic purposes. Remove totally dead trees, cut away all dead branches, and seal off cuts with bituminous paint. Clear away nettles, brambles, etc.

Pruning certainly improves the performance of old trees. The basic rule is to open up the tree so that light gets in and the centre is not just a congested mass of twigs and branches, impossible to pick the fruit from anyway. Branches which overhang so much that, when full of fruit, they may break, should also be pruned back and the general shape of the tree should be made good, neither too wide nor too tall.

Apply bands of vegetable grease to apple, pear and cherry tree trunks in October to prevent wingless female winter moths climbing up to lay their eggs. Spraying should only be done when you know exactly what pests are present, and these can only be identified as the year goes by, and appropriate action taken. Too much pest control can result in problems created by the destruction of useful predator insects. Good cultivaton and pruning will result in surprisingly big crops of apples from old trees, which seem to resist naturally many of the pests of younger orchards. It is a terrible mistake to chop down old apple trees until you are certain they cannot produce fruit.

Overhanging Trees If your fruit trees over-

hang a neighbour's land, or your fruit falls upon it, it still belongs to you, and with his permission you may go and collect it. If he refuses permission, you may go anyway, but not by force, nor may you do any damage.

Apples More than six hundred distinct varieties of apple are registered with the National Fruit Trials centre. However, commercial apple growers limit themselves to a few proven varieties that look good, crop well and keep well. Private growers have a far wider range in their gardens and orchards, and some old orchards still contain prized and cherished trees of older types. If you have an old tree which you cannot immediately identify, don't chop it down, it might turn out to be one of a rare variety worth protecting from extinction.

Apples should be picked carefully, and each one placed, not dropped, into the picking bag. If they are to be kept, reject any with blemishes or maggot holes. Store the fruit in a cool dark place. Use special storage trays or slatted shelves, or shelves covered with newspaper. Place each apple carefully so that it does not touch its neighbour. Check the shelves every week or so and remove any rotting or bruised fruit. On the whole, the later the apple is harvested, the longer it will keep. Early varieties do not keep well.

To keep a few apples in first-class condition, put them in the vegetable compartment at the bottom of your fridge.

Cherries Cherries like deep, free draining, fertile soil, and light summer rainfall, but plenty of water through the rest of the year. They should not be planted where frost is likely to form pockets as they are extremely susceptible at blossom time. Cherries do not like soil with a high lime content. There are many types of cherry and these form groups within which trees will cross pollinate each other, but if trees come from incompatible groups they will not cross pollinate. Some cherries, such as the Kentish Red (Scarlet Morello), are self fertile, but most varieties will crop better if cross pollinated.

Because of the fondness of birds for the fruit, cherries must be protected by bird scarers if they are to be grown on any scale.

The Ministry of Agriculture bulletin (see below) lists the compatible groups, and gardening books will also give full planting and pruning information. Cherries do not need a great deal of pruning. They can be grown as orchard trees, either fan trained or free standing, as wall-grown trees, as single cordons, or even in large pots.

Pears Pear trees like nice fertile soil and a frost-free, protected site, where they can blossom before the apple trees in safety. Conference, Williams, or Bon Chrétien are probably the best varieties to plant for domestic use. Cultivation and pruning is, broadly speaking, the same as for apples, and is well covered in fruit growers' books and bulletins. (See also *Fruit*.)

Useful Address: John Scott & Co, The Royal Nurseries, Merriott, Somerset (for uncommon varieties).

Further Reading: Ministry of Agriculture bulletins: No 207, *Apples*; No 119, *Plums and Cherries* (HMSO); Grounds, R., Ed, Complete *Handbook of Pruning* (Ward Lock); Genders, R., *Complete Handbook of Fruitgrowing* (Ward Lock); Oldale, *Growing Fruit, 1001 Questions Answered* (David & Charles); Simmons, *Potted Orchards* (David & Charles).

Ordnance Survey The Ordnance Survey produces maps of various scales of the entire country and keeps these as up to date as possible. These maps, based on the National Grid reference system, provide a most accurate coverage of the country for all purposes.

1:25,000—approximately 2½in to the mile—are useful for walkers, archaeologists, and property owners as they show in great detail all features including field boundaries, individual buildings and ancient monuments. In the 'First Series' each covers an area of 10km (approx 6¼ miles) square. These are being replaced by the 'Second Series' which are right up to date, include the same detail, but are more colourful and cover 20 x 10km.

The Outdoor Leisure Maps pay great attention to the mapping of particular recreational areas such as the Lake District, cover 20 x 26km and include details of such things as caravan sites.

1:50,000—replacing the old one inch maps—are revised regularly and give detailed topographical pictures with all roads shown. These have not yet been produced for the whole of the north and Scotland, and the old one inch maps are still on sale for these areas. As the new maps are being produced, leisure and tourist activities are being catered for by the introduction of new information and symbols.

Quarter-inch scale maps are also available for entire areas, (south east, south, south west, etc).

Useful Address: Ordnance Survey, Romsey Road, Maybush, Southampton S09 4DH (provide a catalogue giving details of all maps published).

Ornithology See *Birds*.

Otters (*Lutra lutra*) The otter is a member of the weasel family which lives on fish and all kinds of water creatures. It does damage to fish hatcheries and takes salmon and trout. For this reason fishery bailiffs and others dislike otters and the otter, once common in our rivers, is now rare and has retreated into the quiet places of the hills, moorlands and deserted western seashores. Otters are delightful animals, and it would have been a pity if hunting, allied with river pollution, had caused them to disappear altogether. Since 1978 the otter has become a protected animal and it is an offence to kill or hunt it.

Further Reading: Maxwell, Gavin, *Ring of*

173

Bright Water (Longman); Williamson, H., *Tarka the Otter* (Bodley Head).

Outhouses Outhouses may look and smell filthy and rotten, but it is surprising what a good clean up can do. Remove all rubbish, and dirt and burn it. Remove ivy and weeds growing on walls or roof. Brush down dust and cobwebs with a yard broom and replace missing tiles, or add new sheets of galvanized metal or plastic to let in light. Reglaze windows where necessary, and give all interior woodwork a spray or paint of 2 parts creosote with 1 part of tractor paraffin if available—it makes the creosote go further.

Spray or paint the walls with limewash—powdered lime diluted with water to the consistency of milk (or thicker for painting). Both creosote and lime act as disinfectants.

If you wish to use the outbuildings for purposes other than farming or gardening, then emulsion paint can be used on the walls, provided they have been thoroughly brushed down. This lasts longer than limewash and does not flake or rub off so easily.

Rotten or wormeaten timbers can usually be cut out and renewed without the whole building being torn apart. But heavy worm infestation should be treated as it would be in a house.

The floors are usually beaten earth, which can be scraped and swept, or brick and concrete, which should be thoroughly drenched in water and disinfectant and brushed as clean as possible.

To lay concrete floors in outhouses, first put a 4in (100mm) layer of hard core (brick rubble is best), broken down to golf-ball sized pieces, on top. Then make a mix of 1 part of cement to 5 parts of sand, with enough water to make it easily spreadable. Put this directly onto the hard core, tamp it down with the back of a shovel, and then screed it with a piece of wood. The concrete should be about 3in (75mm) thick. Be sure that there is a fall to any interior drains or gutters, or out through the doorway, so that water cannot puddle on the floor if the buildings are used for stock (Fig 90).

Fig 90

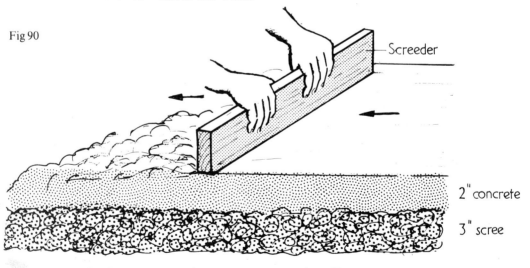

For large areas make a two man screeder with a handle at each end

P

Paraffin This is a most useful and comparatively cheap fuel for lighting, heating and stimulating bonfires! It should be stored in drums with taps, or in cans with proper pourers, preferably not in the house. If the can is brought into the house to fill lamps or heaters, always stand it and the appliance on a newspaper so that any spills are blotted up and can be removed. Wash your hands after using it as the taste and smell are very unpleasant and persistent, and easily transferred to food or cooking utensils.

Paraffin does not have the high flash point of petrol, but nevertheless, be careful when putting it on a hot bonfire, especially a smouldering one, as it will vapourize and then suddenly ignite. (See also *Lighting*.)

Partridges Two species of partridge live in this country, *Perdix perdix*, the native grey partridge, and the red-legged *Alectoris rufa*, commonly known as the Frenchman. Apart from its red legs the Frenchman is distinguished by a cream and black face pattern, a red bill and distinctive bold bars on its flanks.

The most noticeable mark of the grey partridge is the inverted, deep chestnut horseshoe on the lower breast. Not as common as they once were, partridges nevertheless persist, and it is to be hoped that the species will not be almost wiped out by indiscriminate shooting. Partridges are believed to mate for life. (See also *Game* and *Shooting*.)

Party Fences and Walls See *Boundaries*.

Paving Stones See *Algae*.

Peacocks Peacocks are difficult birds to rear and keep, and can appear perfectly well one day and be dead the next. The best way to breed peacocks is to give two eggs to a bantam hen to hatch; she will make a better job of it

Partridges in the snow

Peacock in full display

than the peahen. The birds should be fed on turkey pellets and young birds do require pellets containing antibiotics to have much chance of survival.

Peacocks roost on trees or walls, and do not take kindly, on the whole, to being shut up at night. This means that they are vulnerable to foxes; but are usually alert enough to avoid them. Unfortunately, the hens at breeding time become slightly dopey and it is then that they may be taken. If it is possible for the birds to live in big enclosures, then they can be protected from foxes, but to remain healthy they do need clean fresh ground and the enclosures must therefore be rested from time to time.

However, once established, the birds are

fairly hardy and do well. Especially in the spring at breeding time, and at roosting time, the peacock lets out the most ear-splitting and heartrending cry, a kind of OOOOOOOOH on a rising and falling inflection. This tends to annoy the neighbours. (See also *Poultry*.)

Pears See *Orchards*.

Peat Peat is a surface layer of decaying organic matter partly decomposed, very wet and acid. It forms in waterlogged places where the water has come through granite or sandstone and contains little lime to neutralize the acids formed by decomposition. Peat stays in a much more solid and matted form than ordinary decomposing humus and soil in non-waterlogged areas, because the water keeps out oxygen. It is cut out in brick-sized pieces and left beside the cuts to dry. When it no longer drips water, it can be stacked for further drying and will burn readily with a quiet glowing flame and a lovely smell, giving out plenty of heat.

Peat in less acid areas can, by liming, be turned into extremely fertile farmland. It has extensive horticultural uses for seed growing and potting, for it retains moisture while not becoming muddy. It is usually free from weed seeds and fungus.

Look for peat in fenland areas, in mountains and on heaths; anywhere where ground is waterlogged.

All the larger broads in Norfolk are flooded peat cuttings, where, during the Middle Ages, peat was taken from the marshes beside the slow-flowing rivers.

Pesticides Pesticides, in the form of sprays, are in common use for the control of all kinds of insects and weeds in fields, gardens and orchards. These are subject to stringent regulations and employers *must* provide protective clothing and use the chemicals properly, as some can cause damage to humans as well as to bees and other beneficial insects, and to growing crops.

Leaflets on the use of pesticides are available, free of charge, from the Ministry of Agriculture and the Safety Executives' Agricultural Inspectors.

Further Reading: *Approved Products for Farmers and Growers* (HMSO); Mellanby, K. *Pesticides, Pollution* (Collins).

Pests Most serious forms of infestation—rats, wasps, hornets, etc—can be dealt with by your local authority pest officer, and you should check first with him before taking expensive private action. Although it varies from place to place, the work is often done for nothing, and only nominal charges are made for sprays, etc. It is a relief to have these unpleasant pests removed by experts, but be very wary of the self-appointed expert who

says he will get rid of them for you. His way may be to put down dangerous poisons which can result in multiple killings of pets and domestic animals. Trapping should only be done using legal traps, and care must be taken to cause as little suffering as possible. (See also Individual entries and *Traps*.)

Pheasants Most pheasants nowadays are reared by gamekeepers for shooting, and in fact this does ensure a much larger population than would otherwise be the case. The common pheasant struts shining and handsome in our countryside, so confident and tame as to be a garden nuisance in some rural areas. The large and crested Golden Pheasant has become established in East Anglia's brecklands and in Kircudbright in Scotland, and the Lady Amherst's Pheasant, with black and white head and neck plumage and dark green and white body (of the male), is also established in the south-eastern Midlands after escaping from the Duke of Bedford's collection at Woburn.

It is not illegal to take a pheasant which is in your garden, but if you do so you will not be popular with the farmer, gamekeeper or landowner who reared it.

It is calculated that about half the pheasant population is reared and released for shooting, and of that half about 10 per cent survive to become true wild pheasants in their second summers. (See also *Game* and *Shooting*.)

Useful Address: Pheasant Trust, Great Witchingham, Norwich.

Further Reading: Delacour, *Pheasant Breeding and Care* (TFH Publications); Ministry of Agriculture leaflet STL 145, *Pheasant Incubation* (HMSO).

Photography See *Birds*.

Pigeons *Domestic* If you have a pigeon loft which you wish to use, then buy some already mated pairs from a pigeon keeper, and put

Pheasant

them into the loft, although for three weeks they must not be allowed to fly. They should be kept in a wire netting enclosure from which they can see out, and fed with grain and dried peas. After three weeks they may have their freedom, and will remain with you. Pigeons can be destructive in gardens, and neighbours may grumble. Take squabs—young pigeons—from the nest to eat when the underside of the wing is fully feathered. Kill, pluck and cook them like little chickens. Silver King is a good breed if it is squabs that you want, but there is only a limited market for the sale of squabs and one gets rather sick of eating them.

A few pairs, for decorative purposes, can be kept without much trouble. Pigmy pouters, dragoons. nuns, archangels and modernas, and of course the fantail, are all good decor-

ative breeds. Should you wish to keep racing pigeons, that is an art all on its own and there are many books available on the subject. Practical help and instruction from a pigeon fancier is of course invaluable and there is probably a racing-pigeon club in your district.

Wild Wild pigeons are a menace to crops and gardens and are best kept under control by shooting. *Don't* shoot a resting racing pigeon in your garden. If you see a pigeon on the ground by itself, and it has a leg ring, it is a racer. Feed it water and grain and it will probably soon recover and fly on. Should such a bird die, take off its leg ring and send it with details of where and when it was found to the Royal National Homing Union, Major L. Lewis, The Reddings, Cheltenham, Glos. (See also *Shooting*.)

Further Reading: Allen, W., *How to Raise*

and Train Pigeons (Ward Lock); Stovin, G., *Pigeon pair*
Breeding Better Pigeons (Faber); Magazines:
The Racing Pigeon; *The British Homing
World*; *Pigeon Racing News and Gazette.*

Pigs 'Cats look down on you, dogs look up to
you, but pigs is equal.'

Contrary to popular belief, the pig is the
cleanest of animals if given a chance to be. It
will always dung in a corner of its pen away
from its sleeping area and advantage can be
taken of this by building a dunging passage
(Fig 91) into the pigsty.

A pig kept for fattening and slaughter
should be housed in a sty, and not encouraged
to run around all the time, as this only uses up
food energy which should be making the
animal fat. Pigs eat up all household waste
(swill) and if you can get hold of good swill
from a hotel or some such place, then it must
(by law) be boiled for at least one hour to

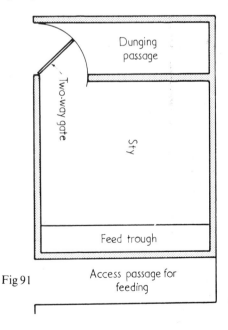

Fig 91

A simple pigsty made in an old open-fronted shed. The dunging passages with their two-way doors are behind the pigman and pigs are fed over the other end wall into concrete troughs

sterilize it, preferably in an outhouse in an old copper or something similar. Keep it apart from raw swill and other feeding stuffs and keep utensils clean and disinfected. Feed pigs on stale bread from a bakery, surplus or skimmed milk with barley or proprietary pig nuts (expensive) and stock feed potatoes (cheap). Specially grown fodder crops if you have some ground, such as fodder beet, potatoes, kale, carrots or Jerusalem artichokes, are marvellous for pigs as they can be let out and strip grazed on it, using an electric fence, the fence being moved on only a little each day. The pigs will clear the fresh food, then continue to root at the previously used areas and do a wonderful job of cultivating them almost ready for replanting.

If you want to run pigs in orchards or paddocks and do not wish the ground to be torn

apart, then they must be ringed. Use small nose rings, clipped in the top edge of the pig's snout with a special tool for fatteners, or larger copper rings put right through the membrane between the nostrils of breeding stock. This is not difficult to do when the pig is small and easily restrained, but is quite a job (and noisy and painful) if the pig is fully grown.

Breeding stock thrive out of doors, provided they can get into dry shelter when they wish (Fig 92). If they are always in concrete pens, they become far more liable to disease and to virus pneumonia (in piglets), worms, etc. Give them a couple of pounds of pig nuts each per day, and if they have access to crops, or can run in a wood, then they will keep themselves fit. Provided pigs are moved to fresh ground every six weeks or so, they should not get worm infested. Keeping a breeding sow is fine if you get a good mother who will farrow without difficulty and not overlay her piglets, but pig breeding is not

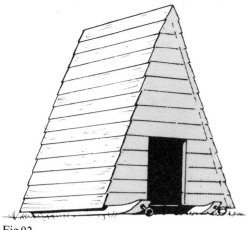

Fig 92

something for the beginner to launch into without experience as there can be problems.

Pigs are highly intelligent animals, and a breeding sow can become a great pet. Their very intelligence means that they are adept at breaking out and raiding other people's fields and gardens. So fencing must be good, and electric fencing can be used for strip grazing, set up at about 1ft 2in (350mm) from the ground.

Slaughtering Your house pig can go to the nearest abbatoir for slaughtering and be returned as meat; or there is usually a local man who will kill a pig for you at home for a small fee, but it is an unpleasant business and, if the pig has become a pet, can put you off pork for life. It doesn't end at slaughtering, the pig must be scaled, scraped and butchered, and the intestines washed, etc. Probably the best way to cope is to get a local butcher to do the whole job, if you can find one who still does some slaughtering. He will also joint it for freezing or curing, as required.

Further Reading: Peck, W. D., *Pig Keeping* (Faber); Ministry of Agriculture leaflets: AL 104, *Pig Feeding*; STL 68, *Practical Pig Feeding* (HMSO).

Pinioning See *Ducks*.

Planning Permission Planning permission is necessary nowadays for almost everything, even for small garden sheds and greenhouses. All extensions or alterations to buildings require planning permission and so does any change of usage of land or buildings, except for agricultural buildings which only require planning permission if they are within 80ft (25m) of a classified road, occupy more than 5,000sq ft (465 sq metres) or are more than 40ft (12m) high. Otherwise the exceptions are so few and so small that if you contemplate any alteration to your property, inside or out, it is best to contact the planning officer of your local council, if possible with rough plans of what you intend before getting down to detailed plans or any actual work. Aerial surveys are carried out which show up new buildings, etc, and, on the basis of these, planning authorities may check on what you have done and insist you restore the land or take the building down.

Plant Hire See *Contractors*.

Poaching A poacher is someone who takes or disturbs game on another's land, or takes salmon or trout by illegal means.

Occupiers of the land, gamekeepers or constables may ask anyone they catch on the land, whom they suspect to be in pursuit of game, for his name and address and tell him to get off the land. If he refuses either request, then he can be arrested. The punishment for daytime poaching is a fine, for night-time poaching it can be up to fourteen years' imprisonment!

If a constable catches someone on a public highway adjoining land and suspects him of poaching, he may seize any game and weapons found and these may be confiscated if there is a conviction.

Poaching, like smuggling, was always looked upon with sympathy by the general public, if not by the landowners. Maybe that was fair enough in a time when many people died of starvation and malnutrition; but it is not an acceptable attitude when this is no longer the case. It is stealing, and sometimes highly organized stealing.

If A chases his own game from his land on to B's land and takes it, that is not poaching. If A's game is on B's land and B takes it, neither is that poaching. Wild birds and animals do not understand about boundary fences, so a pheasant in your garden is your pheasant as long as it stays there. However, should you entice that pheasant into your garden, you could be unpopular to say the least. If you are driving along in your car and hit a pheasant, you break no law if you pick it up, but should you have a gun on the back seat and be searched on suspicion by a policeman, you might have the greatest difficulty in persuading a court that you were not poaching or intending to poach.

Polish See *Furniture* and *Leathercare*.

Pollution This can take so many forms, but, in the country, water pollution is the commonest and most damaging. Great care should be taken not to allow anything harmful, and that can include an excessive run-off of fertilizer, to get into streams. Chlorinated waste from swimming pools, crop sprays, sewage effluent, excessive use of drinking places by stock, can all pollute streams to the detriment of downstream users, fishing, etc, and it behoves all users to make sure that they do not allow streams to become polluted if they can help it. Remember that all ditches, drains, etc, eventually carry water to ponds or streams, and pollutants go with the water.

Riparian laws protect the water which passes across your land from pollution by others. (See also *Riparian Rights*.)

Further Reading: Rothman, H., *Murderous Providence, Pollution in Industrial Societies* (Hart Davis); Mellanby, K., *Pesticides and Pollution* (Collins).

Ponds See *Dew Ponds*; *Fishponds*; *Riparian Rights* and *Lakes*.

Ponies See *Horses*.

Pony Traps See *Horses*.

Poultry *Hens* This is not the place to discuss intensive poultry keeping of any kind, which has unfortunately been forced upon the poultry industry by economics. To produce enough eggs for the average household, plus a few to spare in early summer, a couple of dozen hens kept on free range in orchards, yards or paddocks (not the garden) are the best bet. As long as the hens have access to a shed or a movable house containing some good nest boxes, in which they can also be locked up at night, there should not be too much trouble from foxes, or from hens laying away in their own nests in hedgerows. Run a cockerel with your hens and then outlayers may turn up with a brood of chicks anyway.

Free-range hens should be fed on a handful or two of grain a day and given household scraps and some protein mash or pellets in a container so that they can help themselves.

Light Sussex or Rhode Island Reds are first-class birds for this type of poultry keeping. The other specialist breeds may produce more eggs in batteries or deep litter houses, but are not so good on free range.

Hens bred for deep litter or battery houses are unlikely to go broody, as this charac-

Polluted marina

Rhode Island Red crosses

teristic has been carefully bred out. Even on free range they do not revert. Therefore, if you wish to raise chicks of any kind, from hens to geese, the best possible mothers are bantams, always noted for this purpose. Although their size means that they cannot take very many eggs at a time, they will incubate even goose eggs successfully.

Geese Two geese and a gander is the usual 'pen'. They can run in paddocks or orchards and, although they enjoy it, don't need any grain at all. Geese only need extra feeding when being fattened for the table. In February–March the geese will begin to lay and the eggs should be taken away as soon as laid, and put under a broody hen. A hen will brood six goose eggs and rear the goslings. Goose eggs under a hen must be splashed with water every day (as the goose would do). A good goose will lay a lot of eggs, and the surplus can be eaten; they make excellent omelettes. Or the goose can finally be allowed a clutch of about twelve to fourteen to brood herself. Protect a sitting goose from foxes, if necessary by building a temporary wire-netting pen around her. It is safest to shut the geese away from foxes at night, although on free range they make marvellous burglar alarms, setting up a terrible racket if disturbed.

183

Geese will make do with very little water

If the goslings are reared to be eaten, then leave them on free range until Michaelmas. Then put the doomed birds in a pen and give them as much barley as they can eat for three weeks before killing. Hang them for at least a week before cleaning and cooking.

Ducks Khaki Campbells or Buff Orpingtons are best for laying, Aylesbury for eating. Keep laying ducks in at night. They will lay their eggs in one noisome heap, and they must be washed very clean immediately. Hens brood and rear ducklings better than ducks do, but do not impart oil to the baby feathers from their own, so hen-reared ducklings must not go near water until they have grown a few proper feathers.

Ducks will eat scraps and should be fed in the same way as hens. Fatten them up with as much meal as they will eat for a fortnight before killing.

Ducks

Guinea fowl

Turkey gobbler in full display

Turkeys Very delicate creatures, they are hard to rear. They need shelter, dry ground and medication to prevent a disease called blackhead. The losses you will almost certainly incur will not be covered by the one or two birds that survive to be killed and eaten. Leave turkey keeping to the expert unless you are prepared to specialize and learn by experience.

Guinea Fowl They are known as 'comebacks' because the noise they make sounds like that. They roost in trees where they are safe from foxes, so do not have to be housed. They should be fed on the same food as hens, and, if possible, given extra meal to fatten them for a fortnight before killing. Guinea fowl make very good eating. (See also *Ducks*; *Geese* and *Peacocks*.)

Useful Address: The Poultry Club of Great Britain, 72 Springfields, Great Dunmow, Essex.

Further Reading: Ministry of Agriculture leaflets nos: AL 397, *Rearing Turkeys for Meat*; AL 427, *Feeding Turkeys for Meat*; AL 342, *Free Range and Semi Intensive Egg Production*; AL 112, *Goose Production*; AL 43, *Natural Hatching* (HMSO); Holmes-Eliot, R., *The Right Way to Keep Hens, Ducks, Geese and Turkeys* (Right Way Books); *Poultry Keeping* (Foyles Handbook).

Preservation Orders See *Trees*.

Preserving Food Although many people only think in terms of deep freezing everything these days, there are other and often better ways of preserving food which retain more flavour, or even add flavour, and, although they may take a little time and trouble, are well worth doing. Recipes for fruit jellies and for jams and chutneys may be found in good cookery books, especially *Farmhouse Fare*. There are dozens of guides for deep freezing produce.

Bottling See any good cookery books specializing in jams and preserves of all kinds.

Drying Herbs can be dried satisfactorily by hanging them in bunches in an airy place, or by laying them out on trays in an airing cupboard (with no damp clothes in it). Keep the temperature high for twenty-four hours (at 90°F, 32°C) and then reduce it or remove the trays to a warm room at about 70°F (21°C). Do *not* dry herbs in direct sunlight as this seems to bleach them and reduce flavour. Herbs should take about a week to dry, and they can then be shredded from stalks, etc, and put into airtight jars or brown paper bags (not plastic).

The trick is to dry quickly at first, and then steadily, without humidity.

Apples can be dried successfully. Peel, core and cut into thin rings, thread on a string and dry over a stove at 65–70°F (18–21°C) for twenty-four hours or so until they are crisp. Put them in an air-tight container and store in a cool place.

Other fruit and vegetables may be dried, but on the whole it is not as satisfactory a method as freezing or bottling.

Home Curing Not so very long ago most country people cured their own bacon, ham and pork, and smoked it in the wide chimney over a wood fire. While fresh pork can be kept in a deep freeze, bacon and ham must still be cured and there are many recipes for doing this.

Basic Bacon Pickle: Put 8lb (3¼kg) of rock salt, ¾lb (340g) saltpetre, ¾lb (340g) moist brown sugar into 4 gallons (18 litres) of water and boil it for twenty minutes, removing the scum as it forms. Put this into a container and, when cold, immerse the bacon in it. Turn it every day for ten days. Remove, wipe dry, wrap in greaseproof paper, put into butter muslin, and leave it to dry out in a cool place before use. Do not leave too long, or the meat will take on a reasty flavour.

Basic Ham Pickle: Rub the ham well with rock salt and leave for a day, dry it with a cloth and rub in 1oz (30g) of saltpetre. Mix together 1lb (500g) of salt and ¼lb (115g) of black pepper, and rub the ham with these every day for the next three days. The ham should be in a big container. Then pour 1lb (500g) black treacle over the ham. Baste the ham with the mixture in the container each day, and turn it. After one month, drain the ham, bag it in muslin and hang it up to dry for three months.

Large oval earthenware crocks are best for home curing, or small spotlessly clean wooden tubs or half barrels. These crocks can sometimes be found in country junk shops.
Home Smoking Small home smokers which take just a few fish or pieces of bacon, sausages or poultry, come in several sizes and are most convenient if you only wish to do small quantities at a time for fairly immediate consumption. Made by a firm called Brook (and others) these can be bought at good kitchen utensil shops.

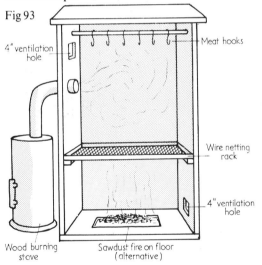

Fig 93

4" ventilation hole

Meat hooks

Wire netting rack

4" ventilation hole

Wood burning stove

Sawdust fire on floor (alternative)

To set up a smokehouse on a big scale for cold smoking to preserve food, you need a small wooden hut like a 'privy' (Fig 93) with a concrete floor, a wire-netting rack inside, about 4ft (just over a metre) from the floor, on which to lay the produce, and a wood-burning stove. This can be set up just outside the hut with a chimney directly into it, so that

cool smoke fills the hut. If such a set up is impossible, then a wood-burning stove inside the house can be used to provide smoke for the hut set up against the outside wall. If hotter smoke is needed, then a fire can be lit on the floor of the smoker, using wood chips and sawdust. If a fire is to be set on the floor of the smoke house, then two ventilation holes must be made to create enough draught to make the fire burn. Each should be 4–6in (100–150mm) square, with sliding flaps. One should be at floor level, the other high up on the opposite side. Once the fire has been lit, adjust the flaps until it is smouldering but not blazing (Fig 94).

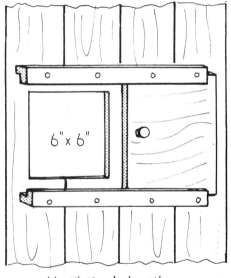

6" x 6"

Fig 94   Ventilation hole with sliding flap

The sawdust should preferably be from hardwood, with some oak in it. Two bucketfuls per twenty-four hours should be enough. A little birch sawdust, and perhaps some fir cones, improve the flavour. Light a twist of paper and feed sawdust onto it in a heap till the smoke is rising nicely. Keep an eye on it to see that it remains alight but does not burn away too quickly.

If you have an open hearth and a wide chimney and burn nothing but wood, then

187

produce can be smoked in the traditional farmhouse way, hung up in the chimney for a week, on rods set across the chimney at differing heights according to the heat wanted, but this is hard to control.

Cold smoking means that the temperature on the surface of the food being smoked should not go above 120°F (50°C), between 100 and 110°F (38–43°C) is ideal. Hot smoking at from 150–200°F (65–93°C) cooks the meat as well as smokes it, but it must be eaten within a few days. In North America and Germany hot smoking is common and the beautiful smoked bacon, etc, which one slices thinly and eats without further cooking is done this way.

Fish should be cleaned and boned before smoking and sprinkled with rock salt. After twelve hours, wash and dry it with a cloth and lay it on the rack to smoke. Small fish will be nicely smoked in twelve hours, but a large fish will take up to twenty-four. Be sure the smoke is not too hot or it will cook the fish rather than smoke it. Once the fish is smoked it should be brought indoors into a warm room to dry off properly, before being wrapped in greaseproof paper for keeping in the refrigerator. Smoked fish can be deep frozen.

Further Reading: Slight and Hull, *Home Book of Smoke Cooking* (David & Charles); *Farmhouse Fare*, country recipes collected by *Farmer's Weekly*, Hulton Press Ltd; Mrs Beeton's cookery books.

Pumps Take advice from your local Ministry of Agriculture drainage officer about the type of pump suitable for your needs. Where electricity is available, remote-control pumps, which switch on when the water in your storage tanks drops below a certain level, and switch off when they are full, are excellent. Remote-control pumps, with manual on and off switches, are also fine, if a bit more trouble. Hydraulic ram pumps, which work on their own water power, will also serve to

keep tanks topped up where the lift is not too great and only small amounts of water are needed. Petrol or diesel driven pumps, which have to be manually started, are troublesome even if properly housed, as they must be. Pumps sited beside rivers and streams are by their very nature in damp places and, especially if they are infrequently used, can be terrors to start. If water cooled they must also be drained in cold weather, or filled with antifreeze, and in any case will have to be drained after use so that no water is left in the pump to freeze. It is essential to have pumps and motors checked when buying a property, because they are sources of trouble unless fairly new and well maintained.

Drainage Pumps Take advice as above. In low-lying areas you might have problems, although the river boards are in charge of all main systems. Locally, to clear dykes into higher levels, small metal windmills are effective, but expensive to install. (See also *Fishponds*.)

Pylons See *Electricity*.

Quarry Blasting See *Nuisances*.

Rabbits There is a statutory obligation to keep your land free from rabbits, but, in spite of this, it was not until myxomatosis almost wiped out the population of sixty million (more than the human population) that they were got under control.

Young rabbit feeding in early morning

Myxomatosis is still with us, but rabbits have built up some immunity and it is no longer so lethal and numbers are again on the increase. If you find a rabbit with all the symptoms of a terrible cold, swollen face and eyes, running with mucus, and not in the least interested in running away, it has myxomatosis and the kindest thing to do is to kill it, as it will certainly die. Ferreting, gassing, shooting and snaring, and their natural enemies, cats, dogs, stoats, foxes, badgers, weasels, buzzards, owls and hawks take their toll.

To kill a rabbit, hold it by the hind legs, grab its head in the other hand, and while forcing downwards to stretch its neck, twist the head backwards. The neckbone breaks and it dies at once. Small rabbits can be killed by being hit on the back of the neck. Hold the rabbit by the hind legs and deliver a couple of karate chops with the edge of the other hand just behind the head. This should kill it immediately.

Clean young rabbits make good eating, but are not so popular as food since myxomatosis; tame rabbits reared for eating make a cheap and easily reared addition to food supply, and their skins are a useful byproduct. Rabbits do eat a lot and some of the bigger breeds become a problem to keep for this reason, but the medium-sized New Zealand Whites, or Californians, do well on any greenstuffs or roots, and in summer will thrive on grass. A supplement of about 3oz (85g) of ground grain per day will fatten them nicely. A pregnant doe should have up to 7oz (198g) of meal per day, from eighteen days after mating until her litter is eight weeks old, when it will be removed elsewhere for fattening.

Rabbits can be kept in hutches, or hutches with runs, provided they can be moved around. The runs should have netting floors, or the rabbits will burrow out. If rabbits are kept in big paddocks, the netting should be dug 9in (230mm) into the ground to prevent burrowing, and cosy shelter should be provided for them. (See also *Ferrets, Game* and *Skin Curing*.)

Useful Address: British Rabbit Council, 7 Kirkgate, Newark.

Further Reading: Ministry of Agriculture leaflets Nos: AL 544, *Rabbit Meat Production, General Management*; AL 556, *Breeding Principles*; AL 562, *Feeding*; AL 565, *Breeds of Rabbit*; AL 534, *The Wild Rabbit* (HMSO); Forestry Commission leaflet No 67, *Rabbit Management in Woodlands* (HMSO); Sheail, *Rabbits and Their History* (David & Charles); Snow, C. F., *Rabbit Keeping* (Foyles Handbook).

Raspberries See *Fruit*.

Rats Rats are enemies because they carry disease and damage crops and stored food, and must be exterminated wherever found. However, they are brave and intelligent animals, and are natural 'survivors'. Ask for help in extermination from your local authority's pest control officer. If you fail to control rats on your property, notice may be served on you requiring the necessary action. (See also *Pests*.)

Further Reading: Ministry of Agriculture leaflet No AL 516, *Control of Farm Rats and Mice with Anticoagulant Poisons* (HMSO).

Reservoirs Being storage lakes for domestic water, reservoirs are under the control of the appropriate local water authority. No boating, fishing or extraction of water may take place without their permission.

If you wish to build a reservoir for your own use, then planning permission must be sought, and there could be problems with water users downstream. In fact, except for the very smallest reservoir made by damming a stream, you should have the plans drawn up by an engineer, or it is unlikely that any planning authority will consider them.

Any reservoir designed to hold more than 5,000,000 gallons of water above natural ground level must be designed and the construction supervised by an engineer appointed by the Home Secretary, and the reservoir must be inspected every ten years. (See also *Water Supplies*.)

Riding See *Horses*.

Rifles See *Shooting*.

Rights of Way A right of way is a right of passage only. It may be a public or an individual right of way, and there are distinctions as to usage. For instance, a right of cartway does not necessarily include a right of way for cattle. These distinctions must be maintained by evidence as to the original grant, or by the user.

Ownership of land beside a public highway carries with it the right of access to the highway from any adjoining land, except to motorways.

Right of way cannot be acquired just by usage if the owner can prove that usage was not of right, but by permission only or that he registered or interrupted such a use. Unless there is an express obligation to repair a right of way, the owner of the land (the grantor) is not obliged to keep the right of way in repair. The user has a right to enter the land to repair the right of way as much as necessary.

A right of way acquired by a user may lapse if it is not used, but there is no specific period over which this happens.

In any difficult cases, consult your solicitor. Rights of way can be very complex indeed. Most trouble seems to arise from change of usage—someone has a right of way across your land for a specific purpose, or the public may have a footpath or bridleway; the individual starts using his right of way for quite another purpose which may be detrimental to you or your property, or the general public starts driving cars along a bridleway. Almost always they have no right to do this and you can stop them, but check out the facts first.

When buying a new property in the country, do make sure that all rights of way are properly checked by your legal advisors and that you know exactly what the position is. (See also *Footpaths*; *Bridleways*; *Access*; *Trespass*; *Bulls* and *Boundaries*.)

Useful Address: Central Rights of Way Committee, Suite 4, 166 Shaftesbury Avenue, London WC2.

Riparian Rights, Rivers and Streams As far upstream as the tide flows, the bed of the river belongs to the Crown and it is a public navigable river. All rivers above tidal flow are privately owned. The public may have navigation rights on private rivers by usage or by Act of Parliament, but this gives no rights of property or of fishing, only rights of way (which include anchorage).

Riparian rights are the legal rights of a landowner in respect of a natural stream flowing through or alongside his land. If alongside, his rights extend to midstream. Riparian rights include the exclusive right of fishing, so that the owner alone can license others to fish there. A licence to fish includes a right of reasonable access to the water. A riparian owner does not own the actual water, no one owns running water until it is impounded. Every riparian owner has a right to the uninterrupted water in its natural character and quality. The same applies to an underground stream, but not to water percolating through gravel, etc. The owner of the land through which it percolates can appropriate it but may not deal with it so that it flows into a neighbour's land in a polluted state.

A riparian owner may be liable for damage caused by neglect which prevents the free flow of water.

You may not take water from rivers for irrigation or any purpose, or impound it, without a licence from the water authority, except for domestic purposes, including the supply for cattle. You may grant the right to extract a reasonable quantity to others for the same purposes.

There are comprehensive laws against all kinds of water pollution. (See also *Fishing*.)

Road Charges The Highway Act, 1959 (Code 1892), covers the execution of work on unmade or private roads by local highway authorities. When this is done, a proportion of the cost is charged to each person owning property which has 'frontage' on the road, whether they have a gate to the road or not. If you object to the amount you are to be charged, then you must do so within a month. There are various grounds for objection and you should consult a solicitor.

If, when the final bill comes, it is more than you expected, you can again object on grounds that the plans have not been reasonably followed, or that the expenses have exceeded the estimates by more than 15 per cent without sufficient reason, or that the apportionment has not been properly made.

The highway authority may charge you and not others on the street for mending a hole in the road on your frontage. If you feel this is unfair, you may appeal to a magistrate's court.

Rookeries and Starling Roosts Rooks do make an awful lot of noise, and for that reason alone it may be necessary to get rid of them. Of course shooting is the obvious answer, but where this is not practicable, there are other methods such as hosing the nests with cold water, or alternatively poking the bottoms out of them with drain rods. Both these methods often involve climbing the trees, as the nests are usually very high. The birds will probably return anyway. There is really no way to get rid of a rookery except to cut down the trees. Just try to persuade yourself that it is a nice noise to live with!

Starlings roost by the thousand in winter, anywhere that seems to take their fancy,

Rookery in March

which can be quite small woods. Although their congregation and mass exhibitions of aerobatics are marvellous to watch and although no one has the slightest idea how they achieve their unison, they are noisy, dirty and smelly. Their droppings damage small trees and scrub, and the racket, morning and evening, is insupportable. It is extremely difficult to get rid of them. Shooting, if it is persistent, may have some effect, as will bird scarers. The latter cannot, however, be let off through the night if they are also going to disturb local residents. Rockets set off through the trees, and various kinds of noxious smoke, also upset them, but whatever method you try it will have to be repeated for some nights before the birds take the hint.

Build fires in perforated oil drums with smoky slack coal on top, or sawdust—anything that will make smoke—and then put on a loose-fitting lid of sheet metal. On this

put a handful of sulphur, and depart. As it heats, the sulphur smells dreadful and wafts up with the smoke. Creosote mixed with sawdust also produces a vile smell.

Of course, if your wood also contains game, none of these methods are selective, and may disturb game as well as starlings.

Further Reading: Forestry Commission leaflet No 69, *Starling Roost Dispersal from Woodland* (HMSO); Ministry of Agriculture leaflets: AL 208, *Starlings*; AL 244, *Rooks* (HMSO).

Rubbish In most country districts there is a rubbish collection service just as there is in a town, but you do have more opportunity to get rid of at least some of your own rubbish by putting vegetable matter on compost heaps or feeding it to pigs and chickens. Burn all the combustibles, including some plastic waste and dirty paper. Clean paper can be saved for recycling, or your local fish and chip shop. In

192

a few areas bottles are collected, but tin cans and other hard rubbish can only go to the dump.

To attempt to bury your own rubbish is to take on an enormous job and it is illegal to leave rubbish in heaps above ground as it encourages vermin. If you have a real problem, contact your local authority and make a bit of a fuss, and they will probably collect it, but may insist you meet them halfway by taking it to a convenient collecting point.

Most councils will allow you to take big rubbish directly to their dump, or will arrange for a special collection.

Skips—large bins—can be hired and left with you until full, then removed by the contractor. These are very useful if you are doing demolition work and cannot get rid of brick rubble, old timber, etc (see Yellow Pages for addresses). Some councils provide this service.

Rushes Clumps of rushes are a sign of wet and stagnant land so, in severe cases, look first of all to the drainage.

Spray with a selective weedkiller, 2.4 D types, 16–24oz (453–680g) per acre, in dry weather, then cut, rake up and burn. Dress the land with lime and then with potash and phosphate to encourage growth of grasses and clovers. If the ground can be ploughed up after cutting, so that the stools are buried, and is then limed and dressed with phosphates and sown with a good grass and clover mixture, then the resulting pasture should be fairly free from rushes, at least for a few years. (See also *Basketry*.)

Further Reading: Ministry of Agriculture leaflet No AL 433, *Weed Control, Rushes* (HMSO).

S

Safety The countryside is a dangerous place, statistically, but most of the dangers can be avoided with a little knowledge and a lot of commonsense.

Natural Dangers Check individual headings for details of these which are merely listed here: *Snakes*; *Wasps*; *Hornets*; *Lightning* and *Dangerous Plants*.

Man-made Dangers Don't leave tools lying about for the unwary to trip over. Sharp tools, or those with points or prongs, are particularly dangerous. Misuse of tools is responsible for by far the greatest number of accidents—about 100,000 a year. Knives, shears and secateurs should be closed when not in use, and hoes and rakes left upright, prongs facing inwards where people cannot step on them.

When using any kind of cutting tool, make sure that no part of your body is in line with the blade. It is easy to hold a branch in one hand, and hack at it with a hook held in the other hand and cut hand instead of branch (Figs 95 and 96). If tools have to be hand sharpened, always work with the blade held away from the body (Figs 97 and 98). This is a very common mistake made by the inexperienced. Always work a slashing hook away from the body, not towards it.

Water butts, garden ponds and swimming pools are all dangerous to small children. Water butts should be covered with tight-fitting lids and safety nets should be installed on swimming pools and garden ponds if small children are allowed to run unattended in gardens. Do not allow children to play around on haystacks, or asbestos or corrugated iron roofs. All pesticides, all paints, all chemicals should be stored in properly marked containers and kept well out of the way of children. Do not put them into soft-drink bottles. Too

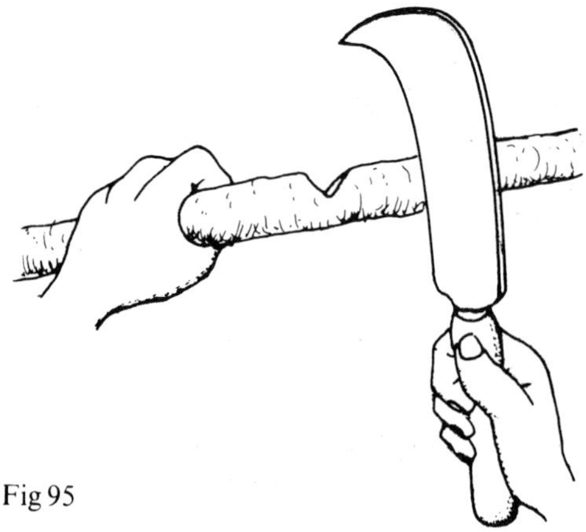

Fig 96

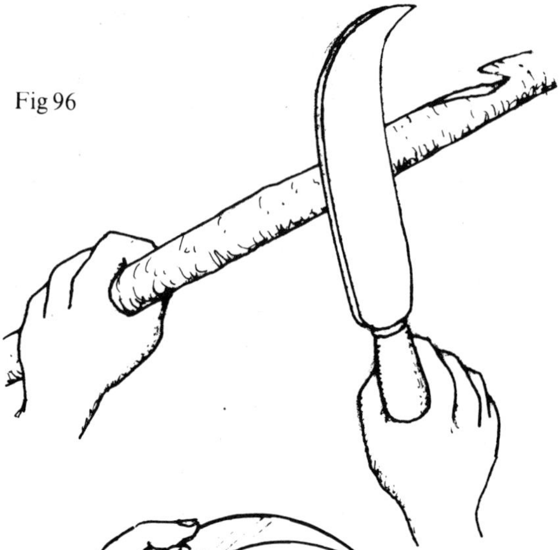

Fig 95

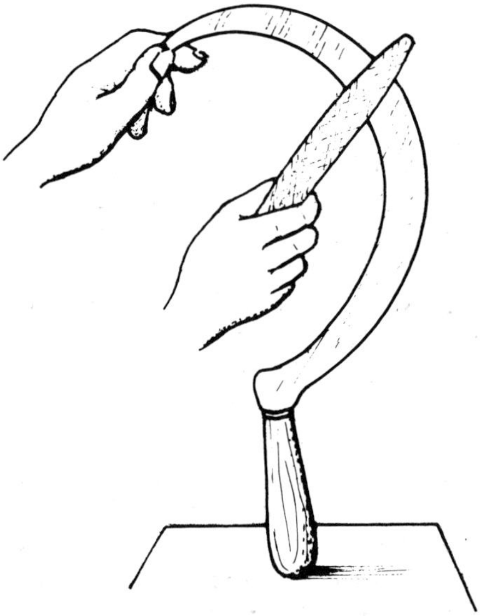

Fig 97   Dangerous

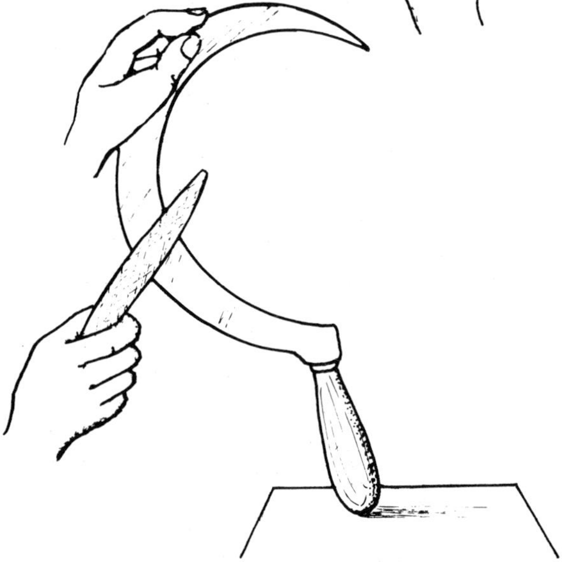

Fig 98   Safe

many people have died from a drink of para-quat out of a lemon squash bottle.

All cuts and punctures should be washed with warm water and Dettol, and anti-tetanus injections should be sought immediately for bad cuts, especially for punctures. Tetanus lives in the soil and thrives away from air, so punctures and closed cuts are especially dangerous. If you are continually working out of doors and cutting yourself, then have

routine anti-tetanus injections. Your doctor will give you one, and there is no reaction.

Don't inhale bonfire smoke. It is dangerous to the lungs if taken in regular doses, just like any other smoke. Be careful when using paraffin to cheer up a smouldering fire. *Never* use petrol.

Always be careful when climbing over a barbed-wire fence.

Be careful when using ladders. Either have a mate to hold the bottom end, or make sure it is firmly set on the ground. If possible, attach the top of the ladder with a rope so that it cannot slide sideways. Never leave unattended ladders where children can climb them.

Algae should be cleaned off stone paths so that they are not slippery (see *Algae* page 8).

Never leave polythene bags, tins or bottles about—they can be death to livestock, quite apart from being untidy.

When dealing with thorny bushes, mind your eyes. It is all too easy to pull a branch across your face. A few scratches from thorns elsewhere are unpleasant more than dangerous, but eyes are very vulnerable.

Mechanical saws, either chain saws or circular saws, are very dangerous and should only be used with the proper safety guards upon them. When cutting up trees, especially old timbers from buildings, for firewood, be sure that there are no large nails or bits of wire or metal embedded in the wood which might break the saw blade with, perhaps, lethal results.

Never adjust any moving or power-driven machinery while the engine is running. It is not sufficient to put it out of gear. Turn the engine off. The same applies to all types of lawn mower. Be sure that all outdoor electrical connections are properly made—of hard rubber. All appliances must be earthed, and don't run over power cables when using lawn mowers.

There are safety regulations about using machinery of all kinds, either tractor-mounted or powered from the tractor by take-off, or belt, or by independent engines, or fixed engines, but all too often these regulations are ignored in the country where there are no factory inspectors to keep an eye on such things. Loose or trailing clothing can be dangerous when using moving machinery, and heavy boots are a great safeguard. Small children should always be kept away from tractors and machinery and not allowed to ride on tractors under any circumstances. The law says that children under thirteen may not ever drive tractors or self-propelled machinery, nor ride on them or on machinery, etc, drawn by them, except on the floor of a trailer or on its load, provided it has four sides higher than the load.

Useful Address: British Safety Council, 62/64 Chancellors Road, London S6.

Further Reading: HMSO leaflets: UL, *Keep an Eye on That Child; Prevention of Accidents*, and many others.

Salting See *Preserving Food*.

Scarecrows Scarecrows do work, at least they help to keep birds off your crops. They are best made to look human, by stuffing an old pair of overalls with straw, and stiffening the backbone with a stout pole, so that he can be firmly planted in the ground. A sack stuffed and tied on top does for a head, and an old hat is always a lifelike addition. Probably the object would be just as effective if it were not in the least humanoid, but scarecrow making is a primitive form of sculpture and the artist must also find the thing satisfying. Some add a stick like a shotgun, others add waving rag scarves; anything which moves, helps. If the arms have been made by using a crossed stick tied to the upright, then a few tin cans, tied together to rattle in the breeze, add an element of noise.

Perhaps the modern scarecrow, a kind of horizontal black and orange windmill on a stick, is just as effective, but it is nothing like so interesting. Bird scarers worked by compressed air, firing a gun every few minutes, are expensive and effective, but can scare everyone for miles, let alone the birds.

The best scarecrows for gardens are cats. The days when one could employ children armed with rattles, for a few pence, are long gone. (See also *Nuisances*.)

Scarecrow on a Suffolk farm

Seashores See *Beachcombing* and *Foreshore Rights*

Sheep To keep lambing ewes on a small scale is neither economic nor practicable. How-

196

ever, should you have an acre or more of paddock or orchard which wants grazing, buy a few store lambs in the autumn; four to the acre is plenty, and these will need some extra hay in hard weather. The lambs can be killed off as you want to eat them, and the spare meat kept in a deep freeze. Lamb keeps well unfrozen, and if you share a beast with a friend, then the half lamb can be eaten up before it spoils.

Be warned that sheep suffer from various diseases and conditions which are all unpleasant, such as footrot, blowfly and liver fluke. Lambing can present problems with which only the expert or a vet can deal, and during lambing time you will have to be there day and night. Shearing is also a job for the expert. (See also *Jacob's Sheep*.)

Useful Address: National Sheep Association, Groves, Jenkins Lane, Tring, Herts.

Further Reading: McCooper and Thomas, *Profitable Sheep Farming* (Farming Press).

Sheep Worrying Many farmers living near towns, who used to keep sheep, have been forced to give them up because of worrying by dogs, and this is a problem even in country districts where people are aware that this can happen. Those new to the country should not get the idea that dogs can be allowed to run free there, any more than they can in town. Sheep worrying is a problem because it is extremely difficult to find the culprits unless they are actually caught at it. Sheepdogs themselves, working the animals by day, and perfectly quiet with them all the time, have been known to go out at night and chase and slaughter sheep, particularly lambs, sometimes working in pairs or groups, while next day butter won't melt in their mouths.

The kindliest and most meek and mild dog can be seized with a savage lust for killing when it gets among sheep, and the more the sheep run, the more excited and murderous the dog becomes. One so often hears the cry '*My* dog could never do a thing like that, he (or she) is so gentle and loving.' There is in fact no dog, large or small, which *could not* be a sheep chaser and killer.

For this reason, the law is strict on the subject, and the local authority may impose an order that all dogs be restrained if sheep worrying is taking place. Only in this way can the culprit be isolated and caught, and at worst the trouble will be contained for the time being.

If your dog is caught savaging sheep by a farmer, you can hardly blame him if he shoots it on the spot, and he is entitled to do this if he can prove it was actually attacking his stock. Otherwise he is committing an actionable wrong (see *Trespass*).

Should your dog be accused of sheep worrying, have him examined by a vet who might (or might not) find some traces which could prove (or disprove) the charge. It really is very important that dogs are restrained at night, especially during lambing time, in the early spring and late winter—and at all times, if there is any question of them being stock chasers.

The owner of a dog which kills or injures stock is liable for the damage under the Dogs (Protection of Livestock) Act, 1953, and this could amount to a great deal of money.

Shoeing See *Horses*.

Shooting *Sporting Guns* Shotguns are smooth-bore weapons of limited range, firing a cartridge containing many round lead pellets which form a pattern of some 20–40in (508–1,016mm) in diameter, depending on range, size of shot and shape of barrel. Shotguns are used by the shooter of wild game and of clay pigeons, and, for all normal sporting purposes for adult use, the double-barrelled twelve-bore is the standard gun. The smaller .410 is a good weapon for dealing with small vermin, especially inside barns or among buildings, and for young people starting to shoot.

The range of makes, types and prices of shotguns is immense. At one end of the scale is the best London-made sidelock, ejector gun, unobtainable even second hand for much under £2,000. At the other is the simplest form of foreign-made, box-lock

Using a twelve bore. High pheasant technique

non-ejector. In no purchase is it more true that you get what you pay for. The difference between an expensive gun and a cheap one is not in fire power, but in quality, durability, beauty and pleasure in use. Never buy a cheap second-hand gun without having it checked by a qualified gunsmith, as it may well be unsafe to use.

Choke (Fig 99) The choke is the degree of thickening of the barrel at the muzzle end which tightens the groupings of the shot in flight. It does *not* increase range, but the tighter grouping is more effective as a killer, as more shot goes into a small area (Figs 100 and 101).

Shot Size The size of the individual lead pellet varies from No 8, the smallest, to No 1, the

Fig 99

OPEN BARREL

CHOKED BARREL

Rifle shooting; deer stalking in Inverness-shire

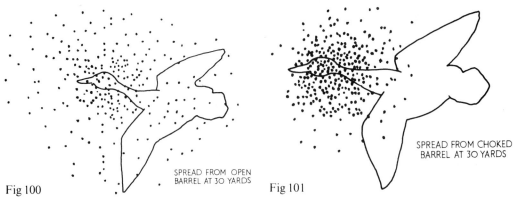

SPREAD FROM OPEN
BARREL AT 30 YARDS

SPREAD FROM CHOKED
BARREL AT 30 YARDS

Fig 100

Fig 101

largest. The smaller the shot, the greater the number contained in the cartridge and, consequently, the denser the pattern. For normal shooting purposes, No 6 is the size in general use, Nos 7 or 8 being used on a day when snipe and woodcock are the quarry, and Nos 1–4 for geese and high duck. (There are even larger sizes numbered by letters, eg, BB but they are not of general interest.)

Rifles A rifle has a rifled barrel to propel a single rotating bullet. It is used for target shooting, and for shooting stationary animals ranging in size from rabbits to elephants. Rifles have a much greater range than shotguns and can be lethal up to a mile or more. Never fire a rifle where there is any possibility of overshooting into a road, buildings or animals. Rifles vary considerably in the size of bullet fired, from the .22, suitable for rabbits and targets, up to the heaviest bullet for big game (not in Britain!). The range of price and quality is considerable, and the use of telescopic sights can make the weapon extremely accurate.

Maintenance Shotguns and rifles, being expensive and cherished possessions, repay care and attention. Avoid damage in use, through carelessness. Never lean a gun up against a fence or wall where it might fall over. Never leave it unprotected and uncovered in the back of a car. Keep the gun clean and oiled to prevent fouling and rust. Always clean after use. Rain or salt-laden air can cause havoc.

The Law You must have a firearms certificate for a rifle and, to obtain this, without which you cannot buy ammunition either, you must apply to your local chief of police. He will expect a very good reason, as firearms certificates are not issued to all and sundry. Certificates are issued to members of a proper rifle club which fires solely at targets, but the police are rightly very careful about the issue of certificates for such lethal weapons. It is an offence to supply, give or lend a firearm to anyone under fourteen.

You must have a shotgun certificate for a shotgun, obtainable from the local police. You may use a borrowed shotgun without a licence for shooting at artificial targets on private premises. Under the age of seventeen, it is an offence to buy or hire a shotgun. Under fifteen, it is an offence to carry an assembled shotgun, except in the company of someone over twenty-one. It is an offence to supply, give or lend a shotgun to anyone under fifteen. It is an offence to own a shotgun with a barrel less than 24 inches (609mm) long.

Airguns are also subject to the law. Under the age of fourteen, it is an offence to have an airgun. It is an offence to have an airgun in a public place except in a cover, if you are under seventeen. It is an offence to supply, give or lend an airgun to anyone under fourteen.

Safety The rules of safety were never better expressed or explained than in the following famous poem. They should be engraved on every sportman's heart.

A Father's Advice to His Son

If a sportsman true you'd be
Listen carefully to me.
Never, never, let your gun
Pointed be at anyone.
That it may unloaded be
Matters not the least to me.

When a hedge or fence you cross
Though of time it cause a loss,
From your gun the cartridge take
For the greater safety's sake.

If twixt you and neighbouring gun
Birds may fly or beasts may run,
Let this maxim e'er be thine;
Follow not across the line.

Stops and beaters oft unseen
Lurk behind some leafy screen;
Calm and steady always be,
Never shoot where you can't see.

Keep your place and silent be,
Game can hear and game can see;
Don't be greedy, better spared
Is a pheasant than one shared.

You may kill or you may miss
But at all times think of this;
All the pheasants ever bred
Won't repay for one man dead.

Commander
Mark Beaufoy

Different Types of Shooting You may shoot at live game (with a shotgun or rifle), clay pigeons (with a shotgun), or a target (with a rifle). Game shooting is non-competitive and appeals to man's primeval hunting instinct to provide food for his family. Clay pigeon and target shooting are essentially competitive tests of marksmanship which exist as sports in their own right and appeal to many who also shoot game. Far from being mutually exclus- ive, the two sports complement each other and overlap.

Clay Pigeon Shooting All that is needed is a small field, or perhaps a lakeside, where over- shooting cannot be dangerous, launching equipment and someone who knows how to use it, and a few enthusiasts to form a club. From then on the limiting factor is cash, for cartridges and clay pigeons are expensive. There are many 'shooting schools' with clay pigeon equipment which provide elementary and advanced instruction. For the complete novice, clay pigeon shooting provides a use- ful introduction to the essentials of game shoot- ing. It teaches the effective use of shotguns, and the essentials of safety and respect for the weapon and its potential. The game shooter does not mind his neighbour's inaccuracy, but he is very upset by dangerous conduct or

Clay pigeon shooting with a twelve bore

gun handling, and by lack of proper precautions.

Game Shooting This is a country sport of immense variety, ranging from the most expensive organized shoot, with keepers and other paid staff designed to produce a large bag of birds, to the individual sportsman, to whom a gratifying day's sport means a hunt with his dog, resulting in a single mallard duck or a couple of rabbits to take home at the end of it.

The principle game birds with which the shooter is likely to be concerned are the pheasant, partridge and grouse, the woodcock, snipe and woodpigeon, and the various species of wild duck and goose. Ground game describes the hare and rabbit. Depending partly upon geography and season, partly on farming policy and terrain, and partly on the effort consciously and expensively made by the landowner or tenant to improve the shooting potential, one or more of these will be the objective. The one certain factor is that demand for shooting rights always exceeds the supply.

The more sophisticated, organized and expensive form of shooting is 'driving', when the birds are driven over the line of standing guns by beaters. The birds offer a difficult and challenging target, and one may stand about for long periods, getting cold, just for a few moments' exciting action.

Less ambitious and less costly is 'walking up', when the guns and their dogs walk in line, hunting up game as it is found. The shooting is less difficult, but it is fascinating to watch the working spaniels, and the excitement as the birds explode from cover is considerable.

How to Get Started Shooting rights (except coastal, see page 203) are the property of the owner of the land and are a valuable asset. There are various ways of gaining access to these assets if you are not born to rich parents owning a large estate, or do not have a prosperous godfather.

Take a lease of shooting rights. This may be difficult to find and, if the sport is good, extremely expensive. The number of privately owned and organized shoots has declined dramatically as the result of rising costs and increased taxation.

Join a syndicate. This is an informal association of a specified number of like-minded shooters who run and share the costs of a shoot. You must get to know a member of a syndicate and persuade him that, when there is a vacancy, you are a desirable candidate with the necessary experience of handling a gun with complete safety.

Obtain permission from a local farmer, or be invited to shoot rabbits or pigeons on his land, or join up with someone who has that permission. Always report to the farmhouse before going onto the land, and also check if anyone else is out there shooting. Take care of the farmer's gates and fences as though they were your own.

Offer your services as a beater or picker-up to the organizer of a shoot or his gamekeeper, and study what goes on and how everyone behaves. In time you may be rewarded by an invitation to shoot.

Join a gun club, usually organized by a branch of the Clay Pigeon Shooters Association, which is an association of shooters which rents rough shooting where it can, and guarantees to the owner of the land that a proper standard of behaviour will be maintained by its members.

Wildfowling Coastal wildfowling for duck and geese is a winter sport, and a lonely one, and involves long hours, usually at dusk or dawn, out in the cold and wet in all weathers. It can be terrible, or infinitely rewarding, and for the addict is the finest sport of all. He may have a companion, but is frequently alone apart from his dog, and success is achieved by patience, knowledge and endurance, as well as by being a good shot. The size of the bag is the least important factor. Wildfowling on mud flats, saltings and foreshores involves knowing a great deal about the terrain and the

No comment!

habits of the many species of ducks and geese. A novice should never go wildfowling without an experienced companion, and should always carry a compass. Ignorance of local conditions, tides, etc, can lead to disaster.

Anyone may shoot along the tideline, below the normal spring tide high-water mark, between 1 September and 20 February. Nevertheless, other people are also free to use the same areas and one is not allowed to carry a firearm in a public place, and theoretically one could be prosecuted. However, the Wildfowlers Association of Great Britain and Ireland have arranged, with the Crown Commissioners, immunity for members of their own association or clubs affiliated with it, so it is important that you join the association. The spring tide limit does, of course, include many areas of saltmarsh and estuary which are below that limit. However, nowadays many of these areas or parts of them are

bird sanctuaries of various kinds, and the greatest care should be taken not to interfere with these in any way.

Useful Addresses: British Field Sports Society, 26 Caxton Street, London SW1H 0RG (for information on all field sports); Game Conservancy, Fordingbridge, Hants (for information on all aspects of game conservation); Wildfowlers Association of Great Britain and Ireland, Marford Mill, Rossett, Clwyd LL12 0HL; Clay Pigeon Association, 107, Epping New Road, Buckhurst Hill, Essex IG9 5TQ.

Further Reading: Marchington, John, *Shooting—A Complete Guide for Beginners* (Faber); Marchington, J., *The Practical Wildfowler* (A. & C. Black); Ruffer, John; *The Art of Good Shooting* (David & Charles). Periodicals: *The Field; Shooting Times; Shooting Magazine* (for clay pigeon shooters).

Shrews See *Mice.*

Silverfish This is a small fish-shaped silver insect always found in houses, where it scavenges at night for tiny scraps of food. It can do a lot of damage to books and papers which it loves to eat. Use insect powder to eradicate the pest.

Skin Curing Skins for curing by a pelt dresser should be cleaned of fat and pinned out on a board in an airy place to dry. When the skin has partially dried, any remaining lumps of fat can be scraped off with a blunt knife, but do not remove the tissue. Pack pelts in pairs, fur to fur, wrap in newspaper and send them immediately to a pelt dresser.

However, should you wish to cure a pelt at home, soak it thoroughly in successive baths of tepid water for about three hours, until it is soft and pliable. Lay the skin over a roller or rounded surface and remove all flesh and fat and a thin layer of surface tissue with a blunt knife. This is quite a skilled job as the skin should be left an even thickness all over. Then rinse in lukewarm water and squeeze until there is no grease left in it. A little white spirit on a rag will remove any stains or dirt and the last of the natural grease. The skin is then ready for dressing.

Dissolve 4oz (113g) alum in 2 pints (1 litre) water and 1oz (28g) of washing soda and 2oz (56g) common salt in another pint (0.5 l). Pour the alum solution slowly into the salt and soda solution, stirring vigorously. Mix ½lb (226g) plain flour with a little water, and then add the alum mixture to make a thick paste, stirring thoroughly, adding more flour if necessary. Pin out the skin on a board and paint a thick layer of the paste on to it, being careful not to get any on the fur. After twenty-four hours, scrape off the paste and put on another coat. Leave again for twenty-four hours and repeat the pasting. This time leave for three days before scraping. Then work and rinse the skin in water, with borax added at the rate of 1oz (28g) per gallon (4¼ litres). Then wash in clean tepid water until every trace of paste has gone. Squeeze out the pelt, but do not wring it, and pull it into shape with your hands before tacking it out, flesh side up, on a clean board. Paint a coat of neatsfoot oil all over the skin and leave it to dry.

Fig 102

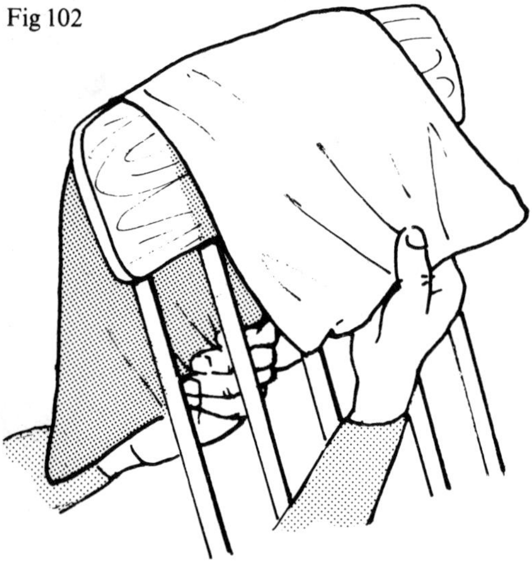

When the skin is almost dry, but still just pliable, unpin it and work it backwards and forwards over the back of a chair until it is supple. This may take quite a bit of time and elbow grease (Fig 102)!

Once the skin is soft all over, put it into a shallow receptacle and cover it with dry hardwood sawdust. Work it about in the sawdust with the hands, pulling it gently in all directions. Then hang it in a cool airy place to dry out completely before use. Never heat skins at any stage to dry them, it merely makes them go hard.

Further Reading: Snow, C. F., *Rabbit Keeping* (Foyles).

Slow Worms See *Snakes.*

Slugs and Snails Slugs and snails are voracious and destructive to plantlife and will eat their way through almost anything in the garden. They like damp dark places and cluster under ivy, stones and damp rubbish. Put down slug pellets to eradicate them.

All species of British snails are edible. It is best to feed them on lettuce leaves for a few days to 'clean' them. Eat only the muscular foot which protrudes below the shell.

Smells See *Nuisances.*

Smoking Food See *Preserving Food.*

Smooth Snakes See *Snakes.*

Snakes *Adders (Vipera berus)* Also known as the viper, it is distinguished by having elliptic pupils like a cat, but do not risk getting near enough to check. Adders have a dark zigzag line right along their backs and are usually greyish or brownish, occasionally greenish or reddish-brown, and slaty-blue underneath. Males are brighter than females, growing up to 2ft (600mm) long. Both bite. If your snake is considerably longer it is *not* an adder.

The adder is the only poisonous snake in Great Britain (there are no snakes at all in Ireland) and is the only species in Scotland. It follows that a Scottish snake *must* be dangerous. Adders prefer dry grasslands, commons, sandy woods, stacks of firewood, etc. They are not aggresive, or there would be far more cases of cats, dogs and farm animals being bitten, which is extremely rare. Hedgehogs keep adders under control, so encourage them if you have too many adders about the place.

All animals (including humans) are very wary of snakes. The adder does little harm except when taken by surprise, trodden on, or cornered.

Snakebite can be very unpleasant indeed, even occasionally fatal to small dogs or small children, rarely so to large animals or adults. Dogs usually get bitten on legs or head, humans on the lower legs or hands. The only evidence of the bite will be two small punctures in the skin, with little drops of blood and

An adder

A grass snake

venom showing where the fangs entered. The bite should be sucked out immediately and bathed in warm, soapy water if possible, but do *not* apply a tourniquet, cut the wound, or bathe it with chemicals. Keep the victim still and support the bitten limb as if it were fractured. Get a doctor or a vet as soon as possible. Reassure the patient who, particularly if he is scared of snakes, will be rather shocked. The area of the bite will swell, redden and hurt a lot. The victim may be sweaty, giddy and sick, may have diarrhoea and may collapse, depending on how much venom has been absorbed and how big and healthy he is. Rest for at least a couple of days after snakebite. Take painkillers to relieve the pain.

Grass Snakes (*Natrix natrix helvetica*) They grow up to 3ft (nearly 1m) long, greeny-olive-brown on the upper side, with vertical black bars along each flank and yellowish crescent-shaped patches at the back of the head with two black triangles behind it. The most important difference from the poisonous adder is that the grass snake has a *round* eye pupil. Totally harmless, it lives on small rodents, frogs and birds' eggs, and is a good swimmer. It lays its eggs in warm places such as the base of an old haystack.

On being picked up, the snake will hiss and carry on, but never bite. It may exude an unpleasant smelly fluid onto you. Failing all else, it shams dead, opening its mouth, going limp, and flopping onto its back. It gives itself away, however, because, if righted, it immediately turns over onto its back again.

Smooth Snakes (*Coronella austriarca*) Rare but occasionally found in Hampshire, Dorset, Wiltshire, Surrey and Sussex, in dry sandy heaths and open woodland with water nearby. Very smooth grey, to red or rich brown, with dark spots along the back and dark patches on each side of, and on top of, the head. Non-poisonous.

Slow Worms (*Anguis fragilis*) These are in fact lizards and not snakes. They grow up to 18in (450mm) long and have movable eyelids (unlike snakes). The body is smooth with close greyish-brown scales. Females have a dark back stripe and occasionally slow worms have bluish spots. They are found mainly in quiet dampish places, hedgerows, rubbish dumps, etc. Like ordinary lizards, slow worms can shed their tails if picked up by them, so, if the tail falls off, it is definitely a slow worm and not a snake.

Further Reading: Appleby, L. G., *British Snakes* (John Baker Ltd); Smith, Malcolm, *British Amphibians and Reptiles* (Collins).

Soil Testing See *Fertilizers* and *Lime*.

Solar Heating The heat of the sun can be used at all times of the year to provide domestic hot water. One has only to stand in a greenhouse on a sunny day at any time of the year to feel the amount of heat trapped under the glass, and it is the absorption of this heat which provides the energy. As we live in a climate where the sun cannot be relied upon to pierce the clouds all day and every day, any solar heating systems must incorporate thermostatically controlled electric immersion heating to produce a constant level of heat.

Much research is going on into this source of heating, which is non-pollutant, and free (after the initial capital expenditure of installing equipment), except for minimal maintenance and the running and servicing of a small pump. Reasonably efficient units are on the market, which will provide a normal household with all the hot water it needs in the summer and will cut winter fuel bills by heating mains water several degrees (more or less according to weather) before the electric or gas heating cuts in.

The collectors consist of large copper panels, containing copper piping, with a black painted surface, covered with glass. These are set up on a sloping roof facing south to catch the sunlight, and water is circulated through, absorbing the heat as it goes (Fig 103). This heated water passes into an ordin-

Four solar heating panels which provide enough hot water for this big house in the summer, and a very useful backup amount in winter. This photograph was taken in December, and even in pale intermittent sunshine was registering a water temperature of 70°F (21°C)

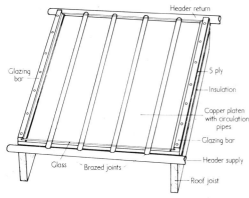

Fig 103

ary domestic hot-water tank, if the system has no pump, and works by the thermo-syphon principle that hot water rises. This can only work if the collector panels are installed below the level of the tanks. Otherwise, using a small circulating pump, water from a header tank passes through the collectors, which may be above or below the house tanks, and a heat-exchange tank linked to the normal domestic hot-water tank (Figs 104 and 105).

Obviously the number of panels installed directly affects the amount of hot water obtainable. A good rule of thumb is to provide between 1 and 1.25 sq feet (0.093–0.12 sq metres) of panel for each gallon (4.546 litres) capacity of the storage tank. Thus for a 25 gallon (114 litres) storage tank, two or three panels 10 sq feet (0.93 sq metres) each would be needed.

In northern latitudes 43 sq feet (4 sq metres) of collectors will heat 30 gallons (136 litres) of water up to 140°F (60°C) in summer weather and over 40°F (4°C) on a clear winter day, which should provide an annual average of 40 per cent of all domestic hot water.

Installation is easy as the panels can be built directly onto existing roofs, and the plumbing presents no problems. It can be done by any efficient handyman at great financial saving, but is normally done on a contract basis by specialist installers. If you employ an efficient installer he should set thermostat switches and pumps properly, so that water is not circulated during times when the outside temperature is cold, for instance at night, when heat would be lost rather than gained.

As far as swimming pools are concerned, only a comparatively low water temperature is required, and this can be provided by solar collectors set up in banks conveniently near the pool (see *Swimming Pools*). An area of panels, equal to half the surface area of the pool, will provide water warmed up to 10°F (5°C) more than it would be without heating. The pool water is circulated by pump directly through the panels.

Solar heating is also being used very successfully to provide a constant supply of warm water for fish hatcheries, trout farms, etc, and there are doubtless other applications of the principle.

If you are thinking in terms of recovering the capital cost of installing solar heating, then it will take quite a few years of reduced

fuel charges to do this. But the saving on fuel bills will certainly more than offset the interest charges on capital used, and, when building a new house or putting in heating where none exists, the economics become very attractive. Especially, taking a long-term view, as electricity, gas and oil will become steadily more expensive, to the point of being ruinous, as the North Sea bonanza fades out before the end of the century.

Useful Addresses: The Solar Installations Co, 27 Lovelace Close, Rainham, Kent; The Solar Centre, 176 Ifield Road, Chelsea, London SW109AF.

Fig 104

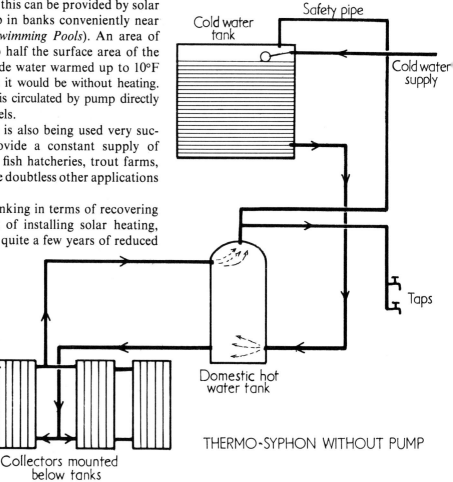

THERMO-SYPHON WITHOUT PUMP

Collectors mounted below tanks

Domestic hot water tank

Cold water tank

Safety pipe

Cold water supply

Taps

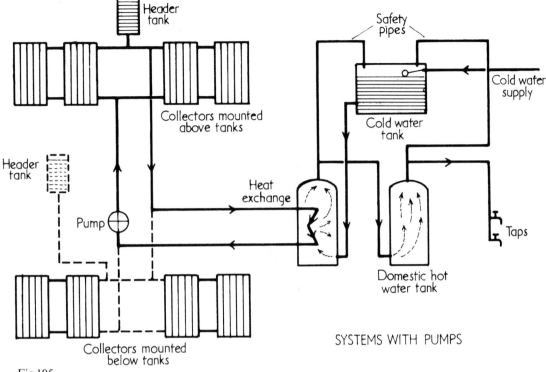

Header tank

Collectors mounted above tanks

Header tank

Pump

Heat exchange

Collectors mounted below tanks

Safety pipes

Cold water supply

Cold water tank

Domestic hot water tank

Taps

SYSTEMS WITH PUMPS

Fig 105

Solid-fuel Stoves Rising fuel costs have made more and more people look for ways to heat their homes and cook, which will not use oil, electricity, gas or coal. There are solid-fuel boilers which will burn absolutely anything combustible, and which will, according to size of unit, cope adequately with all demands. 'Passat' boilers will burn wood, straw (better than burning it in the fields), sawdust, turf, paper, cardboard, in fact anything combustible. Because the combustion chambers are big, they can be filled with large chunks of wood, bales of straw, etc, and stoking need only be done once or twice per twelve hours, according to the fuel used. The saving on fuel costs is enormous—disadvantages are that the stove has to be let out and cleaned about once a week, and that fuel must be brought in and stored somewhere. Installation is simple, and it is well worth investigating, especially if

you have a constant supply of fuel to get rid of. One bakery runs a boiler on breadcrumbs and packaging; and a turkey farm burns turkey droppings and sawdust!

Wood-Burning Stoves Scandinavian wood-burning stoves, which run on logs, are becoming popular. Those which include ovens look like the old-fashioned kitchen ranges, but those intended for room heating come in various shapes, sizes and colours, and look well in modern settings. They are made of cast iron and have flue pipes which must be led into a chimney, and they have *bas relief* motifs all over them (Figs 106, 107 and 108). Again, they do have to be cleaned out, the fuel must be carted, cut and stored, and the stove must be stoked once every twelve or twenty-four hours. Some models have opening doors so that you can have an open fire when required. Most have hotplates on top. The heat output

209

Fig 106

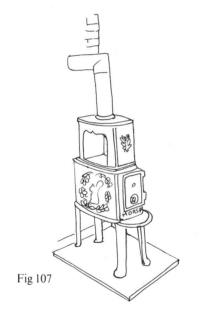

Fig 107

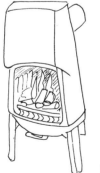

Fig 108

is considerable, as the stove itself gets very hot and radiates warmth throughout the room. Not recommended without guards, or except within the bounds of a big fireplace where there are children about. The stove must not be installed too near to combustible materials, although the fire risk is not great—after all these stoves have always been used throughout the world, particularly in forest areas where fuel is cheap and where most houses are built of wood anyway.

Solid-Fuel Stoves for Cooking Apart from those mentioned above, there are various solid-fuel stoves on the market, all proved by long use to be effective. Agas and Rayburns are famous for their efficiency, both for cooking and water heating. Do not be tempted to get too big a stove. A small stove will provide all the cooking space and water heating that is necessary for a small family.

Courtier, particularly, specialize in grates using slow burning fuels, and Rayburn make hooded grates with chimneys for open hearths. (See also *Fireplaces*.)

Useful Addresses: The Wood Stove Shop, SETS, Bullockstone Road, Herne, Nr Herne Bay, Kent CT6 7NL (for details of Passat boilers and wood-burning stoves); The Heating Centre, 34 Mortimer Street, London W1.

Further Reading: Department of the Environment Guides to Good Building: No 31, *Installing Solid Fuel Appliances*; No 2, *Room Heaters, Boilers, Cookers*; No 50, *Chimneys for Domestic Boilers* (HMSO); Harrington, *Woodburning Stove Book* (Collier/MacMillan).

Spiders There are six hundred species in the British Isles, not one of which is harmful to man. Spiders catch insects, including flies, so are, in the main, actually beneficial. There is no reason to dislike or to destroy these fascinating creatures. If a spider could encircle the world with a single thread of silk, it would weigh less than 6oz (170g) which accounts for the fact that they have no difficulty in floating their silk sideways across enormous gaps to anchor their webs.

'If in life you wish to thrive, let the spider run alive.'

Useful Address: British Spiders Study Group, c/o British Arachnological Society, Pear Tree House, Blenner Hasset Green, Carlisle, Cumberland.

Further Reading: Tweedie, *Pleasure from Insects* (David & Charles); Linssen, E. F. and Newman, L. Hugh, *Observer's Book of Common Insects* (Warne).

Spinning, Dyeing and Weaving If you keep more than four sheep for their wool you must register with the British Wool Marketing Board.

In a sheepfarming district there should be no difficulty in getting hold of a fleece for spinning, dyeing and home weaving. Quite a lot of wool can be collected from fences, fields and hedges in summer time, and that can be spun into wool after it has been teased out into a light fluffy ball, like cotton wool, or carded. Carding is done with scratch card mounted on wooden bats (Fig 109). Put a

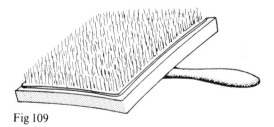

Fig 109

layer of wool across one bat and draw it out with the other until the fibres are evenly distributed. They are then removed with the empty carder and rolled into a loose ball (a rove) for spinning (Fig 110).

The wool can be spun on a hand spindle. This takes a little practice, although even the beginner's wool, which tends to be thick and

Fig 110

thin by turns, can knit up into most attractive clothes.

Take a 1ft (300mm) long piece of $\frac{3}{8}$in (9.5mm) dowelling and a wooden disc 3in (75mm) in diameter and $\frac{1}{2}$in (12mm) thick, with a hole in the exact middle to take the dowel. Run the dowel through so that it sticks out about 1in (25mm). Cut a notch in the dowel $\frac{3}{4}$in (20mm) from the top of the stick, sloping upwards. Take a handful of fleece and pull some out, twisting it with your fingers to make a yarn. Tie this end of yarn to a convenient hook and, holding the fleece in your hands, pull it and roll it and twist it so that the yarn gets longer and longer, always twisting in the same direction (Fig 111). When this

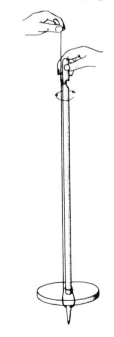

Fig 111

211

Spinners at an agricultural show

piece is 18in (450mm) long, unhook it and tie it to the spindle just above the disc. Pass the yarn down over the disc round the protruding bit of dowel, up to the notch, through it, round the dowel under the rising thread, and so up to the hand above holding the fleece. Twist the spindle sharply clockwise with the right hand, move the fingers up the yarn to just below the fleece and hold as the spindle turns, then pull upwards with the left hand to bring out more yarn from the fleece just as the rising twist reaches the right hand. Release with the right hand and spin the spindle again. When you have reached arm's length, unhitch the yarn from the top and bottom of the spindle and wind it on criss-crossing up and down to make a cone shape. Re-hitch and then repeat, till the spindle is full. Wind off the wool into a ball and start all over again with the last 18in (450mm) of spun yarn.

Spinning wheels can be bought new, and

212

old ones can usually be put into working order. There is no space here to detail the method, but it is not difficult, and is a more sophisticated mechanization of hand spinning as described above. Spinning is a restful and rhythmic operation which allows one to think of other things while working. It is becoming very popular and there are local spinning and weaving societies in most areas who will welcome you and help you to get started.

Spun wool must be washed by winding it into skeins and soaking it in a bowl of hot water and pure soap for twenty minutes. Then wash it out gently, but thoroughly, with your hands, puddling and squeezing, but not wringing or twisting it. Rinse it in warm water with a few drops of ammonia in it, and then spin dry, before continuing with the dyeing.

Many natural dyes can be made from the

A very large loom in a very small room

bark of trees, and fruit, such as blackberries, leaves and flowers. Lichens and walnut dyes remain fast on wool, but, for many dyes, it must be prepared by 'mordanting', treating the wool with chemicals before it is dyed. Different mordants produce different colour tones from the same dyes. Thus it is quite an art, and, although the processes are not at all difficult, they are too complex to be described here. The colours of natural dyes are those of the countryside around us and are never harsh and 'chemical'. It is the natural dyes which give their wonderful colours to real Scottish tweeds and wools.

Weaving The end processes of spinning and dyeing are knitting and weaving. Weaving

213

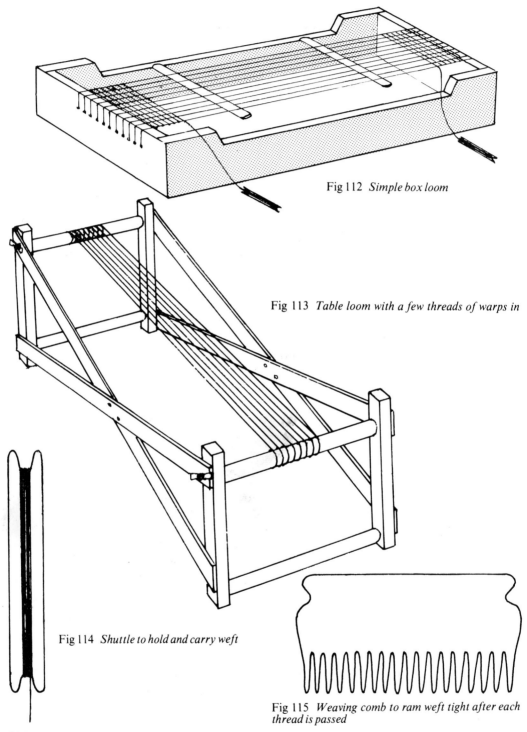

Fig 112 *Simple box loom*

Fig 113 *Table loom with a few threads of warps in*

Fig 114 *Shuttle to hold and carry weft*

Fig 115 *Weaving comb to ram weft tight after each thread is passed*

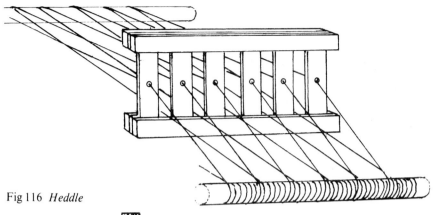

Fig 116 *Heddle*

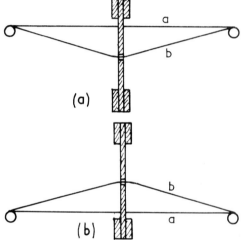

Fig 117 *Action of heddle: lifts alternate threads of weft to make shed through which to pass the shuttle*

can be done on almost any frame on which threads can be set up, right through to enormous complicated hand looms which need a room to themselves. There are several types of small table looms on which excellent work can be done, although the web (finished weaving) will not be very wide. Those with rollers incorporated allow long pieces to be made, as the finished work is wound round and round the roller. The beginner should start on a small table loom before thinking about getting a big expensive one. Any handyman can make a simple loom (Figs 112, 113, 114, 115, 116, 117a and b).

Courses in weaving are run at almost every adult education centre, and you should enquire at your local library to find out what is available in your area. There are many excellent books on the subject, and books of weavers' patterns which give full details and charts of how to set up looms.

Useful Addresses: Amalgamated Weavers Association, 1st Floor, 74 Corporation Street, Manchester M4 2BX; Association of Weavers, Spinners and Dyers, Mrs Laycock, Five Bays, 10 Stancliffe Avenue, Marford, Wrexham; The British Wool Marketing Board, Kew Bridge House, Brentford, Middlesex (purchase of fleece); Peter Teal, Millhouse Studios, Parracombe, Devon (spinning equipment); National Sheep Association, Groves, Jenkins Lane, St Leonards, Tring, Hertfordshire (purchase of fleece); Midland Hand Weavers Association, 51 Westridge Road, Birmingham 15 (mordants, dyeing equipment); Harris Looms, Northgrove Road, Hawkhurst, Kent (looms).

Further Reading: Marret, E., *Vegetable Dyes* (Faber); *Hand Weaving on Two-way Looms* (Dryad Press); *The Weaver's Craft* (Dryad Press); Chetioynd, H., *Simple Weaving* (Studio Vista); Tovey, J., *The Technique of Weaving* (Batsford); Znamierowski, N., *Weaving* (Pan Books); Tovey, J., *Weaves and Pattern Drafting* (Batsford).

Grey squirrel

Spray Damage See *Nuisances*.

Squirrels The grey squirrel which infests some areas is a pest, although extremely attractive to watch. The main damage he does is to young trees and seedlings, by nibbling the bark. He carries surplus seeds and nuts about and buries them, thus usefully propagating trees and bushes. Continual attempts are made to exterminate squirrels by shooting, etc, but they are too widespread and adaptable to be got rid of easily. If numbers are kept to a reasonable level they do not really do very much damage.

Red squirrels are much shyer and prefer conifers, so are rarely seen in gardens. The growth of artificial pine forests is favouring

Red squirrel

216

them. They were *not* exterminated by the imported grey squirrel, but were hit by a lethal epidemic. Numbers are now increasing steadily.

Grey squirrels become very tame, and a table placed by a window, supplied with nuts, bits of toast, or bread, will attract them right up to the house. They will raid bird tables and can reach almost anything as they are excellent climbers.

Further Reading: Forestry Commission leaflets; No 56, *Grey Squirrel Control*; No 101, *Red Squirrel Control*; No 29, *Wild Life Conservation in Woodland* (HMSO); *The Observer's Book of Wild Animals* (Warne); Harrison Matthews, L., *British Mammals* (Collins).

Stabling See *Horses*.

Stags See *Deer*; *Hunting* and *Game*.

Starling Roosts See *Rookeries*.

Stings and Bites Never scratch stings or bites, as this inflames and infects the area. Dab with antiseptic such as TCP or diluted Dettol, and put on anti-histamine sting cream which can be bought from a chemist, and should always be kept in the first aid kit. In severe cases go to a doctor, who will probably prescribe anti-histamine cream or pills. Few of the old traditional remedies for stings and bites do any good at all.

There are those who are extremely allergic to insect bites and who should certainly seek immediate medical treatment. When a wasp or bee has stung the inside of the mouth, it is best to seek medical help (or veterinary help for a cat or a dog), in case swelling interferes with breathing.

For snakebite treatment, see *Snakes*. Snakebite (adder) is the worst bite of all in this country, but is rarely lethal. The stings of some jellyfish and some types of seashore rock fish can be very painful indeed for an

hour or so, but are not lethal. Reassure victims on this point.

Any sting or bite which has become inflamed and badly swollen is probably infected and immediate medical treatment should be sought.

Multiple wasp or bee stings can be very painful, and medical help should be sought, but, unless the subject is allergic to them, they will be uncomfortable rather than dangerous. The subsequent itching a couple of days later, as the stings get better, is less supportable than the actual pain of the stings!

Insect repellent creams are effective if used before exposure to midges, etc. (See also *Mosquitoes* and *Snakes*.)

Stoats and Weasels *Stoats* (*Mustela erminea*) Growing up to 17in (430mm) long, reddish-brown with a black tip to the tail, this member of the ermine family is very common (called ermine in the north where they go white in winter). They feed on small animals and birds, mainly rabbits and hares who are terrified of them. Gamekeepers dislike stoats and owls and hawks also prey on them.
Weasels (*Mustela nivalis*) A small and extremely vicious version of the stoat, up to 10in (250mm) long but without the black-tipped tail. It hunts mostly at night, and lives on mice, voles, shrews, frogs, etc. Gamekeepers kill weasels as vermin as they take pheasant and partridge chicks.

Further Reading: *The Observer's Book of Wild Animals* (Warne).

Strawberries See *Fruit*.

Swimming Pools While you will probably have your pool dug and installed by a contractor, there are one or two considerations to make before placing the order. The first essential is a good site, nowhere near trees which continually drop bits and pieces into the water. Preferably the ground should not slope towards a dwelling house, and a level

Solar heating for swimming pool

site is best. A pool cut into a big slope means that the downhill side must be particularly strong to withstand the water pressure behind it, which will add to cost.

Secondly, water supply; the pool will only have to be filled once a season, or if it is drained for any reason, but topping-up water is always necessary.

Thirdly, drainage; this is important. The pool will only rarely be completely drained, but overflow must have a safe outlet. Swimming-pool water contains chemicals and must not be put into cesspits or into streams or rivers where it can damage plant or fish life. Those downstream from you could be very angry indeed if you chlorinated their water, however briefly or slightly. Even the main drains are not always suitable, and you should check with your local drainage officer before using them.

Fourthly, heating; solar heating is entirely

adequate for swimming pools, unless you want to swim in mid-winter, and, after the initial cost of buying and installing panels, only the running and maintenance of a small pump to circulate the water is necessary. The solar panel area should equal half that of the surface of the pool. This will keep the water about 10°F (5°C) warmer than it would be without heating in fine weather. The panels should be sited as near the pool as possible, but can be hidden behind a fencing screen or put on a convenient roof.

Conventional heating units will need to be housed in a shed near the pool with the filtration unit.

A swimming pool needs maintenance, it must be kept clean by skimming and 'hoovering', and the water must be tested and sufficient chemicals added to keep it safe. The more use the pool has, the more chemicals are needed. These are not cheap, nor is the power to run the plant. Contractors tend to underestimate running costs, and you can probably add a bit to any figure they give you. There can be a lot of expensive extras for a swimming pool, not least what it costs to provide refreshment for all those new-found friends. If there are small children about, then the pool must have a safety net on it when not in use, and there will be problems with the neighbours' children who come to use your pool, which no child should ever do without adult supervision. So think carefully.

The small above-ground pool, made of metal framing with a plastic lining, is the cheapest way to get a swim, but maintenance costs are still high, safety is still a problem, and they are very unsightly.

Useful Address: Swimming Pool and Allied Trades Association, 74 London Road, Croydon, Surrey.

Further Reading: Beedell, S., *Water in the Garden* (David & Charles); Wills, N.D., *Build Your Own Swimming Pool* (John Gifford Ltd).

Tape Recording Nature See *Birds*.

Thatch Surely the most beautiful roofing material that there is, thatch, either of straw or Norfolk reed, is durable and warm. It moulds itself over the roof timbers and round the windows and gables, and overhangs the walls of a house as if it had been poured there. It looks as right as a well-groomed head of hair.

Although for a time thatching was a dying art, it is now flourishing, and there are plenty of thatchers working, although they are all fully occupied and you will have to take your place in a queue for their services. It takes about three weeks to thatch a small house.

Three types of straw are used: long straw, ordinary wheat or rye, now very hard to come by as almost all crops are grown with short straw for combine harvesting; combed wheat reed which comes from a 'reed-comber' at the back of the threshing machine, tied in bundles ready for making into thatchers' yealms (bundles), also a rarity these days; and Norfolk reed, cultivated for the purpose, which is far and away the best material. Cut in winter in bitter cold, it will last as thatch for at least sixty years, twice as long as straw.

Fire danger is not really very great. The reed can be dipped against fire before it is laid, or sprayed when in position (see *Fire* for recipe). Insurance companies often demand that this be done regularly. In the old days, people kept long hooks with which to drag burning thatch off roofs, and, as oak roof timbers were slow to catch fire, there was usually more mess than damage and a new thatch set things to rights. Nowadays it is the paint and varnish and panelling inside the house which catches fire and sets the roof going from below. The sensible precaution is to have fire extinguishers handy, a hose which can throw water onto the roof and a long ladder. If the roof timbers will support it, asbestos sheeting, fixed on the inside of a thatched roof, will externalize any fire from chimnney sparks, lightning or bonfires.

Thatch can be patched, and where birds have caused damage this may be necessary. Very often a new ridge of thatch will give an old roof a new lease of life. Birds pull out straw for their nests and some species, particularly tree sparrows, will nest right in the thatch. The only way to protect thatch from birds is to cover it with fine-mesh wire netting. Take the advice of your nearest thatcher. (see Yellow Pages and also *Fire* and *Insurance*.)

Useful Addresses: Master Thatcher Association, c/o G. E. Dunkley, 25 Little Lane, Yardley Hastings, Northants; Norfolk Reed Growers Association, 15 Chaplefield East, Norwich.

Further Reading: Woods, K. S., *Rural Crafts of England* (E. P. Publishing).

A weaver's cottage with 'Aunt Maud' in straw spinning on the roof. Built in 1530 this cottage must have been thatched 15 or 20 times

(opposite left) *Turning a corner. Note the U-shaped spars or pegs holding the long hazel 'sways' which pin down the thatch. Also the metal thatcher's needles, and how the layers of thatch are built up*

Note the ridge roll and the reed ends left untrimmed
to be woven in

(right) *Norfolk reed stacked inside a sixteenth-
century barn*

Thumbsticks See *Walking Sticks.*

Ticks See *Fleas* and *Dogs.*

Timber See *Trees.*

Toads See *Frogs.*

Tracks Tracks are not always what they seem, melting snow soon makes a cat's footprints as big as a tiger's, and a dragging tail leaves a distinct mark. Some bounding animals place hind feet down before fore feet. Many natural history books do give tracks of animals and birds, and it is best to go tracking armed with one of these. Look for birds in estuary mud, on wet sand, and in snow. Look for animals in mud, snow and sand.

Further Reading: Bang and Dahlstrom, *Collins Guide to Animal Tracks* (Collins).

Traps There are stringent laws about trapping. Only traps of a type approved by the Ministry of Agriculture are permitted. Traps for rabbits may only be set with the plate inside the mouth of a rabbit hole, under the overhang, and must be inspected at least once a day between sunrise and sunset. Approved traps, unlike the old illegal gins, kill outright, and were they to be set in the open, would be a menace to cats as well as rabbits.

Traps may not be set for deer.

Snares may be set for foxes. Get advice from someone who knows how to do it, and be sure the snare has a stop so that it cannot continue to tighten each time the animal moves, thus inflicting dreadful agony. A snare should hold a fox which can then be shot. Always set snares low, and cover the top with brushwood in such a way that no deer or other large animal can step into them by mistake. Use Bowden cable, not wire, as the latter breaks too easily.

There are various kinds of spring traps of differing sizes. In these a pair of arms comes up when the trap is sprung, and these catch the animal by the throat and kill it instantly. Fenn traps may be set in artificial tunnels or in runs for taking stoats, weasels, rats, mice and other small vermin.

Box traps, for squirrels, kill the creature immediately upon entry.

Cage traps for mink can be borrowed from the Ministry of Agriculture.

To kill animals caught in cage traps, put the whole cage in a fertilizer bag or close-woven sack. Pour carbon tetrachloride on a pad of cotton wool and put it in the sack. Tie the mouth tightly. The chemical will kill the animal quickly and painlessly. (See also *Mink*.)

Useful Addresses: S. Young & Sons (Misterton) Ltd, Crewkerne, Somerset (rabbit traps); F. H. T. Works, High Street, Astwood Bank, Redditch, Worcs (Fenn traps); Fuller Industries, Marepost, Pondtail Road, Horsham, Sussex (squirrel traps).

Further Reading: UFAW, *Instruction for Dealing with Rabbits*, from 7a Lambs Conduit Passage, London WC1; Forestry Commission leaflet, *Traps for Grey Squirrels* (HMSO); ICI Game Services advisory booklet no 17, *Enemies of Game, Some Control Methods for Ground Predators.*

Treasure Trove Any money, coin, gold, silver, plate or bullion found buried or hidden, whose owner is unknown, is treasure trove. It belongs to the Crown and if you conceal it you are guilty of a common law misdemeanour. Report any such finds to the police. The local coroner will hold an inquest to decide whether or not the find is treasure trove, but has no power to apportion its value to anyone. Items found must be submitted to the British Museum who, if they wish to retain them, will pay the finder. If not retained, it is the finder's to do what he likes with.

Trees The need to care for our trees has been highlighted by the present epidemic of Dutch

Springtime beeches

elm disease. It takes such a long time to replace trees that the whole look of an area can be completely altered, and its ecology along with it, by indiscriminate tree felling.

The scars of the motorways across our countryside, where all trees have gone and few of any consequence have been replanted, show only too well what I mean. On a much bigger scale, consider the Mediterranean countries, most of which were forested in classical times, now denuded and eroded.

Knole Park sycamore. A protected tree

Land for new housing estates is often cleared of all trees before building is begun, when at least some could be left. Because trees do not live for ever, continual replanting must take place, not only of fast-growing, but also of slow-growing and long-lived trees. The Forestry Commission and amenity committees of county councils encourage tree planting, from large estates to small spinneys, but eternal vigilance is necessary to prevent unnecessary felling. Local groups make it their business to exercise this vigilance, to

undertake tree surveys so that all trees in an area are recorded, and to get tree preservation orders imposed where necessary. Only a local planning authority can make a tree preservation order, so local amenity societies must work closely with them.

Tree Preservation Orders Once a tree preservation order has been made, the tree may not be lopped, topped or cut without permission from the local authority and heavy fines can

Ash tree in winter

be imposed if it is done. Some trees are exempt from preservation orders: those on Crown land, cultivated fruit trees in a garden or orchard, and trees planted with the aid of Forestry Commission grants. Trees in conservation areas are automatically protected by requiring the owner to give six weeks' notice of his intention to cut the trees in any way.

All this amounts to two things: 1) you should not cut established trees without checking whether or not they are subject to preservation orders; 2) if you see anyone else cutting trees, check with the local authority or amenity society immediately to find out if they have permission. You may be called a busybody, but it is too late once the damage has been done.

Forestry Grants Considerable grants are available for tree planting under schemes approved by the Forestry Commission to whom application should be made through the local

Forestry Conservancy Office. These include Dedication Schemes (Basis III) for large areas. The grants are big, but the owner, in return, must accept a continuing obligation to manage the woodlands in accordance with Plans of Operations drawn up with the Forestry Commission.

There are grants for the management of established plantations, and planting and management grants for existing unproductive woodlands.

For areas of less than 25 acres (10 ha), there is a 'Small Woods Scheme' which provides grants for areas as small as 0.25 hectare. This is to encourage the planting of copses, spinneys, etc, for aesthetic and amenity value as well as for timber.

Shelterbelt grants are available under Agricultural and Horticultural Capital Grant Schemes, administered by the Ministry of Agriculture.

The Countryside Commission and some county councils are interested in replanting and also administer approved grants for planting in areas of less than ¼ acre (o.25 ha). Check with your county amenities and countryside committee at county hall. Special attention is being paid at the moment to areas where Dutch elm disease has done its worst.

In all cases, the grant must be approved and planting in areas of less than ¼ acre (0.25 ha). useless to apply for grants after doing the work. The work must be done and management continued up to Forestry Commission standards.

The Forestry Commission publish a wide range of bulletins, booklets, leaflets, etc, on all aspects of forestry, woodland and wildlife, and their catalogue is a vital reference book.

Tree Felling A licence is required for the felling, or sale for felling, of growing trees.

Make application to the local conservator of forests, who will inspect the trees. The commission may impose replanting conditions for the issue of a felling licence, which may qualify for grant aid as above.

If a tree felling order is in force for the trees concerned, it is usually necessary for the local planning authority that made the order to be consulted, and exceptions (a) – (d) below may not apply.

Felling orders are not required for:
a) Trees in gardens and fruit trees;
b) Any trees below 3in (76mm) in diameter, measured 5ft (1½m) from the ground;
c) Underwood below 6in (150mm) in diameter, measured 5ft from the ground;
d) Thinnings below 4in (100mm) in diameter measured 5ft from the ground;
e) Dedicated woodlands, provided the felling is in accordance with the agreed plan of operation, and the positive covenants of the deed of agreement are applicable.

In addition, an owner may fell up to 825 cubic feet (23 cu metres) of timber (hoppus measure) per quarter of a calendar year, for use on his own property, with a felling licence. Of this quantity he may, if he wishes, sell, without licence or other formal permission, up to 150 cubic feet.

Timber There is no reason why you should not use wood from your own property for constructional purposes; rebuilding sheds, making gates, etc, but it takes long-term planning because the wood must be allowed to season. Quite small ash, larch, elm, walnut, sweet chestnut, oak, beech, Scots pine, and spruce trees may all yield quite large amounts of useful timber, as well as plenty of firewood.

Fell and trim trees in the autumn when the sap is not running. The logs can be taken to the nearest sawmill and cut up according to your requirements, or, in some country areas, a contractor will come to your place with a tractor-driven saw. The wood must be stacked when cut as it comes off the saw; each plant or piece separated by a spacer so that the air can circulate (Fig 118). Timber normally needs to be seasoned for at least eighteen months, standing undisturbed, before it is

Mountain birch in autumn

fit to be used. Some woods take much longer. Wood which is not completely seasoned will warp, shrink and twist after use. In some cases, for rough work, this does not matter, but for any kind of decent carpentry or joinery, there is no point in using improperly seasoned wood.

Always replant at least two new trees for every tree felled. Sweet chestnut takes a lot of beating for many purposes, and is a quick-growing handsome tree. (See also *Boundaries, Conservation, Dutch Elm Disease, Firewood* and *Trespass*.)

Fig 118

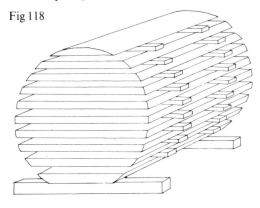

Further Reading: Countryside Commission publication No 103, *Grants* (HMSO); The Forestry Commission booklet on grants (as from August 1977) from HMSO, or direct from Alice Holt Lodge, Wrecclesham, Farnham, Surrey GU10 4LH; Arboricultural Association leaflet No 6, *Trees and the Law*, from 59 Blythwood Gardens, Stanstead, Essex; leaflets and instructions on record keeping from The Tree Council, Room 202, 17/19 Rochester Road, London SW1; list of approved contractors from the Association of British Tree Surgeons and Arborists, 11 Wings Road, Upper Hale, Farnham, Surrey; Forestry Commission leaflet, no 38, *Common Trees*, and many others (HMSO); Edlin, H. L., *Trees, Woods and Man* (Collins); Guides to Good Building, Nos 55 and 56, *Timber Sizes for Small Buildings*; No 29, *Care in the Use of Timber* (HMSO); British Research Establishment leaflet No 181, *Timber, Efficient and Economic Use*; Gorer, *Trees and Shrubs*, (David & Charles); Deal, *Growing Trees for Profit* (David & Charles); Findlay-Crosby, W. P. K. *Timber Properties and Uses* (Lockwood Staples).

Trespass To put up a notice reading 'Trespassers will be Prosecuted' is rather an empty gesture, because although theoretically trespassers can be *sued* for a civil wrong it is unlikely that any court would award more than a nominal sum unless it could be proved that damage had been done. Only when a crime has been committed (poaching, malicious damage, etc) can a prosecution follow.

It is a trespass to go on someone else's land, without permission, to retrieve game shot over your own land. It is a trespass to use a footpath for any purpose other than passage. It is a trespass to go on your neighbour's land in order to repair your own walls, etc, without permission.

The owner of an animal is liable for damage done by that animal if it trespasses. If someone else's cattle trample all over your garden, that is trespass regardless of whether or not you had a fence. The onus is upon the *owner* of the cattle to keep them out of your garden. This does not apply to cats which are natural strayers and the law accepts that they cannot be prevented from doing this. Therefore no one can kill a neighbour's cat, however much of a nuisance it is. Generally speaking, domestic pets may not be killed or injured in any way.

To kill a trespassing dog is an actionable wrong. Only if it can be proved that it was attacking you or your stock can killing it be legally justified. Dogs which attack game, if the owner knows that they have a tendency to do this, *are* committing a trespass, and you might be able to bring a case.

For purposes of the trespass laws, poultry count as 'cattle' and therefore the onus is on you to prevent your poultry from straying onto your neighbour's land.

Cattle being moved along a highway are not reckoned to be trespassing if they get onto your land, unless the owner can be proved negligent, and this is obviously very difficult. Never leave drive or garden gates open in case this happens.

For a person to enter or walk through your property is a trespass, and if it happens frequently it is a wrong against which an injunction can be obtained. Thus someone who continually used your garden as a short cut could be stopped. You are allowed to expel trespassers using as much force as is necessary to do so.

Trees can trespass. If branches of an overhanging tree damage your property, then the owner of the tree is liable (see *Trees*).

If people trespass on your property and pick cultivated crops of any kind whatsoever, then they are stealing and committing a trespass and could be sued for damages. But if they pick mushrooms, blackberries, or wild plants of any kind, it is no offence, as these things belong to no one until they are gathered and then only to the gatherer. (See also *Rights of Way*; *Access*; *Boundaries*; *Sheep*

Worrying; *Footpaths* and *Bridleways*.)

Trout Farming This is a highly specialized business. Primarily it requires a supply of absolutely unpolluted and clean stream water which must be led through a series of artificial pounds. It also requires knowledge and experience and considerable capital outlay. The high-protein food which must be fed to the trout is expensive. If you contemplate going in for trout farming, ask your local Agriculture Advisory Service for advice. Grants are available for fish farming on a commercial basis.

Further Reading: Sedwick, *Trout Farming Handbook* (Seeley Service).

Turkeys See *Poultry*.

V

Valuers In country matters, local estate agents and auctioneers will act as valuers or will help you to find a valuer for anything.

Useful Address: Central Association of Agricultural Valuers, Estate Office, New College, Oxford.

Vegetables (Wild) A few wild plants are poisonous so it is best to be sure of identification before trying them on humans, although this applies to berries more than to leaves. Use one of the books mentioned below.

Outstanding among wild vegetables are seakale (*Crambe maritimum*) which can be found on some shingle beaches. Samphire (glasswort) which grows in saltmarshes (*Salincornia herbacea*) is a real delicacy. Another cliff cabbage which grows round the south-east corner of England is *Brassica oleracae*. There are others, such as ordinary nettle (*Urtica dioica*) shoots which cook up

Seakale. The early shoots are salty and succulent

Cliff cabbage

like spinach, but they are not to everyone's taste. Several wild plants make good salads, such as young dandelion crowns (*Taraxacum officinale*) and young chickweed (*Stellaria media*) as a salad or eaten like mustard and cress with brown bread. Wild garlic (*Allium vineale*) grows everywhere in rough grass on sand dunes.

Many other herbs grow wild; fennel, marjoram, mint and sorrel, and horseradish roots come from one of the commonest weeds.

Always be sure to pick wild herbs and vegetables where they cannot have been polluted by fumes or dust from motor cars, and away from agricultural crops which have been sprayed with weed killer.

Further Reading: Keble Martin, W., *The Concise British Flora* (Ebury Press & Michael Joseph); Beedell, S., *Pick, Cook and Brew* (Pelham).

Vermin See *Pests* and individual headings.

Veterinary Matters Country vets differ from town vets in that their main job is dealing with large animals rather than domestic pets, although of course they cope with these as well. The vet in a country district is very much part of the scene. He knows everyone who keeps stock, he is deeply involved with such things as local agricultural shows, point to points, local hunts, pony clubs, gymkhanas, horse shows, etc. He is always on hand on these occasions.

Nowadays vets usually have group practices covering a wide area, two-way radios in their cars so that they can be reached quickly for emergencies, and are on call all hours of the day and night. Surgeries do not form so big a part of country practice as they do in towns because you can't take a cow to the surgery!

Veterinary science has advanced enormously and a great deal of immunization and vaccination is done, but the heavy work of dealing with animal accidents and maternity cases still remains as tough as it always was. You will be expected to help your vet with this if necessary; to help restrain animals, to provide supplies of hot water, and sometimes brute strength. Sometimes you will need a strong stomach and a hard heart. He is the surgeon and you must be the nurse. In veterinary work it may be necessary to be cruel to be kind in the long run. Those who cannot face unpleasantness should not keep animals.

If your vet has to come out of a warm bed on a cold night, or has to work outdoors in bad weather, don't fail to have at least a good cup of tea or coffee for him when he is done. Something a little stronger may not come amiss. Treat your vet very well, he deserves it!

If, unfortunately, you have a dead animal to dispose of and it is not infected in any way, give your local hunt kennels a ring and they will gladly come and pick it up. They are always grateful for anything which keeps their costs down.

Further Reading: *Black's Veterinary Dictionary* (A. & C. Black).

229

Village Life The modern conception of the village as a community bears little relation to what it was in the first half of this century. Communication was slow, and the communities much more isolated, intermarrying, dependent upon themselves for most services, or at best upon area market towns. Money was scarce and entertainments homemade and unsophisticated. Community functions, such as there were, grew from circumstances not from choice, be they Sunday School outings or the village flower show. The paternalism and patronage of the 'Big House' was much more evident than it is today.

Nowadays the village community is a kind of devolution, a small nationalism in a large and impersonal society which provides its members with identity and cohesion in the face of many disruptive outside influences;

Piano smashing. Teams from rival villages compete to see which can pass the pieces through a 1ft (0.3m) diameter hoop the fastest. A dying sport as even the oldest piano is worth money nowadays

home rule for Nether Churchington, determined to run its own affairs within the law of the land, and to run them better than Up Churchington. This in turn leads to village rivalry, and so to a further strengthening of the community principle. From the point of view of the new country dweller, it does mean that some village clubs, societies, etc, will welcome him or her because the village needs all the strength and all the new ideas that it can get, and is rarely conservative in outlook when it comes to local pride.

There are various focal points, primarily church, chapel, pub and school. A good parish hall encourages the formation of clubs

230

Hit the disc with a tennis ball and a bucket full of cold water empties over the 'miscreant'. This sideshow became very popular when the vicar took his turn in the stocks

and societies; Women's Institute, Mothers' Union, men's groups, dramatic societies, choral societies, keep fit classes, young wives' groups. It provides a venue for whist drives and socials throughout the winter, flower shows in the summer, and jumble sales all year round. Additionally there will be cricket clubs, football clubs, darts clubs and even angling clubs, according to the size of the community. The annual church fête, village fair, or revel is the high spot of village life.

The Women's Institute, highly organized on a national scale, is usually the main meeting point for women, and provides all kinds of activities, social and educational. It is non-denominational, non-political and classless, and is unquestionably an absolutely first-class organization. All are welcome. The Mothers' Union and young wives' groups are run by the church and chapel. Men are not usually so well catered for in this sense, but do have far more sporting activities open to them.

There is a saying that if you want anything done in a village, go to the busiest person. This may be anyone at all, but it is surprising how often the same people crop up in positions of responsibility in different organizations. This occasionally leads to power struggles as newcomers or young people develop to replace the old, but that is all part of community life.

Village life is not a bit private. People do not run in and out of each others' houses any

231

more than they do in towns, but, because the population is relatively small, because many families are interrelated, and because the doings of other people are always of supreme interest, everything about you, including your hithertofore intimate habits, become common knowledge by a kind of bush telegraph. Your comings and goings will be known to everyone and even your latest purchases will be discussed. This of course cuts both ways and you can be as well informed about your neighbours as you wish to be. The reason for this is partly that it is impossible to hide in the country; lost among thousands in a town, you will be noticed by twenty people the first time you walk down the village street. Movement tends to be regular in the country, to work and home, to school and home, shopping and home, and any break in routine is very noticeable. Anything unusual, any unaccounted-for movement in the countryside itself will usually be spotted by someone. This is not inquisitiveness, but much more protective in origin. It is rare for an old person living alone to come to much harm or to die alone in a village. Someone will always be keeping an eye open for a change in the pattern which could indicate trouble.

There are usually feuds and hatreds in the community which have nothing whatsoever to do with the outsider, and may be of many years' standing, and the newcomer must beware of putting his foot in it. If you suspect anything of the kind, ask a third party and you will probably get the full details and can thus avoid trouble.

On another level, although local authority districts now embrace huge areas, parish councils still exist and there are church councils, parish hall councils, even amenity and ratepayers societies, and various other organizational and political bodies which run the non-social affairs of the village. The newcomer will have to work his passage and prove his true allegiance to the village before he can hope to participate at this level.

Community life of any kind is difficult; when people try to live together under the same roof it is usually disastrous, except under the most rigid of disciplines. The population of a parish does not live under one roof, but it is nevertheless a community and if you wish to be part of it you cannot flout its unwritten rules. When it becomes irksome, it is easy enough nowadays to get away from it for a time at least, provided you have your own transport. Public transport in the country has degenerated to the point where it has almost disappeared from some areas. In some places villagers are running their own community transport, and this movement may gain ground during the next few years. It is all part of self-sufficiency. (See also *Difficulties of Country Living*.)

Vineyards Grapes for wine were widely grown in southern England in medieval times. Viticulture then died out completely to be reintroduced with some success in the last twenty-five years.

Vines like south-facing slopes on lime rich but thin soil with well-drained subsoil. It takes several years to establish a vineyard and no crop of grapes should be taken before the third year. An acre of established vines should produce an average of 2,000 bottles a year—but there are so many variables of weather, etc, that no certain figures can be given.

The successful growing of grapes and their quality depend largely upon the hours of sunshine the fruit gets. There are strains of grape which do well with less sunshine. The sunshine determines the amount of sugar in the fruit. Bad weather during harvest time can also have a serious effect on the crop and September–October weather is not to be relied on in this country.

Riesling, Sylvaner, Siegerrbe, Siebel 13053 and Precoce de Malingre are all grapes which will do well out of doors here and are suitable for wine making.

Anyone interested in planting a vineyard,

either for their own use or for commercial wine producing, should first contact The Viticultural Research Station, Rockfield Road, Oxted, Surrey.

Further Reading: Hyams, Edward, *Vineyards in England* (Faber).

Voles See *Mice*.

Walking Always be well shod, whatever the time of the year, and carry a light water- and wind-proof nylon jacket at least. An extra jumper, light in summer, heavy in winter, can come in useful if the weather suddenly gets colder. Check your route on a map before you start if the country is unfamiliar to you, and carry the map and a compass if you intend to go more than a little way. If you mean to go right off the beaten track, up onto hills or moors, then you really must observe more stringent rules—those of fell walkers which involve quite a lot of special clothing, food and equipment, and the carrying of heavy rucksacks. Join a group or a club which does this sport, and they will put you in the picture.

If you go on your own or in a family party in a car, intending to leave it and wander in wild places, remember that a sudden mist could lose you just a few yards from your car, and so do not go without proper equipment and clothing, and at least a little know how.

Never take short cuts which involve climbing up or down cliffs or rocks; they are always steeper than they look. Following hill streams downwards in the hope that they will lead you to lower ground, may just lead you over a precipice, although this is a safer principle in lowland walking.

Useful Address: Ramblers Association, 1/4 Crawford Mews, London W1H 1PT.

Further Reading: *Mountain Rescue Handbook* (from sports shops which sell climbing gear); Greenbank, A., *Walking, Hiking and Backpacking* (Constable).

Walking Sticks and Crooks The making of walking sticks is a simple craft which allows for some individuality. Hazel wood is the best, but holly, ash and thorn are also commonly used.

The blocks for the sticks must be cut at least a year before use, in late autumn when there is little sap in the wood. Look for straight sticks (although kinks can be steamed out). For a thumbstick you need a long straight piece with a Y-fork at about 45 degrees (Fig 119);

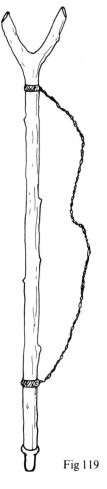

Fig 119

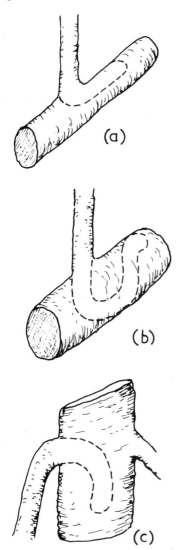

Fig 120

try your thumb in it before cutting. For crooks only a straight pole is needed because you are going to put on a horn handle. For sticks with rounded or shaped heads, part of the main branch or root must be included and the block must be cut a foot above and below the anticipated handle length, to avoid splintering and cracking as the head dries out. These are the hardest to find.

Wait till the wood has seasoned before cutting off any surplus. Then sketch in the shape of the handle you have decided upon and cut out surplus wood to shape with a bow or a coping saw (Fig 120a, b and c), and file and sandpaper the rest away until you are satisfied with the result. Cut off knots with a sharp knife, but don't sandpaper the stick down too smoothly or it will look like a broomstick. Sand off any loose bark and give the stick a couple of coats of clear varnish or sealer, and then a good rub with wax furniture polish.

A walking stick must have a ferrule or it will splinter and spoil at the bottom. Metal ferrules can be bought which are put on with a hammer and punch, but rubber ferrules, which just slip over the end, are much easier to fix (Fig 119).

To make the tops of crooks, or walking-stick handles, use ramshorn. The ram must be at least three years old for the horn to be large enough. Scots blackface, Wiltshire and Dorset horn breeds provide the best.

Heat the horn in a pressure cooker or in a saucepan of water until soft, and then place the thick end in a vice. Using a ring spanner over the tip, bend the horn round carefully until it is parallel with itself, tie the tip down and leave it to cool (Fig 121). Drill a vertical

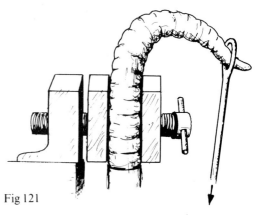

Fig 121

hole in the thick end of the horn, big enough to take the top of the stick or pole. It should be about 2in (50mm) deep and $\frac{1}{2}$in (12mm) in diameter. Shape the stick to fit this hole

234

tightly, and glue it into place on the shank. If the horn needs to be bent again, spot heat it with a blow lamp, but be careful not to burn it. File off the outer horn with a rough file and finish with finer and finer sandpaper.

Cut a ring of hollow horn which will fit over the horn handle and stick to make a collar. It should be heated in a pressure cooker or saucepan and slid up from the bottom of the stick to fit tightly over the join.

Horn can be carved with a sharp pocket knife and fine files.

A lanyard, nicely plaited out of leather strips and held by whipping or a leather collar, is most useful on a thumb stick, as you can sling it on your back when climbing over gates, fences or rocks when you need both hands (Fig 119). A detachable rope lanyard may come in handy for a dozen purposes.

Walnuts See *Nuts*.

Wasps and Hornets *Wasps* (*Vespula vulgaris*) Wasps ask for trouble because they will not leave people alone, which is a pity, for most of their lives they are entirely beneficial to man, eating up quantities of other insects, some of them pests. Unfortunately, towards the end of the summer, wasp colonies begin to disintegrate as the queen stops laying. The workers are deprived of the sweet saliva of the grubs and go off to find other sweetness, eating fruit on the trees, and jam on the picnic sandwich. Wasps are not really aggressive unless harried, yet the occasional one stings for no reason at all. The sting is painful for a short while and some people are more allergic than others. Anti-histamine cream usually relieves the pain. Should anyone receive a lot of stings at the one time, or know themselves to be allergic, then immediate medical help should be sought.

Hornets (*Vespa crabo*) These are very large wasps, the queens being more than 1in (25mm). Hornets are brown and orange, rather than black and yellow. They build nests in hollow trees, holes in banks, or in outhouses, and make a loud hum as they zoom past. But rarely do they attack or sting unless taken by surprise or provoked. When they do, the sting is very painful indeed and should be treated as a wasp sting with anti-histamine cream.

Do not attempt to eradicate wasps' or hornets' nests; send for the local pest control officer, who will arrive suitably equipped and clad. (See also *Stings*.)

Watercress Watercress is a very common plant which grows wild in streams and ditches wherever there is a good flow of water. It can be picked and eaten, but it should be thoroughly washed first, and do check very carefully that the stream is not polluted by drains from farms or cottages, from animal droppings, or by a run off of pesticides or weed killer.

To grow watercress commercially, a constant supply of clean running water is essential; straight out of the ground, ideally from chalk or greensand formations. This water will emerge at about 50°F (10°C) which is ideal for watercress. Water which travels too far above ground before use may be much warmer in summer or much colder in winter. Next, there must be enough room on the stream, or beside it, to make several beds in which cress can be grown at different stages of development. On a commercial scale, like anything else, watercress demands quite a lot of work and expertise.

There is no reason why you should not make a shallow bed and plant watercress to supply your own domestic needs if you have a convenient clean stream. Sometimes the bunches of watercress bought from a greengrocer have roots still on them. Plant these out in early summer and they should crop well. Make a shallow area beside the stream, preferably with a bed of clean sand, through which stream water can be diverted to flow gently without washing the plants away (Figs

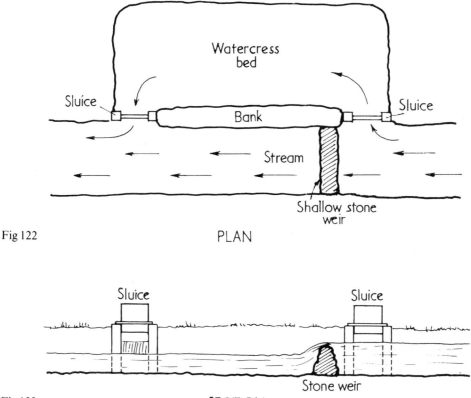

Fig 122   PLAN

Fig 123   SECTION

122 and 123). Install a simple sluice gate (see page 63) to shut off the area when there is heavy rain and flooding. Once watercress has rooted, it will survive quite severe flooding remarkably well. In times of frost, allow more water to enter your watercress bed so that it is deeper and the plants are submerged and therefore protected.

Further Reading: Ministry of Agriculture leaflet No 136, *Watercress* (HMSO); Beedell, S., *Water in the Garden* (David & Charles).

Water Divining See *Dowsing*.

Waterfowl See *Ducks*, *Geese* and *Shooting*.

Watermills Between five and six thousand watermills were recorded in the Domesday Book. Primitive watermills, with the paddle-wheel set horizontally in the bed of the stream, and a vertical shaft passing up through a bedstone on a framework across the stream, and carrying a runner stone on the top, were in use throughout northern Europe long before that. The Romans developed watermills which worked in much the same way as these still in existence in this country. A horizontal axle carries a vertical paddle wheel at one end and, at the other, is geared to work sets of millstones. The paddle wheel is turned by the force of the water falling upon it from an impounded stream (Figs 124, 125 and 126).

The flow of water being controllable, and

(opposite) *Crabble Watermill at Dover; a nineteenth-century mill on a centuries old site*

236

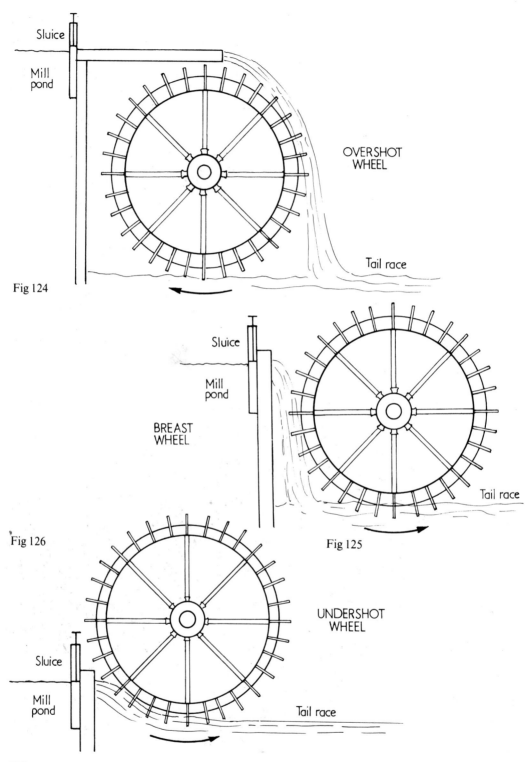

Sluice

Mill
pond

OVERSHOT
WHEEL

Tail race

Fig 124

Sluice

Mill
pond

BREAST
WHEEL

Tail race

Fig 126

Fig 125

UNDERSHOT
WHEEL

Sluice

Mill
pond

Tail race

therefore constant, meant that watermills were always built in preference to windmills where water was available. Water power can, of course, be harnessed to work machinery other than grindstones, and there is a famous mill at Sticklepath, in Devon, which still turns out agricultural implements and other ironwork, using the water to work hammers and other machinery. Not so picturesque outwardly as windmills, nevertheless the tall mill buildings straddling a stream, and reflected in the still millponds beside them, are often most attractive and much less vulnerable to the elements than windmills. They do make good subjects for conversion, provided they are in good condition and not undermined by damp or rot. Unfortunately they are usually rather large for the modern small family and expenses for conversion, restoration, or maintenance can run very high.

The breast shot mill at Crabble

Waterproofs Do not buy clothes marked 'showerproof' and expect them to keep you dry. They only resist the lightest of drizzles. Thin nylon anoraks, coats and overtrousers which can be carried in pockets, haversacks, or rucksacks are not only perfectly waterproof, but windproof as well, and if worn over warm clothes are excellent for walking and outdoor sports. Heavy PVC 'oilskins' are even more weather- and waterproof, but are much heavier and bulkier to carry. Excellent for really wet and cold days when you need to wear them all day, the latest material is vinyl bonded to a thin knitted base which stretches a little—this breathes and so reduces condensation.

Waterproofs tend to get damp inside from body sweat and condensation if worn for any length of time, especially if you are doing anything energetic. They should always be hung up in a warm airy place to dry out, but not put too near heat.

A room where coats, boots, etc, can be kept, preferably with a radiator or hot pipes in it, is an essential part of a country home. Mud and dust, carried in from outside, can be shed in there and not carried further into the house.

Aerosol sprays can be bought which render almost any material showerproof. A coat of silicone spray all over the surface of the garment does reject a certain amount of damp, but it will not keep out anything but light rain. This is extremely useful for light showerproof jackets which have to be cleaned or washed and have lost their proofing. Any closely woven material will certainly be more showerproof after spraying, but loosely woven tweeds, woollens, etc, don't benefit much, as the spray cannot form a waterproof skin. Most dry cleaners run a re-proofing service.

Waterproof headgear is a problem. The traditional sou-wester acts as a droopy portable umbrella (as does any wide brimmed hat)—essential if you wear glasses. Anoraks have hoods, a woolly cap with a peak keeps out mist and drizzle and the hood can be pulled over it. Or try a plastic golf peak worn under a woolly cap and hood to keep the face dry. The hood protects the other vulnerable area, the back of the neck. (See also *Boots*.)

Water Supplies If you are connected to a mains water supply the Water Authority is obliged to make water available. Water rates entitle you to receive clean water for domestic use. If you take water from the mains for other than domestic purposes—irrigation, supply of water for lakes, ponds, swimming pools, etc, it may have to be metered and you should contact your local water authority before taking it for granted that you may use the water. During times of water shortage there may be stringent local rules against its use for gardens, washing cars, running fountains, filling swimming pools, etc, carrying fines if they are ignored.

Water from rivers, streams or springs, for other than domestic use, may not be taken without a licence from the water authority.

For years, when I was dependent upon a hand-pumped well-water supply, my visitors had to pump so many strokes each time they pulled the plug. Always they had to be restrained from habitual water wastefulness. Only rarely is the town dweller forced by drought to think about saving water, as the countryman may have to every summer if he is not on a mains supply. (See also *Dowsing*; *Riparian Rights* and *Wells*.)

Weasels See *Stoats*.

Weather See *Meteorology*.

Weaving See *Spinning*.

Weeds Should you be plagued by weeds spreading from a neighbour's land, ask your local authority to do something about it. Under Section 36 of the Town and Country Planning Act, 1962, land must be kept according to the rules of good estate management. If the nuisance from weeds is severe, the local authority may serve a notice on the offender to clear things up. The Ministry of Agriculture may do this on agricultural land.

Control weeds on your own property. Weeds in grassland can be sprayed with selective weedkillers, or be cut, raked and burned. The latter is the preferable treatment, if not the least trouble. If grassland weeds are cut a couple of times at least during a year and not allowed to flower, it does much to control them. Weeds in arable land or gardens must be cultivated out or pulled. Spot treatment with weedkiller is sometimes the only way to get rid of persistent weeds. Such things as couch grass, ground elder, and bindweed, which run underground and send up a myriad shoots, have to be rooted out inch by inch by hand. Cutting and chopping the roots merely spreads the weeds.

Kill brambles, gorse and other woody-stemmed weeds or bushes with brushwood killer. This takes a little while to work, but is effective. Large weedy areas can be cleared quickly with a flame gun. Used in late summer when the weeds are tall and dry, it has a dramatic effect, but is really just a quick way to get rid of rubbish so that the weed roots can be dug out and the ground cultivated.

The organic farmer insists that weeds should not be burned or killed with weed killers, but should merely be hoed out and left to die, eventually forming humus in the soil. This is a counsel of perfection and hoeing will only supress weeds when they are young and when the weather is dry enough to shrivel the young plants. In wet weather they merely lie on the surface and send down new root shoots. And once weeds have got to the flowering stage, they will probably spread seeds everywhere, even if cut and raked up and burned.

Ground left fallow will grow a crop of weeds and this can certainly be ploughed in as green manure to enhance the fertility of the soil. However, next year their offspring will grow with redoubled vigour on the enriched ground and must then be eradicated somehow if food crops are to be grown.

Further Reading: Salisbury, Sir Edward, *Weeds and Aliens* (Collins); Ministry of Agriculture leaflets: AL 46, *Weed Control, Docks*; AL 51, *Thistles*; AL 89, *Couch*; AL 280, *Ragwort*; AL 433, *Rushes*; AL 190, *Bracken* (HMSO).

Wellingtons See *Boots*.

Wells Existing wells are rarely in use these days, and are usually thoroughly polluted by rubbish thrown in from the top. If a well is yielding water, either via a pump or a bucket, then have the water tested by the public analyst; if it is all right nothing need be done. A well full of stagnant water should be pumped dry, using a small portable pump, and then investigated. First lower a powerful light on a rope. Then put a ladder inside and climb down. There may be a pocket of lethal gas in a foul well, so descend slowly, checking the walls as you go, and always have a rope round your waist, held by a helper up top just in case of trouble. At the slightest feeling of dizziness or breathlessness, return to the surface. If there is an inflow of water through the rendering near the top, it should be possible to see where it is coming in, and any bad pollution will have left telltale smears of filth on the walls. This is more likely to be found near the surface, as water entering lower down should have filtered itself clean through the surrounding subsoil of rock, chalk or sand. The upper layers of the well lining must be pointed and impervious, and only lower down should the bricks be unpointed to allow water to run in. Make good the pointing where necessary. Keep the water level down and scoop rubbish and sludge into a bucket for hauling to the surface. Once the well has been cleaned out, allow it to refill naturally and leave it as long as possible, to settle, before using the water.

At one time I was dependent upon polluted well water and the local expert threw large lumps of lime down the well to 'sweeten' it. This could do no harm and probably had some disinfectant effects.

The Digging of a New Well Once a water supply has been found, a shaft must be sunk well below the water table, and lined. This used to be done by making a wooden framework which was extended downwards and the brick or stone lining installed as work progressed. Nowadays, concrete rings are used and these drop down as the soil is cut away inside them, new rings being added when necessary (Fig 127).

The sides of the well must be impervious for a depth sufficient to avoid the possibility of pollution from cesspools, ashpits, etc, in the surrounding ground. In addition, the surface

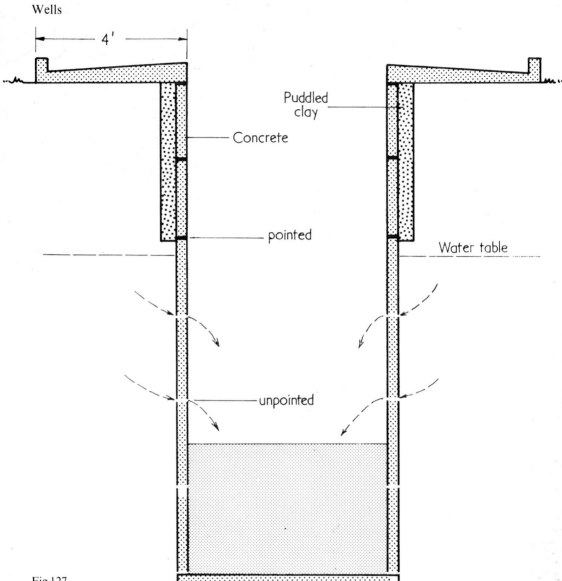

4'

Puddled
clay

Concrete

pointed

Water table

unpointed

Fig 127

of the ground, for a distance of 4ft (1m), round the well must be covered with impervious paving and have a raised kerb to prevent any surface water from entering the well. Puddled clay must be put behind the concrete lining until the water table is reached. Old-type wells were lined with pointed brick or stone, behind which was the layer of puddled clay. Once the water was reached the clay was

omitted and the bricks left unpointed.

Water engineers contract to build wells or to sink bores. This is an expensive process, but the one most commonly used nowadays. Once water has been reached it can be pumped to the surface mechanically when

(opposite) *Shipley Mill, owned and restored by Hilaire Belloc, this wooden smock mill is in perfect working order*

242

required, or a metal wind pump can be installed, emptying into a large tank. A wind pump (see *Pumps*) will work for years with little maintenance, and using free wind power.

Two points: go down well below the water table so that there is no danger of running dry in a drought; make sure that the well is properly covered, with a locked lid that cannot be removed by children, through which not even the smallest animal can find its way, and which excludes all surface rubbish.

Useful Address: The Well Drillers Association, Windsor House, Temple Row, Birmingham.

Wildfowling See *Shooting*.

Wild Fruit See *Fruit*.

Windmills There are few windmills left which work commercially, but ever-increasing numbers are being restored to the point where they do work, if only for the benefit of enthusiasts and visitors. Once there were thousands, a windmill every two or three miles, turning whenever the wind was blowing, and a whole industry of millwrights, stone dressers and

(opposite) *Barham Mill, a smock mill, with a typical Kentish bluff cap*

millers serviced this essential equipment for grinding grain and pulses. In marshy areas windmills by the hundred pumped water from ditches and dykes into main streams. Steam, diesel and electric pumping engines inevitably superseded the drainage mills, first in the fens of Lincolnshire and Cambridge, and later in Norfolk and Suffolk. Rolling mills, mechanically powered, took over large scale flour production in the last century, and one by one the country grinding mills went out of action, as farmers no longer had grain ground locally, and as the general public demanded white flour of a fineness (not necessarily of a goodness) that windmills could not produce.

Many mills were pulled down as they became derelict, and many remain derelict now, or the towers alone stand. Local windmill societies, county societies, the Society for the Protection of Ancient Buildings (wind and watermill section), and some local and county authorities are now concerned to save and restore what is left. Private individuals who

Putting new sails on Sandwich Mill

own mills usually do what they can but costs are very high. If you are interested in this work and in windmills generally, contact your local society, or write direct to SPAB. Your help will be welcomed.

Of all the things from the past that remain with us, there is nothing more beautiful than a windmill with its sails turning. It projects a sense of natural power and balance, like a ship under sail. But what is lacking now is the old bustle and purpose of people using the mill. It is too much to hope that more than a handful will again grind grain for general use, but it is a shame that restored mills should just stand there, picturesque but useless, until once again they rot.

Windchargers Much research is going on into alternative sources of power, and it might

Chillenden open post mill, the last to be built in Kent. This mill has no fantail so had to be 'winded' by pushing on the tail pole which can be seen through the ladder at the back

seem that windmills could harness the enormous wasted energy of the wind to produce electricity. Even using modern technology, a very big and expensive windmill, with probably two enormous propeller-like blades, is needed to produce anything worthwhile. Small windchargers (see *Electricity*) can provide a certain amount of power for domestic use and, especially in windy areas, justify installation costs. The problem with large scale wind power is that the wind is so inconstant that it cannot be relied upon to produce direct power all the time. Power must therefore be stored while the wind is blowing to

Cross in Hand post mill with a closed-in trestle making a round house

balance the supply when it is not. If the electricity generated by the windmill is turned into another form of energy which can be stored, then there is something to be gained. For instance, water can be pumped up into reservoirs from which it descends through hydro-electric generating plant. There are other ways, but all of them require enormous capital expenditure which could probably only be justified if there were no other ways to produce electricity, such as the harnessing of tidal or solar power.

In any case, banks of ugly monsters on great metal towers, dominating the hilltops of our land, would look terrible, not a bit like the gentle creatures of the past made from, and part of, the countryside. (See also *Pumps*.)

Useful Address: Society for the Protection of Ancient Buildings, Wind and Watermill Section, 55 Great Ormond Street, London WC1.

(opposite) *Sibsey Trader, a fine Lincolnshire brick tower mill with six nails and an elegant wrought-iron stage, ogee shaped cap and knob*

Further Reading: Beedell, S., *Windmills* (David & Charles); Wailes, Rex, *The English Windmill* (Routledge & Kegan Paul); Freese, S., *Windmills, Millwrighting* (David & Charles).

Wine-making Wine can be made from almost any non-poisonous flower, fruit, leaf or root plant. Perhaps the easiest and most successful are those made from mayflowers, elder-flowers, blackcurrants, blackberries and elder-berries. These produce delicious white and red table wines, not, perhaps, of the standard of expensive château-bottled wines, but certainly better than the equally expensive (for its quality) 'plonk' that passes for wine these days.

Keep your methods simple, use simple equipment and don't fiddle about too much with the wine at any stage. Keep the air from it after the very first stages, and don't drink it too soon after it has been bottled.

You will need a plastic bucket for making the 'must', a plastic strainer and funnel, a glass demijohn, fermentation locks, plastic tube, a cork flogger, hydrometer, and clean wine bottles; also corks for the bottles and corks both with and without holes for the demijohns.

Special wine-making containers and air locks can be bought and are most effective, but make a start with the basic equipment above.

Pick clean blossoms or fruit, away from roadsides; a third of a bucketful of fruit, or blossom pressed down a little, is, roughly speaking, enough for one gallon of wine. Cover this with boiling water as soon as possible after picking, and crush the berries with a wooden mallet (a steak mallet will do) or a plastic potato masher. Put the lid on the bucket and leave for two days. Crush again, and then strain the juice into a demijohn. Boil up some more water, pour it over the contents of the bucket and strain this with the other juice. The jar should be a little over half full. Put 2½lb (1kg) white sugar into a saucepan with just enough water to dissolve it and bring just to the boil. Allow to cool and add to the demijohn, bringing the level up to the curve of the jar. Add 1oz citric acid or the juice of two lemons, ¼ pint cold tea, and half a teaspoonful of yeast nutrient. Put a level dessertspoonful of dried yeast in a bowl with a spoonful or two of the juice and sugar mixture and leave it for an hour or two. When the contents of the jar have cooled to blood heat—the jar feels

Picking elderflowers

Fermentation jars with locks

Siphoning wine from demijohn bottle in the simplest way

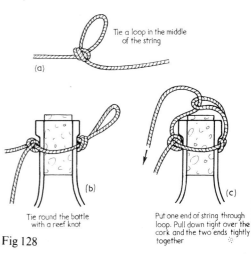

Tie a loop in the middle of the string

(a)

Tie round the bottle with a reef knot

(b)

Put one end of string through loop. Pull down tight over the cork and the two ends tightly together

(c)

Fig 128

neither hot nor cold to the palm of the hand, add the started yeast. Put in a cotton wool plug and stand the jar in a big bowl in a fairly warm room. For a couple of days fermentation will be fierce.

When it begins to subside, put in a fermentation lock, and, each day, top up the jar with a little boiled water until it is about 1½in (38mm) below the bottom of the cork. Leave to ferment until the wine clears, which should be from three to six weeks. Remove the lock and siphon the wine off into another demijohn, leaving the sediment behind. Top up with boiled water, and put the lock back in. When you are sure all fermentation has ceased and no small bubbles can be seen rising, put a tight cork in the jar and leave it for another month. Siphon off (rack again) into another jar and add a crushed Campden tablet to stop any further fermentation. Leave the jar to stand, well corked, for another two months. Then bottle the wine by siphoning it into clean bottles.

Cork with clean corks using a 'cork flogger' and tie them down (Fig 128a, b and c) Store the bottles in a cool place, on their sides. Drink no sooner than six months later. Wine which ferments at all after it has been corked

250

will be sparkling when opened, but may burst the bottles.

This is a very basic recipe and method, and there are many wine recipe books available which may give slightly different instructions, and, of course, different ingredients may require different methods. Many advocate leaving the must in the bucket for longer and adding the yeast at that point. This is all right, but can lead to too much air getting into the wine at an early stage, causing a rather unpleasant taste in the finished wine.

To measure the sugar content of wine at any stage, both before adding sugar and during fermentation, use your hydrometer according to its instructions. It can be a useful guide as to how much sugar to add in the first place, and to how sweet or dry your finished wine is. As a general rule, 3¼lb (1½kg) sugar per gallon will produce a sweet wine, 2¼lb (1kg) a medium wine, and 2lb (901g) a dry wine. (See also *Vineyards*.)

Further Reading: Beedell, S., *Home Winemaking and Brewing* (Sphere).

Wireworms Wireworms are a species of beetle which, in the larval stage, live underground and eat the roots of plants. If you see flocks of rooks pecking away in short grassland, they are probably looking for leatherjackets and wireworms. When the ground is ploughed and sown to root crops, the wireworms do a great deal of damage by burrowing right into the roots of the vegetables. Carrots and parsnips are particularly subject to wireworms which also eat seedling roots. The symptom is the yellowing of leaves. Fork gamm-BHC dust into the soil before planting or sowing.

Wood See *Trees*.

Wood-Burning Stoves See *Solid-fuel Stoves*.

Woodworm and Death Watch Beetle The woodworm, which makes the telltale shot holes in timber, is the larval stage of the wood-boring beetle (*Anobium punctatum*). The death watch beetle (*Xestobium rufovillosum*) also lays eggs in decaying wood and the larvae live for a long time, feeding on the wood, before turning into adult beetles. The holes left by the emerging beetles are, of course, a sure indication of the presence of the creatures at some time, but if there are traces of yellowish dust left by the insects' voracious appetites, this indicates live infestations. The whole of the attacked woodwork eventually becomes completely riddled with holes and soft inside, losing its structural strength to the point of collapse. Any evidence of wood-boring beetles at work in house timbers or furniture (they spread from one to another) should be taken seriously and eradication treatment carried out immediately. Contractors do a comprehensive job of lifting floorboards, skirtings, etc, and spraying and painting every possible place; and it is always best to have this done before moving into an old house for it is almost certain to have some woodworms somewhere. It is not a job which can be done in rooms full of furniture.

The death watch beetle is not so common in houses. Its natural home is dead tree stumps and infestation was usually begun when it was taken into a building in timber sawn from infested trees. This is not likely to happen nowadays as wood is treated before use.

Softwoods are not so prone to wood-boring beetle attack, which means that modern soft-wood house framing is not at risk, although there is some evidence that wood-boring beetles, deprived of hard wood, are adapting to soft wood.

If you can see the large flight holes of death watch beetle in old timbers—they thrive on damp and decay—check them for interior soundness by running in the fine bit of an electric drill. At first, as it penetrates the hard surface wood, considerable pressure will be needed and greenish shavings will emerge, but if the bit suddenly runs soft and a fine brown powder comes out, then the whole interior may be soft and the beam must be replaced.

Useful Addresses: Rentokil, 945 London Road, Thornton Heath, Croydon, Surrey CR4 6JE; also addresses in the *Damp* section.

Further Reading: Guides to Good Building, No 42, *Woodworm* (HMSO).

Wool See *Spinning*.

Wrought Iron Wrought iron has many uses and nowadays decorative wrought-iron work is done by blacksmiths as the main part of their business. Small foundries and smithies exist which do nothing else. Gates, garden furniture, railings, balustrades, banisters, grates, fire baskets, partitions, curtain rails, weathervanes—all these and more can be made by a smith who works wrought iron. He works in the traditional way with furnace, bellows (electrically powered), hammer and anvil, and because his products are not mass produced, they take time and are expensive. He has also to be a designer, according to his talent, so the work he produces will be beautiful or just plain utilitarian. Even if he is not a creative designer, he will have books of patterns for all kinds of things which he can copy and adapt

Modern smithy with electrically fanned fire

(left) *The martyrdom of Thomas à Becket designed and made by Mike Cooper Smith in his modern smithy*

Elegant but strong garden furniture

252

Wrought-iron balcony inside a house

(right) *Hammering over the first curl*

Wrought-iron lamp brackets

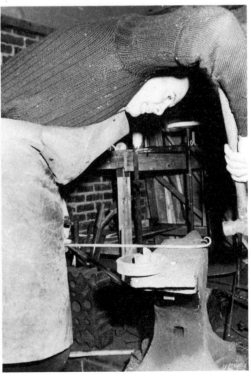

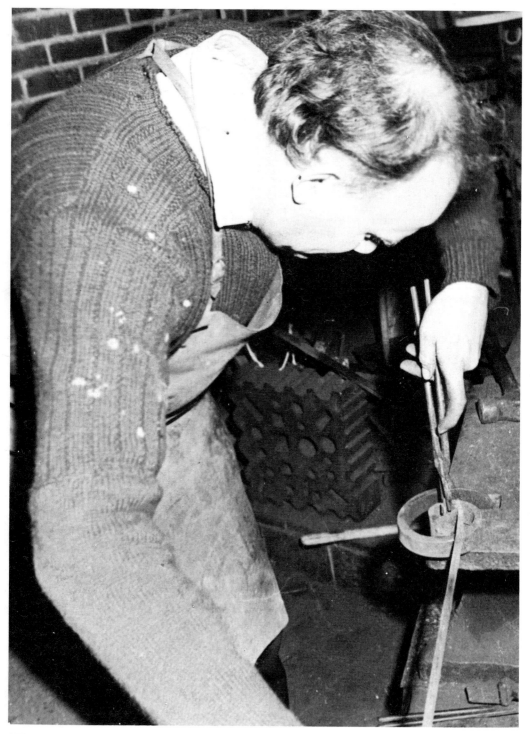

Wrought-iron curtain rail and fittings

as you wish, and he will be prepared to work to your designs within the limitations enforced by the material he works in. The basic metals are in strips and rods which are hammered and twisted to create scrolls, leaves and flower shapes, or figures and animals. He may also use expanded metal to block in large areas and show different colours.

Useful Addresses: Wrought-iron Tool Kits, J. C. Wood (Wirecraft), 303c Hull Road, Anlaby Common, Hull; National Master Farriers and Blacksmiths Association, 48 Spencer Place, Leeds.

Further Reading: Underwood, A., *Creative Wrought Iron* (Batsford).

(opposite) *Making the scroll on a special form*   *Wrought-iron gateway*

Illustrations

Suzanne Beedell took all the photographs with the exception of the following:

Mistle thrush—Eric Hosking; boot beetle—B. Hargreaves; peacock butterfly—R.C. Revels; red deer stag and deerstalking—John Marchington; roebuck—Manfred Danegger; Yellow Labrador—G.L. Carlisle; pointer—John Tarleton; golden retriever puppies—B. Hargreaves; Border terriers, Norfolk terriers and Jack Russell—Sally Ann Thompson; lurchers—B. Hargreaves; Percheron stallion—F.H. Meads; ferrets—John Marchington; flyfishing for salmon—William Marchington; primroses—Philip Johnson; fox—McSweeny; toads—John Marchington; frogs—Sean Hagerty; hunting—Frank Meads; barograph—John Tarleton; fat dormouse—John Markham; blue butterfly—Ray Kennedy; partridges—Fritz Siedel; pheasants—George Quedens; scarecrow and 12-bore—John Tarleton; rifle shooting—John Marchington; grey squirrel—V.L. Bissland; training a puppy—Ivor Ashmore; nest box for breeding ducks—B. Hargreaves; Shire Horses—H. Ilsley; Rosehips and Haws—Popperphoto; heather burning—John Topham; results of heather burning—John Marchington; hedgehog and young—L. W. Newman; prize-winning turnout—*Birmingham Post and Mail*; young rabbit—John Marchington.

All the diagrams were drawn by Suzanne Beedell, finalised by Victor Welch.